Chinese Canadians

VOICES FROM A COMMUNITY

Evelyn Huang with Lawrence Jeffery

Chinese Canadians

VOICES FROM A COMMUNITY

Evelyn Huang with Lawrence Jeffery

Douglas & McIntyre
Vancouver/Toronto

92 93 94 95 96   5 4 3 2 1

Douglas & McIntyre Ltd.
1615 Venables Street
Vancouver, British Columbia V5L 2H1

Canadian Cataloguing in Publication Data

Huang, Evelyn.
Chinese Canadians
ISBN 0–55054–034–3
1. Chinese Canadians—Interviews. 2. Chinese Canadians—History. 3. Chinese—Canada—Interviews.
4. Chinese—Canada—History.
I. Jeffery, Lawrence, 1953–
II.Title
FC106.C5H82 1992971'.004951   C92–091260–5
F1035.C5H82 1992

Calligraphy by Irene Christine Chu

Corporate sponsorship for Michael Lee supplied by Vistek Ltd. in conjunction with Kodak, Canada Ltd.

Editing by Brian Scrivener
Design and production by RayMahDesign,Inc.
Jacket design by RayMahDesign,Inc.
Printed and bound in Canada
by D. W. Friesen and Sons Ltd.

Printed on acid-free paper

Contents

To my husband Michael
and our beloved family.

I began this project in the hope that I might be able to bring to Canadians an insight into the community of which I am a part. The policy of multiculturalism wishes to encourage the diverse cultures of this country to thrive in harmony. But culture and community are words that remain abstract concepts for most. I have brought these Chinese Canadians together to offer their experiences and insights because I believe that we can only come to understand a community through the lives of its individual members.

It is perhaps unfashionable for me to say how much I love Canada, but I can't help wanting to celebrate the nation that offered my husband and me a new life in 1967 and is the birthplace of our four children. Canada is a nation of many different cultures whose future may seem more optimistic in light of the sentiments expressed by the Canadians in this book.

Evelyn Huang

We began this project by reading every book we could find that had anything to do with the Chinese in Canada. With the exception of a few young Chinese Canadian writers of fiction and poetry there was little in all that we read that struck us as being personal. What we missed was the voice of individual experience. We chose the interview format in part because nothing brings history to life as well as its impact on the lives of those who survived it. From Sam Eng who paid the head tax to enter Canada in 1905, to Selwyn Au-Yeung who came from Hong Kong on a student's visa in 1982, we have been fortunate to assemble a diverse group whose personal experiences illustrate the major events in the history of the Chinese in Canada in the twentieth century. This format allows these individuals to stand at centre stage, and though the interviewers' presence can be felt in the questions asked and the topics explored, we tried to keep our influence to a minimum. Personal anecdote exposes character and the dynamics of the subject's relationship to society better than any description and analysis penned by another author.

It was always interesting to see how the people whom we interviewed used language and shaped sentences, and how rhythm of speech is like a fingerprint—no two being alike. They tell us a great deal about themselves by what they choose as the significant events in their lives and speak volumes by what they choose to omit. The careful reader will learn much between the lines. It was always a surprise when we were asked to turn off the tape recorder because people did not want their opinion made public, or when fear of some sort of censure led them to have neither an opinion on a particular incident, nor even acknowledge its existence. Such reticence was confined by and large to the older generation: it is the discretion of the oppressed. The best responses were the most spontaneous—sparked as if an electric charge had passed between us. Those screened by too much thought or that came back at us as if a button had been pushed were of the least interest and were often dropped from the final text. The most skilled storytellers animate each character with a unique voice, while others control the narrative with their own. We found that the young are not quite ready to tell the stories that explain who they are as they are perhaps too busy living them, the middle aged have had time to pasteurize them, and the old abandon them—their character becomes their story.

David Lam and Adrienne Clarkson were obvious choices for such a collection; others were selected carefully but capriciously. While it is important to add that there are many Chinese Canadians whose achievements equal or surpass those of the individuals in this book and whose stories are perhaps more compelling and of greater historical interest, each of those whom we have chosen added something of value, a brushstroke in a growing portrait.

It took us a great deal of time to match the appropriate Confucian analect to each subject. We wrote new translations for the analects and are grateful to Irene Chu for doing the calligraphy. We then gave each subject an opportunity to speak of that which has brought them the most satisfaction or made them most proud. These sentiments are placed at the end of each interview.

Following the interviews comes an essay on the history of the Chinese in Canada, written for us by Dr. Peter Li, which provides a fascinating though somewhat disturbing counterpoint to the grace and optimism expressed by the interviewees.

It is folly to think that any one book can tell the whole story of the Chinese in Canada. But we have—from our very different backgrounds—learned much from the experiences and insights of the individuals included in this collection. Whether it is to place oneself in the shoes of a citizen denied the vote, or to look at our current national crisis in light of the obstacles faced by Chinese Canadians, all Canadians, whether or not they are of Chinese descent, can learn something about themselves from reading this book.

Evelyn Huang
Lawrence Jeffery

Dock Yip

Born in Vancouver in 1906, the seventeenth child of Yip Sang, one of the city's wealthiest merchant princes, Dock Yip studied at the University of British Columbia, Columbia University and Osgoode Hall, and in 1945, was the first Asian Canadian called to the bar. In mid-life, he was a member of a committee that travelled to Ottawa to present a brief concerning changes in the Immigration Act. Now, in his late eighties, when most are happy to lead quieter lives, Dock Yip continues to practise law and pursue his new career as an actor. The front room of his home in Toronto's East York is full of books, photographs and mementos from a long, eventful and still very active life. Among the many family photographs adorning the walls is a large portrait of his father. It was used as a prop in the film The Year of the Dragon, in which Dock Yip played a pipesmoking Tong leader. Dock Yip told us if we included his father's picture, hundreds of his relatives would be sure to buy the book, so we hung it on the wall behind him before taking his photograph.

子曰知者不惑
仁者不憂勇
者不懼

THE WISE MAN IS NOT CONFUSED,
THE BENEVOLENT FREE OF ANXIETY,
AND THE BOLD HAS NO FEAR.

When I was born at my father's home in Vancouver, 51 Pender Street, in 1906, a very famous Chinese scholar by the name Kang Yu Wei was staying at our house. My father asked him to give me a name. He called me Yip Kew Dock. My name is from Confucius—it means teacher. Kang Yu Wei was the prime minister at the end of the Guang Sui Empire; he advocated the constitutional monarchy with Guang Sui as king and the Parliament elected by the people following the English pattern. But the Empress Dowager ordered him arrested. He escaped to Vancouver to establish an association among the overseas Chinese in North America. My father was an ardent supporter of the reform movement and invited him to stay in our home.

How did your father come to Canada?

Well, go back to ancestors—my great grandfather. He was known as Cock–Eye Wah. In 1845 he was operating a small store in a marketplace called the Do Fook, in the district of Taishan, Guangdong province in South China. He was selling bean curds; we call it tofu. A group of men came and gave him ten or twelve baskets and asked him to safekeep them. But they never came back. After many years, he opened the baskets and saw they contained gold, silver and jewels. It is possible the men were bandits. My family were honest people—for generations honest people—and it was possible he was safekeeping for the bandits without knowing they were bandits. So there was a saying that the five devils transferred the treasure to him.

I have been practising law for fifty years and I have never done one dishonest thing. I did not cheat one time. That's in our genetics. We are always honest people. My great grandfather and his brother lent money to the officials of the Ching dynasty, in order to get interest. But in 1860 the Tai Ping Rebellion occupied the whole of China south of Nanjing. All the government officials ran away. We lost all our money. My father had to sell his land and then went to San Francisco for the Gold Rush. By the time he got there, the gold was all gone. He worked in a cigar factory rolling cigars and he also worked in Montana as a cook for some cowboys. He made some money and went back to China. In China he got into merchant trading between Do Fook and Macau. All his life he liked trading—he was a born merchant.

Our family, for generations, were merchants. I really belong to the merchant class. But my father went back to San Francisco. At that time the United States was overpopulated. So, he sailed on a China clipper from San Francisco to Victoria. That was about 1880. Then he took the ferry boat from Victoria to New Westminster. There was no Vancouver then.

Your father worked for the CPR*?*

Yes. He became the paymaster for the Chinese. He brought them over to work on the railroad. When the railroad was finished he bought land in Vancouver. He bought empty land and built houses on it. He also had an import business, a Chinese store, which sold goods for the Chinese.

When did he marry your mother?

He was married four times; he had four wives. His first wife was very weak; he needed someone to look after her. So he got a concubine, a second wife, to look after the first one. The first one died. Then he married my mother. When she came into the house, she had to recognize the one before her as being first, number one, so she acknowledged her by placing a flower in her hair. And then later my mother played politics; she brought in another wife. We call them all mother.

And how many children?

Twenty-three in all: four girls and nineteen boys. I'm number seventeen. Number one, number two, number three were born in China. The rest in Vancouver.

How did he support all these women and children?

He was a great man, one of the richest Chinese in Canada. His name was Yip Sang.

Mr. Yip Sang and children 1906 (Dock not present).

You were born in 1906. What are your childhood memories?

I remember I was living in a ghetto—Vancouver's Chinatown was a ghetto then. Pender Street was for Chinese only. White men didn't come down there. In the ghetto everybody spoke Chinese. The road was made of wood, blocks of wood packed together. Everybody spoke Chinese. That's why when I speak English, I speak with an accent even now. I knew one Chinese living there who had never left Chinatown his entire life.

How many people lived in the building at 51 Pender Street?

Many people. Cousins and grandsons. Afterwards my father built another six storeys. My father not only looked after his own children, he also looked after all the cousins. Many of them he brought over from China.

How old was he when you were born?

Sixty. My mother was forty.

What sort of school did you go to?

I went to central schools. When I was in grade four, they put me in the Chinese class. It was all Chinese. So the result is that I'm very strong in the Chinese language. Chinese is my first language. I think in Chinese. I can't think in English, even now. I don't know if that's an advantage or a disadvantage. Is it an advantage to me or a disadvantage?

How many of your clients are Chinese?

Most of them.

Then it's an advantage.

That's a very good answer. . . . I can swear in Chinese better than I swear in English. In any language, you always learn the swear words first. I learned how to swear in both English and Chinese. The Chinese don't know much English, but they know how to swear. Some Chinese sometimes don't know how to talk but they can always swear.

Do you remember the riots in Vancouver against the Chinese?

No, no, no. I was born after the riot. But I could see the effects of the riot. I saw boards covering the windows. Wooden boards. We were afraid they would do it again.

What else do you remember about that time?

The white people didn't come down to Chinatown.

When did you first meet white people?

When I went to school.

When was that?

Well, they kept me home. For God's sake, they wouldn't let me go to school. I don't know why. In 1914—I was eight years old, son of a bitch!

Your father kept you home until you were eight years old?

Yes, this is a crime I think.

You started school in 1914. Do you remember the First World War?

Little bit.

What do you remember?

I saw some soldiers in the streets, that's all. . . . Gradually, Chinatown changed. After 1923 the Chinese Immigration Act came into effect. No more Chinese were allowed to come to Canada, so we gradually mixed up with the white people. For instance, we played soccer and football with them.

Who won?

We won—we were champions in Vancouver in 1925.

What do you remember of the Exclusion Act?

In 1923 I attended some Chinese mass meetings against the Exclusion Act. Joseph Hope—Ying Hope's older brother, a businessman—tried to oppose it but he couldn't do anything. My brother was studying medicine at Queen's University. He went to Ottawa to protest. He couldn't do anything either. He was in the gallery at the House of Commons and just watched as they passed the Act. I was at a meeting where Joseph Hope spoke after they passed the Act. We called it humiliation day, July 1st, 1923. I listened to him. Maybe that inspired me to help change the Act when I finished law.

Is that what motivated you to go into law?

Absolutely. I wanted to fight for Chinese rights.

What else?

I'd spent one year at Columbia University in New York City. I began to see the big world.

When was that?

1928. I went as a provincial boy from Vancouver. We were very provincial. New York is a cosmopolitan city. All kinds of people there. I'll tell you a funny story. I was living in a dormitory for foreign students. It was known as International House, built by J.D. Rockefeller. One day I was having a conversation with a man. Afterwards my friend asks me, "You know who you were talking with?" "No. I don't know," I answered. "You were talking with John Dewey." I said, "Who's John Dewey?" He nearly died! In the United States John Dewey is a god. Everybody knew him. My friend nearly died. He got the biggest shock in his life. John Dewey told a story. He said that in every man's life there are three women. One, you love but she won't marry you. One, she loves you but you won't marry her. And then you marry the third one. How true. You just think about it.

Did your father send you to Columbia?

He was dead. He died in 1927.

What happened to his businesses and buildings?

Well, the buildings went to his eldest son to look after. Then after 1931 the Depression came. There were two things that made us lose our fortune. Firstly, the Depression. No doubt about it. Secondly, the immigration. Our family based its business on the Chinese immigration. When that stopped, it killed the business.

How did you come to choose Columbia?

My father wanted me to study pharmacy. I took the boat to Seattle, then the train to Chicago. I met up with a friend there and then we went to New York. I had finished two years at UBC already. You see, at that time it was the style to study in the United States, both the Canadians and the Chinese studying at Columbia University had prestige.

It must have been expensive.

Yes. Two thousand dollars a year. Today, twenty thousand isn't enough for Harvard or Yale.

How long did you stay at Columbia?

I only stayed half a year.

Why?

New York is not a place to study, I am telling you. Too many distractions!

How many of Mr. Dewey's three women did you meet in New York?

Well, I met one. There's some interesting women in New York. I could speak English. Not many Chinese could speak English in 1928. I met a Tong leader. He controlled Mott Street and Pell Street. He invited me to a nightclub. He brought his own girlfriend and one for me. We had dinner. After we finished the dinner, the girls said, "You excuse us. We go to wash up our hands." So the two girls left, and just the Tong leader and me were left. He wanted me to join the Tong, the Hipsing Tong. Good pay. And then I remembered I came to study not to be in a Tong. My life would be in danger; they were always shooting at each other . . . . So that girl was one woman. Another was the daughter of a Hong Kong millionaire. One day she asked me, "Dock, come and have tea with me." So I went to have tea with her. Nobody took tea with her so I had a lot of tea with her. I don't know if she had intentions for me or not. She may have had intentions for me . . . but I missed it. She was a multi-millionaire's daughter. Maybe I blew it! Maybe another reason is that she was a multi-millionaire's daughter. My father was a coolie with the CPR. Doesn't mix. Maybe that's one of the reasons. I don't know.

You'll never know.

No. My wife, of course, she's number three.

How did you meet her?

Well, I was back in Vancouver. I was very depressed—it was the Depression! You don't know what's a Depression. You're a good time baby. After I finished at Columbia I went to Michigan University for chemistry and then I came back to UBC to study arts. . . . I was at a dance. I was very depressed. I was just standing there and then there she was. Then I sat over there and she sat beside me. I thought, what the hell . . . maybe she's got intentions. So I asked her if I could take her home. She said, "No, I didn't come with you. Some other time." So I took her to a show. And then I married her. I married her in 1941.

What were you doing at this time?

I worked as a secretary in the Chinese consulate in Vancouver. My third brother was a disciple of Dr. Sun Yat Sen. He followed Sun Yat Sen to China to join the revolution. The Chinese consul in Vancouver went to Ottawa to become the consul-general. My brother had connections with the consul-general and he wrote a letter to Ottawa and I got a job as secretary in the consulate in Vancouver. That was 1933 and I worked at that job until 1941. I got married and moved to Toronto with my wife.

In Toronto, I owned a restaurant, with partners, on Yonge Street. There was a restaurant for sale. I put in $500—a lot of money then. So I got a one-sixth share. My wife became the cashier and managed it. She looked after the accounts. And I studied law. The restaurant helped give me food and give a job to my wife. I studied on Sunday. It was a good time.

What do you remember of the Second World War?

I was in the reserve army, the Queen's Own Rifles. You could volunteer. My brother-in-law volunteered to join the Camp X Group. Six of my nephews were sent over to India. My brother-in-law was in the intelligence service with Churchill. He was sent to train in Penticton, B.C. Originally he was supposed to go to Oshawa, but the general was afraid to see so many Chinese walking around Oshawa. From Penticton they were sent to Australia, up in the Blue Mountains. He was supposed to go by submarine, carry gold bars and a radio, and join the local forces and attack Hong Kong.

You were the first Asian to go to Osgoode Hall law school.
Tell us something about that.

One of my schoolmates said to me, "Dock, I wonder why they don't flunk you." Why would they flunk me?" I asked. "Because you're Chinese." "No, I'm not Chinese, I'm Canadian." One day a Chinese, another friend, asked, "I understand that Chinese are not allowed to practise law in Canada, so then why do you go to Osgoode Hall?" "Yes, that is true," I answered, "but I am not Chinese. I am a Canadian and so are you. Yes, racially I am Chinese, but from the point of view of nationality or citizenship, I am a Canadian."

After you graduated in 1945, did you begin to practise immediately?

I set up my office in Chinatown, on Elizabeth Street. I became a storefront lawyer. I'll tell you something about a storefront. It's very good for public relations. You see everybody on the street. Sometimes they just come in to say hello. One time I pushed a client out. He said, "Don't push me out." "I have to—I'm not making a living with you sitting here talking to me," I said. I had to push him out to be able to do my work.

What kind of law did you do?

Real estate law, commercial law and immigration law. I still do a lot of immigration law. I also do some work as an interpreter. Sometimes I'm asked to go do some interpreting out of town. They pay the fare, they pay me something. That's one advantage of being so strong in Chinese, I can interpret.

When did you first become involved in the repeal of the Exclusion Act?

In 1942, when I was with the Queen's Own Rifles, I got rheumatism, and Irving Himmel, another lawyer, he got rheumatism too. We went back to the camp to rest. We did some small jobs, cleaned up. So I told him, "Himmel, I want to do the Immigration Act. I want to do immigration work. They won't let the Chinese in." So he said, "We have to repeal that law." We organized a committee. We enlisted some Occidentals. Dr. Armstrong, the moderator of the United church, and Cardinal McQuigan from the Catholic church. Arthur Martins, who is now a judge, and Colonel Croll. So we went to see Cardinal McQuigan. We had a Protestant minister with us and a minister of a Chinese church, Dr. Neyes. A Catholic priest came in and said to us, "When the Cardinal comes in, you all have to kiss his ring. That's the custom." So Dr. Neyes said, "What am I going to do? I can't kiss the Cardinal's ring." I said, "Dr. Neyes, according to Chinese custom, when you go into a village, you have to follow the customs of that village. You are in a Catholic place, you have to kiss the ring; otherwise you have to leave." And he didn't want to leave. "So you think I should kiss it?" "Yeah, you have to join in." So we all kissed the ring. And it came to Dr. Neyes. He said, "May I?" The Cardinal just lifted him up and said, "Not you!" It was the best show I've ever seen in my life!

The Cardinal helped you?

Yes. Then the Toronto *Star* did an editorial.

And you went to Ottawa?

Yes. There were four people. Dr. Ngai, a Chinese medical doctor; Irving Himmel, a lawyer. He ran all the manoeuvres, Himmel. Me, Kew Dock Yip, I'm the secretary. And Colonel Croll, David Croll, a Liberal MP. Irving Himmel asked me to lead this movement but I thought Dr. Ngai would do it better. He was from Hankow in Hopei province. The people there are noted for gallantry. They seem to be better leaders, so I deferred the position to him and he did a very good job. The law was finally repealed in 1947.

What do you think of the Chinese community in Toronto today? How has it changed from when you first arrived in Toronto in 1941?

In a sense, there's an advancement. There is better education, much better than in my father's time. There are many professionals. In my father's time there was no education. Do you know how my father did his correspondence? He had two secretaries—one English, one Chinese—both very good. He would dictate in Chinese. All the time he would just swear, he'd say, "You goddamn son of a bitch." The English secretary would ask what he was saying. The Chinese secretary would make it up, make up the letter, because my father only ever said, "You goddamn son of a bitch."

You're still practising law. Do you think you'll ever retire?

No! I wouldn't be happy. All my life I've been busy. I'm not a lazy man. All my life I'm busy—work, work, work. If I stop working, I'll die. I warn you. Don't ever stop. Get another occupation rather than retiring.

How did you come to be a movie actor?

By coincidence. When I finished law I took a course in public speaking. I came first in a class of lawyers, businessmen, missionaries, salesmen—in spite of my language difficulties. You see, public speaking is nothing but acting on a platform.

When did you start acting?

Well, it was *The Year of the Dragon*. Michael Cimino, the director, was looking for someone to play one of the Tong leaders. They sent a tape of me to Michael Cimino. He had five assistant directors. They looked at my tape. They thought I might qualify. I went down to New York for an audition with Mickey Rourke, John Long and Victor Wong. They talked to me, they asked me everything. That's how I got the part. Michael Cimino said I'm a diamond in the rough. He said I'm the greatest find in the twentieth century. For God's sake, I'm not. So they thought a lot of me. . . . He's a very good director. He doesn't tell you things to your face. He comes over and whispers in your ear, "Dock, you should be angry in this scene." I enjoyed it. I just love to see myself on the silver screen. You never get tired of it. Furthermore, the pay is good.

What do you hope for the future, for the Chinese community and for Canada?

I hope the Chinese become more Canadian. Take part in Canadian life. Join the Rotary Club, the Lion's Club. Take part, and contribute money to Canadian society. But I also believe the Chinese should retain their ancestral language. For instance, my children, they should learn Chinese and learn the Chinese culture.

Is there anything else you'd like to say?

Yes, I have neglected to tell you that I have served as school trustee for the Toronto School Board for two terms. During my tenure of office, I have accomplished two things. I advocated early education especially for the inner city children. I advocated school should start at three years old. I led a committee from the Toronto Board to see the Minister of Education and the Minister asked me what your program costs, Mr. Yip? No, Mr. Minister, I don't know but no matter what its cost, we must give this program to the children. I did not get the three-year program, but the Metropolitan School Board instituted the junior kindergarten program starting school at four years old. I also instituted the Heritage Program for children of ethnic background to learn the language and customs of their ancestors.

And anything about your life?

As I said, I believe in retaining the ancestral culture, the Chinese, the Japanese, the Italian, the Portuguese, the Greek. If they know something about their ancestral culture they become part of their own ancestors. They won't be lost. . . See, I don't believe in, "One country, one language." Remember, Canada was settled by the French first, you can't forget that.

The Native people first. Let's get this right.

That's right. . . .

In 1945 Dock Yip was the first Asiatic called to the bar in Canada. He later worked for the re-unification of families and changes in immigration policy, and today, he continues to practise law and pursue his career as an actor. His three sons all completed university and have families of their own. Dock and his wife Victoria will celebrate their fiftieth wedding anniversary in 1992.

Three wives of Yip Sang and children 1906
(Dock Yip's mother, centre)

Sam Eng

Sam Eng turned one hundred years old in February of 1991. It is difficult for most of us to imagine what life was like before we were born—it is even difficult to remember what we were doing, whom we were with or where we were ten or twenty years ago. To have the opportunity of having someone who has lived a full century share his memories with us is to be in touch with another world—to experience living history. When Sam Eng was born, Queen Victoria was on the throne of England and movies, airplanes and trips to the moon were science fiction. Some would argue that the scientific and technological developments of the last century have changed civilization more than any other period in history. Yet, for Sam Eng, there has been one constant. It is his family, which has remained most important to him during his hundred years—his children, his grandchildren and his great-grandchildren.

The ancients who wished to set an example of great virtue first put their house in order. To put their house in order they had to put their family in order. To put their family in order they had to cultivate themselves.
To cultivate themselves they had to reconcile their hearts. To reconcile their hearts they had to become sincere in their thoughts. And to become sincere in thought requires great learning. It is from this journey toward knowledge that the example of great virtue is made.

古之欲明明德於天下者先治其國欲治其國者先齊其家欲齊其家者先脩其身欲脩其身者先正其心欲正其心者先誠其意欲誠意者先致其知

I was eight years old when my father left home. He came here as a coolie. He paid the $50 head tax. That was 1897. He was about twenty–eight years old at that time. In 1905, when I was thirteen, I came over. When I came they sent me back; I didn't have the right papers. I was illegal. They sent me back to Hong Kong. I waited for one year. My father got somebody here to get the right papers to allow me to enter . . . I landed in Vancouver and then took the train to Toronto. My father was in Windsor, working for a fellow named Edward Carey, a hotel owner. The hotel was called the Ojibway.

How many brothers or sisters did you have?

I had four or five brothers and sisters. They're all dead. I was the only one to come to Canada.

Why did you come?

My father was over here and I was in China. My mother used to say, "Do you want to make more money?" I said, "Yes." She said, "Why?" I said, "There's only one man to support the whole family; it's hard work." So I left to go and help my father. That's how I got here.

What do you remember of the trip from China?

I felt sick . . . seasick. I'd never been in a boat before in China and I had to go through the Pacific Ocean. It took about twenty-eight days to come through. It was a steamship. The ship was so small the waves almost came over. You rolled on the boat just like a rocking chair.

Did you speak any English?

Not a word. No.

How did you learn?

How did I learn? A miracle! . . . My father didn't earn enough money to send me to school. But he put me in the hotel and the boss, Edward Carey, he said, "That little fellow you've got there, I want to use him." I said, "Can you pay me any money?" "Oh yes, I'll pay you." I asked my father how much. He said, "Let the boss decide that."

What did you do for him?

I was the bell hop and my father was the cook. He would make up the tray and I would carry it up to the room. So I never went to school. Actually, I took my English lessons from a French lady. Her husband worked in a grocery store there. He delivered food to the hotel. . . . I told my father, "I want to go to school." He said, "No, no school. But while you're working as a bell hop at the hotel here, you'll pick up English." I was very sad when he said that. It was that way for the Chinese people. You didn't go to school. Nobody, I don't think.

What sort of hours did you work at the hotel?

I opened up in the morning . . . and at night time I worked from 3:00 P.M. to midnight every night, no let up. I went to the grocer's house during the days to learn English from his wife. Then I worked in the hotel from 3:00 to midnight. I picked up English very fast, in about five or six months. I learned my English very, very fast. It's a miracle.

Were there many Chinese in Windsor at the time?

No. Very, very few. About fifteen people.

How long did you stay in Windsor?

My mother wrote a letter. She said it's been six or seven years now with my son over there. Have him come back. What's the matter with you? My father showed me the letter. I said, "My mother wants me to go home." I was twenty-one or twenty-two. So I went back. I stayed there about six months and then came back to Canada. There was only a limited time you were allowed to leave the country and return. The permit expired after six months and they wouldn't let you back in. . . . The second time I went back they had changed the law and allowed you to leave the country for one year.

BLUEBIRD GRILL, 1960s.

When you entered Canada the first time you paid the $500 head tax?

Yes. $500. But I don't want it back, no.

Why?

The $500? It's a long story. If you want, I'll take that story and I'll give it to you.

Give it to us.

Lately, I hear so much criticism against the government. I regularly read the paper. I regularly read books. I learn everything. I think I have a good memory yet. More than I can tell you right now. I saw the opinion of the Chinese public. It's so confused. Sometimes it makes my stomach sick. The Japanese, now they make the government pay what they were worth before. Canada pays the damage that they suffered through the war because the government took over their property and took away their power so they wouldn't make any funny business behind the lines because Canada was at war with Japan. But for the Chinese, it's different. The Chinese are different fish. The Japanese people didn't pay any head tax; the Chinese people did. Since before the beginning, they got unequal treatment. It's shameful for human beings; we're all one family. Why shouldn't the Chinese come in here free, without paying the tax? They don't make the English people pay the tax, not even the European people, so why should the Chinese people pay tax? It's not fair.

But you said you don't want the government to return the money to you. Why?

I'll tell you. Canada didn't ask that the Chinese people come over here. We came over ourselves. Why? Because you heard that if you come to Canada, you'll find a better living there than in your own country. So I think, you are paying the tax to be allowed to come here to get yourself a life, a living, not only for yourself. Also for your family.

How did you feel at the time?

I didn't know about it. I didn't know anything then. My father paid for it.

Are you angry that you had to pay the head tax? Do you resent it?

No. I was very poor. I'm glad to put my foothold in and make myself a home. It's my country. . . . I'm not talking about race. I'm Chinese. If you don't want a friendship with me, get away from me. If you want me, you see me but not as Chinese. You want to be friends with me? We're very impressed. We're glad to have a friend.

What would you do if they decided to give you compensation for the head tax you paid? Would you accept it?

No. I don't care for it. Some people say that I'm crazy, but I don't think I am.

After your visits back to China did you always return to Windsor?

Not always Windsor. I've been many places. The biggest restaurant that I had was in Hamilton in 1932. At that time, only 50 cents a meal, my restaurant 75 cents. The people said I was crazy, but I made lots of money.

Why did you go into the restaurant business?

Because it was the only business I knew. It was the only business I understood. I hired people, cheap labour from my own country, brought them over from China. Sometimes relatives, too.

When did you stop returning to China?

When my mother died and I forgot about it. She was an old lady and she had a big home in China. My father went home and didn't come back to Canada. He went back to live in China when I was old enough to be on my own. That was 1913, 1914, the First World War.

What do you remember about the First World War?

Terrible, terrible. I see a lot of young ladies crying at the Union Station. Gee, that's tough. . . . All the young men, yes . . . some coming back with only one leg. Why does it have to be like that? Who was gaining? Who got the benefit?

What was Toronto like at that time?

Nothing but farms. North of Eglinton, nothing.

Were there many Chinese?

I would say about thirty, forty Chinese people. Ninety percent laundry people. Chinese scattered here and there. Except a few met at the Chinese gambling house.

Did you meet Dr. Sun Yat Sen when he came to Toronto?

Oh, yes. He was in Toronto to sign up membership. I was a very young man then. He came to raise money to buy munitions and guns and take them back to the revolution.

What was he like?

He was about fifty years old, I think. I understood what he tells me and I almost joined up and went back to China to fight the 'dynasty demon.' He was a great talker. At that time he had to go and visit different individuals, you know. We just had a hall. It was quite a big hall . . . something like a church.

What do you remember most about him?

I remember him. . . . He was a very, very noble man. Very noble to people, race to race. I believe that. The only trouble is he didn't stay here long enough. He comes on Wednesday, leaves on Saturday. We talked but not long enough to learn everything he learned. All his history. . . . We all understand that . . . how he came to be a leader of a country.

Have you continued to return to China?

Not now. I have my family here now. I've got a big family over here now.

When did you get married?

A long time ago . . . a very long time ago . . . I think I've finished my life already. After this, it's their job.

Their job?

My family. I raised all my children . . . my family to make themselves to be 'somebody' themselves—I got that from my father. He said you can be rich or you can be poor if you want to. It's up to you. So I said the same thing to my family. Now I've got eighteen great-grandchildren and thirteen grandchildren. A good family, eh?

Are you tired?

Yes.

Would you rather we came back tomorrow?

Then you ask me more. . . . What is it? What you asked me now . . . we can finish it and be done?

Okay. In 1923 they began the Chinese Exclusion Act. During that time what did you do? Did you go back to China?

No.

But you married?

I went back to China and my wife came with me.

You married her in China. When did she come to Canada?

In 1949, I think, after the Second World War.

What did you think of the government not allowing Chinese immigration for all those years?

You can't blame the Canadian government because they had enough people here who didn't have jobs. There were a lot of people coming in . . . there was no work for them to do . . . who's going to feed them? So, they had a right.

But they only did it to the Chinese. It didn't apply to other races. Why do you think they did it to the Chinese?

I don't know. . . . They came over to make money to support the family, so when they don't have a job to give them so what's the use of coming over? It was a simple reason like that. After the Second World War, they cut that off.

What do you remember of the Second World War?

I was in Sudbury then. I had a restaurant.

During the war there wasn't conscription for the Chinese.

No. I don't think they pictured the Chinese as a fighter. I don't think so.

There was a unit in Vancouver that did go to Burma.

But they volunteered in there, they volunteered. If you want to volunteer yourself, they'd let you.

When did you leave Sudbury?

I stayed there until I could retire. I was seventy-four years already.

What was the happiest time or moment in your life?

I don't think I had a hard time at all. Happy? . . . My family. . . .

Why do you think you've had such a long, happy life?

Well, I succeeded this way. I have my family here. We see eye to eye everyday. Everything I do . . . they know me, I know them. I know where they go, so I don't worry. That's the way I satisfy myself. I'm very happy. They all grow up, though. They don't come around and sit on my knee anymore. . . . I'm happy because they're all grown up, they're educated—what they wanted, they found. They found the way they wanted.

You said your father didn't have enough money to send you to school, but you encouraged your children to get an education?

I swore to myself that I wouldn't let my children down. I'll see that they get a good education. . . . It was a pleasure to reach that goal like that. You wouldn't blame me for that?

Sam Eng worked from the day he arrived in Canada in 1905 until his retirement at the age of 74. He is proud to say that he never collected unemployment insurance or accepted social assistance of any kind.

THE ENG FAMILY AT SAM ENG'S ONE HUNDREDTH BIRTHDAY PARTY.

Lee Bick

When Lee Bick was sixty-five he suffered a serious heart attack and was told by his doctors that he did not have long to live. So he turned his business affairs over to his children and built two greenhouses in the back yard of his home in Vancouver's Shaughnessy district. It was his intention to spend his final days doing precisely as he wished—filling those two greenhouses with flowers and tending his beautifully landscaped garden. Lee Bick is now in his one hundredth year and continues to work eight hours a day in his greenhouses. The only concession he seems to have made to age is some loss of sight. This impairment, however, has had as little effect on his life as the announcement of his imminent demise thirty-five years ago. His son Bob Lee accompanied us to his father's home and stayed with us during the interview, encouraging his father's memories, correcting him and sometimes being surprised by stories he'd not heard before—showing a remarkable respect and a tenderness of affection for his father. It was proof to us of the primacy of the family and the respect for elders that is traditional in Chinese families, all the more noteworthy considering the sacrifices Lee Bick made to provide so well for such a large family.

子曰吾十有五而志于學
三十而立四十而不惑五十
而知天命六十而耳順七
十而從心所欲不踰矩

The Master said, "At fifteen I set myself to learning; at thirty I decided on my course; at forty I was free of doubt; at fifty I knew the Decree of Heaven; at sixty I could receive the truth; at seventy I could follow my heart without fear of transgression."

I came to Canada in 1911. I was about nineteen. Lots of people said that Canada was a good country. They talked about *Kam san, Kam san* [Gold Mountain]. I thought Canada must be better than China, so I came.

From about age seven to fourteen I went to school. Then my father died and I went into the business. It was like a drug store. I worked in the drug store for two or three years, then I came to Canada. I did not pay the head tax. I was a merchant. Canada allowed the merchants to come to Canada without paying the head tax.

Did you come to Canada alone?

Two or three people from my village came; I came with them, by boat, the Empress of Japan. From Hong Kong it took about a month to come to Canada. We landed in Victoria, where I stayed I think about three years. . . . And then I went back to China to get married.

What did you do in Victoria?

I worked as a cook in a restaurant. At that time Victoria was very busy, a lot of people, and very busy. Lots of business. . . . There were a lot of Chinese in Victoria.

When you weren't working, on your day off, what would you do?

On my day off I would go to Christian church. I saved my money. I couldn't start a business of my own at that time because my salary was very small. I couldn't do much with the money I had. So I put my money in a bank, the Imperial Bank.

After three years I went back to China. I went back to get married. A matchmaker found me a wife. I never saw my wife before we got engaged. I never even saw a picture.

How did you choose her?

My uncle said she was a good girl. He wrote me in Canada and said this was a good girl for me, and I trusted him. So I agreed to marry her. Two days before I married her I saw her. I thought she was pretty, but we were married by then. I had already agreed to marry her so I had no choice.

And it worked out alright?

Yes, it worked out okay. She was a very good girl. We were happy. We never fought. We had a good life together. She trusted me and I trusted her. And she raised the children well.

How old was she when you married?

I was twenty-one, she was about nineteen. I was two years older. I was born in 1892, she was born in 1894.

How many brothers and sisters did you have?

One brother and two sisters.

Did they stay in China?

Yes.

Did you bring your wife back to Canada?

I came back by myself. After the wedding, I stayed in China about a year. In 1915 or '16 I came back to Canada, by myself—my wife stayed in China.

Back to Victoria?

First to Victoria for about three months, then to Vancouver. There were a lot of jobs in Vancouver. I worked in a restaurant for about one year and then I worked in a store, import and export. I stayed at the import-export business for two or three years, then I started a business myself.

How did you start that business?

Well, I raised a little bit of money with friends—we all put in together. I was the boss because I raised the money, and I had the idea. I opened the business. A lot of good people trusted me.

Why did they trust you?

Oh, because I worked hard. They thought of me as a good person.

What did you sell in your store?

Oh, a lot of Chinese goods.

What do you remember of Chinatown in those days?

Oh, a lot of things. The Tong. At that time Vancouver was not as good as it is today.

Lee Bick 1920

How did the white people treat you?

Pretty good.

What about the riots, do you remember those at all?

No . . . not quite.

Do you remember some of the big merchants like Yip Sang?

Yes, I remember him. I knew Yip Sang before I came to Canada.

Did he help you when you came to Canada?

No, I did it myself.

When did you start your business?

I started the business in 1920 on Pender Street. I had four or five people working for me.

Was it successful?

Oh, it was a bit hard to get going.

When did it start to be successful?

Well, it did better every year.

Do you remember when the government stopped the Chinese from entering Canada?

Oh yeah, in 1923.

How did that affect your business?

Oh, well, it kept going but I couldn't import anything because of the Pacific trouble, you see. It lasted for about one or two years—Japan and China.

How did you survive?

Oh well, we got things locally. Vegetables, fruit, that sort of thing.

Did you continue to go to church?

Yes, sometimes I went to church. The Presbyterian Church. It used to be on Keefer Street; now it's on Cambie Street. Many Chinese went to that church. . . . I learned my English there on my day off.

Did you go back to visit your wife?

No, I had no time.

What was the community's reaction to the Exclusion Act of 1923?

Oh, I've forgotten all about that.

How did they feel?

They weren't happy.

Were they angry?

Yes.

How did your business do through the 1920s?

It was slow. We couldn't get goods from Hong Kong.

Did you still have five people working for you?

Not so many. I cut down.

When did your wife come to Canada?

1928.

That was during the Exclusion Act. How did you manage to bring her over?

I left her in China too long. So I bought some paper. I bought a birth certificate.... Some people returned to China with their children and their birth certificates. I found out who had one and I bought it for my wife. So she could come to Canada.

How much did you have to pay?

Oh, about $2,000 or $3,000.

That's a lot of money in 1928!

Yeah, but my wife was important, you see. I left her in China since 1914. I hadn't seen her since then. I missed her.

How did you get all the money: that was a fortune in 1928.

I saved it at the bank, the Bank of Montreal.

Why did you choose that bank?

It was the bank closest to my store.

Were there Chinese staff at the bank?

The manager was English; everyone else was Chinese.

Did you recognize your wife after all those years?

Sometimes she wrote me.

Did she send pictures?

Yes.

What did she think of Vancouver?

She was very happy to come to Canada.

Did she help you in the business?

She worked at home. Seven children in nine years. It was very busy at home.

Why did you want to have so many children?

Chinese people like big families. I don't know why. Lots of people had big families.

How did your business do through the 1930s?

At that time, I bought Brown Brothers' florist greenhouse, about 1933. The main business was still import and export. . . . Then I started to buy property. Some friends showed me the greenhouse and the farm. I thought it was very reasonable, so I took it.

How much did they want?

About $40,000 for fifty acres on Grandview Highway. I paid so much down, then paid maybe $4,000 or $5,000 a year to Mr. Brown.

How did you raise the money?

I got some friends together. Oh, five or six friends came together.

And your partners at the import-export business, did you buy them out?

No, it kept going.

How did the greenhouse business do?

I grew a lot of flowers and vegetables. I had good Chinese employees. I grew a lot of flowers and vegetables for the market.

Where did you live at this time?

We had a house on 7th Avenue. We rented the house. After a few years I saved a little money and bought a house on the same street.

Did your children help you in the business?

Oh, yes. When the children got big enough, they helped me. The small ones went to Chinese and English school.

Did you speak Chinese at home?

Yes.

You had two businesses—that's a big job. How did you manage it?

I had good help at the greenhouse, a good manager there. I only worked there sometimes, not every day.

What's the secret? You survived a very difficult period—the Depression—how?

Oh, I think everyone should just keep looking for the future to be better. Just carry on hoping for the best, that's all.

Did you expand into other businesses?

Oh, not really. But I raised money to build a Chinese school. I was with the Lee Association and the YWCA.

Why did you do all these things?

Because I was in Vancouver for so long. I wanted to do something for the young people.

When you went to your friends and you asked them for money to build the YWCA *and the Chinese school, did they help?*

Yes, they helped.

Was it difficult getting them to help?

Yes, it was pretty hard. Things were pretty difficult. The economy was not very good in 1940.

What do you remember of the Second World War?

The Second War? . . . I forget.

Do you remember the discussion in the Chinese community about fighting for Canada or not?

. . . Not quite, no.

Do you remember when they took the Japanese, took away their homes and sent them to the interior?

Yes.

What did you think about that?

Oh, it was because of the war, you see. The government did that because of the war.

But what did you think?

Oh, I can't say very much about that now. There used to be a big Japanese Tong in Vancouver in 1940 or 1941.

Did you have very much to do with them?

No, nothing.

Were you frightened that the government might do to the Chinese what they did to the Japanese?

I don't have any opinion on that. I can't say.

What happened after the war?

It got better.

Did you start to buy more property?

Oh, if it was a good piece of property I would try to find the money to buy it.

Did you continue to raise money through your friends?

Yes, little by little.

When did you buy this house?

1948. I saved a little money and the house on 7th was small and not so good. I sold some of the property around the greenhouse, and with that money I bought this house. I still kept the greenhouse and half the land. I got a good price.

Besides buying this house, what did you do with your money? Invest it?

Yes, I made investments. I sent a little money to Hong Kong. . . . My brother was in Hong Kong; he found a good building to buy there.

What did you think about having your children in the business?

If they wanted to do it and if they could do it, why not?

Were you hard on them?

Yes.

When did you retire?

I sold the last part of the greenhouse in 1956. I retired and came to work here at my house in 1957. I built my own little greenhouse here.

What do you grow in your greenhouse?

I raise orchids and gardenias. I like flowers.

What do you think of the head tax issue? There are some people who want the government to give it back.

Oh, I think forget it.

Why?

Because at that time in Canada it was the law. If you wanted to come to Canada you had to pay the tax—it was your choice. Now it's different altogether. Now it's very good for us. You see, I think Canada is such a good place and I'm very lucky to be here. . . . I think we should just forget about the past, that's all.

Have you ever been back to China?

Not to China but many times to Hong Kong.

What do you think will happen to Hong Kong in 1997?

I think the Chinese will come and take over. It's not a good thing.

What do you think of the Communists?

Oh, I don't like the Communists. Little people can't do anything. It's no good. In China a lot of people are saying it's not satisfactory. A lot of people. They don't let you do anything. In Canada and the United States you are more free. You can do anything in Canada, but not in China, no.

What advice would you have for your grandchildren or great-grandchildren?

Get an education. Be happy. Canada is a very good country. In Canada everything can be okay. . . .

Do you think we could take some pictures of you outside in your greenhouse?

Oh, there aren't many good flowers today. . . .

Can we try?

Yeah, okay. . . .

In his younger days, Lee Bick was chairman of the North American Lee's Association and donated land for the construction of the YWCA *in Vancouver's Chinatown. At the age of 90 Lee Bick became chairman of the fundraising committee for the Chinese Community Centre and Public School. He continues to be actively involved in the community even at the age of 99.*

Working in the garden of his home in Shaughnessy, August 1989

Jean Lumb

When she was sixteen years old she was put on a train bound for Toronto with her eight-year-old sister. Her father gave her a ham, a loaf of bread and one dollar to buy something to drink. Jean Lumb and her sister only spent ten cents; at every stop they would get off the train for a cup of water. We asked her what she remembered of the trip to Toronto: "Hard, hard seats, filled-up seats. . . ." Years later, Jean Lumb travelled again, as part of a delegation to Ottawa in the late 1950s to present a brief to Prime Minister John Diefenbaker concerning changes in the Immigration Act. It was not anticipated that she would play a major role. Unexpectedly, she was seated at Diefenbaker's good ear and the official spokesman at his bad one; since that time she has come to be known as the Chinese community's unofficial spokesperson. She has given generously of herself all her life, whether it was supporting her brothers through school, raising her six children or welcoming patrons to Kwong Chow, the restaurant she and her husband established in Toronto's Chinatown in the late 1950s.

樊遲問知子曰
務民之義敬鬼
神而遠之可謂知

Fan Ch'ih asked about wisdom. The Master said, "To do your utmost to fulfil your duties toward others and to respect the spirits while keeping one's distance can be called wisdom."

I was born in Nanaimo, British Columbia. My father was a coal miner in Nanaimo and when the mine closed in 1928 we moved to Vancouver. He got hold of a hundred-room hotel; it was Depression time but he was doing alright.... I started school in Nanaimo. We had to go to a school called Indian School because that's where the Indians and non-whites went. Italians, Blacks, Natives. We didn't know it was called a segregated school but that's what it was.

How did it make you feel, to be discriminated against?

If I think back . . . there were times that we wished we were not Chinese. We seemed to have managed, but just a little later when we got to Vancouver, we were able to go to a regular school. It was still mostly Japanese and Chinese. You see, we lived on Pender Street which was the Chinese area and the Japanese lived on Powell Street and the school was in the middle.

How did your parents help you to understand this discrimination?

My mother and father told us that the white people were devils. Of course, my parents didn't speak English; my father learned a few words but not much. Where he worked in the mine, they were all Chinese people. I remember as a child, living in the Chinatown area, that we only saw these bad people every now and again. I remember one time the white people came through Chinatown and were real devils. We locked all the doors and closed the lights, they came through and broke down fences and marked on the windows and made all kinds of noises and wore terrible masks—they really looked like devils! We found out later that it was Hallowe'en! So we were taught as children to be afraid of them. We were scared of the white people, scared that they would harm us, so we never thought that we would ever have a white friend. So we stayed in our ghettos and played with our own people and spoke our own language.

Were you friends with the Native people?

Oh yes, in Nanaimo. We didn't learn to be afraid of them. We were told we could go with the children but not with the older ones. We were told we should never follow them because they lived in a different place. We were told that if we went with them, we might get lost and might not be able to find our way home, but we could play with the children. . . . Nanaimo was a small town, it was dirt roads wherever we went. We had to go to a Chinese school—there was the regular school and then the Chinese school. That's how important the Chinese culture was during my growing-up days. My father sent us there. In Nanaimo they had to hire their own teacher. They had to get money together and bring this teacher over from China. But in Vancouver we went to a bigger Chinese school, the Wong School; I was a Wong before I was a Lumb. They had different schools for different families.

When did you start to have white friends?

That didn't come until quite late. My father always felt that we shouldn't fear the white people; this is where we settled and where we were going to stay so we were just going to get used to it. He always taught that education was the most important thing in every person's life. Because he had none. He said he didn't have shoes to wear until he was twelve years old. He was a peasant. There's nothing wrong with being a peasant, but living on a farm where there's nothing growing—that's different. A lot of Chinese people brought over to Canada came as cheap labour. He said coming over to Canada was better than starving in China, because there was a famine in China at that time, in Canton. Most of them came from Canton.

Where did his ideas about education come from?

Confucius. He was very strong in Confucius. I think if you asked what religion my parents had it would be Confucius's teachings. If you really go into the books of Confucius, it's almost like a bible where you teach people to be good and to be kind to one another and to learn, to become educated.

Did your father pay the head tax?

No. My mother did, and my husband. My husband came in 1921.

Did he believe that he should be compensated for having paid the head tax?

No, because we had a choice. The Chinese people had a choice, not like the Japanese people who were shoved into the camps and lost everything. My father said that the government had to stop the immigration of people to Canada. So much cheap labour was coming into the country. If there's not enough work for the people already here then it's a bad thing. My father said you're always happy until your job is being threatened. You may have a very good friend, but if they're after your job, you're going to have an enemy because you're fighting for the same bowl of rice. That's why the government put in the head tax, to try to slow down the immigration. And when that didn't work they put in the Exclusion Act.

Your father supported the head tax?

Yes. He thought that it was the only thing they could do. He didn't come right out and say "I'm for it" or anything like that, but he felt it was the only thing the government could do.

But the Exclusion Act was very unfair and hard for families.

Some moved back to China saying, "I don't want to live in a place like this where we're not welcome." A lot left with their families to go back to China, but he always said how happy and glad he was that he didn't. . . . I was born in Canada, but it wasn't until 1947 that we were finally classified as Canadians.

When I got married to my husband, who was from China, I lost my right to Canadian citizenship. And then in 1957 I had to be sworn in again with my husband to become a Canadian citizen, even though I was born in Canada.

How did it make you feel?

The government was making it right. If it had stayed the same then we would have had a right to go out and make a lot of noise. But it changed. I thought, "What do I have to do to be accepted? I'm always looking in from the outside." I was looking from the corners, peeking in. How does one become 'in there' instead of being 'outside'?

How long did it take before you felt you were inside and not looking from the outside?

When we moved to Vancouver I think I might have lost a bit of that 'looking from the outside.' The other thing was doing things to be recognized as part of the community. Of course, the immigration appeal was something my father passed down to me. He died in 1950 but had had the opportunity to vote twice, one local election and one federal. He told me, "Jean, it's the most important thing, this vote." I think he's the person who told me that the government is people and people are us, and if we don't do our part, we're going to hurt our own people and hurt ourselves. He also thought it was important to go for reunification of the families that had been separated by the Exclusion Act. Family was everything to him. We went through some very bad times. He said I can feed the family on 10 cents a day. I can feed the family with a dollar a day. I can feed the family with ten dollars a day, but one thing is for sure, they'll never go hungry. We went through the Depression—terrible times but we never went hungry. He was that kind of man. I remember the first fight my mother had with my father; it was terrible—fighting openly with him.

You had never seen that before?

No. He had a bit of money tucked away and when someone came along with an idea he'd get into it. He would invest in something, some business; he got involved with a lot of little projects that he didn't know anything about and he lost money. My mother was after him because when things got really bad, he finally had to go to her to get some money to help him out with the loss. My mother held onto her purse strings fairly strongly at that time. When you don't always see money and then you see some, you just keep saving it. That was the time my mother told him off.

She said, "Yes, I know, you don't gamble the money away, but you lost it all and are doing some things that you don't even know anything about." My father said, "Yes, but I've seen men who are such bad gamblers, they'll steal their wife's pants and pawn them to pay their debts." He said, "I've never taken your pants away to pawn them." My mother said, "If you ever do that, I wouldn't punish you . . . I'd get your sons to go after you. Don't you ever lose money any more!"

I know we lost the hotel. Things were bad; it was the 1930s. We couldn't pay the rent because the people wouldn't pay us. We moved into a very small place and father in desperation opened a little fruit store on Robson Street in 1932. I was twelve years old and just going into grade six or seven. My parents said, "Jean, we have to talk to you about school." I said, "What have I done wrong?" My father said, "We have to make a decision. We need another person to go to work in the store. It has to be you because your brother, Robert, is a boy and he has to have a little more education to get on in this world."

So you had to go to work?

Twelve years old. In those days there was no law . . . nobody's going to get after you about not going to school.

How did you feel about that?

I cried. I remember that. My father felt very bad and said, "I didn't think Jean would take it so hard." Mother said, "I know, it's because she likes school. . . . She isn't like the older ones who didn't care if they went to school or not, they were anxious to either go to work or get married, but Jean likes school." I had skipped a class and was in the same grade as my brothers. We studied together and were getting along so well. That was my first cry, my first not being happy. But I understood because I was very close to my father.

So I left school and worked in the store for three years until I came to Toronto in 1934. . . . My older sister got married in Hamilton where they were in the restaurant business. They left that business and went to Toronto looking for a fruit store because fruit and grocery stores were becoming popular.

You were sixteen at the time. How did you feel about leaving your family?

Not only that but my mother came to me and said, "I want you to take Dorothy with you." . . . One less mouth to feed and one less person for her to look after. Dorothy was the next oldest, so she could leave. My brothers were too young. I said to her yes, I can take her, but I felt very badly. When my father found out I was going to be given that responsibility he said, "That's a little bit too much for Jean—she's sixteen and to take care of an eight year old. You shouldn't do that . . . we can manage." "No," mother said, "she's going to take her. Jean will be capable. She'll look after Dorothy." So I brought her to Toronto on the train.

What did you think of travelling across the country?

It's the first we ever travelled . . . hard, hard seats, filled-up seats. Three days and four nights, or four days and three nights, and my father cooked a ham and a loaf of bread and gave me a dollar between us for drinks. That was it. And he paid for the fare. And over here, my sister's husband's family picked me up at the station, Union Station. . . .

The store was on Bloor and it wasn't good. Things were still bad . . . 1935. . . . It was still bad so my brother-in-law, who used to be in the restaurant business in Ingersoll, Woodstock and Hamilton, decided we'd sell the fruit store for whatever money we could get and go north and look for a restaurant. So we went off business hunting.

We had a little car with a little wagon on the back that you pulled. We stopped at all the different places. I always remember that the hardest part was Timmins. When we got to Timmins, it was dark and a dirt road. We stayed there for one night. In the morning we woke up and found that the place was completely empty. It was a mining town. We went back to Sudbury, which we liked right away, with the nickel mine there and things were moving.

We found a restaurant there, a place that was called Wimpy Grill, Wimpy . . . with a big hamburger on the sign. I think we paid about $200. It was empty and the person who was renting it out was glad to have someone rent it. So we went in there and the four of us worked, painted and cleaned up and we changed the name from Wimpy to Hollywood. Real style! Hollywood Grill!

Your name is Jean, your brother's name is Tommy. How did your parents come up with these names?

The church. We went to church when we were children. We lived right across from the church. My name is Gin, Toy Gin, but they gave me the name of Jean when I went to the church.

Your parents gave you Chinese names and the church anglicized them.

Yes.

How long did you stay in Sudbury?

Two years. I liked the job. I packed lunches for the miners. Some of them would take us down the mine and show us around; you can't do that now. But there were nights when it got pretty rough in the restaurant because it was pay night. They'd get pretty wild. In those days we had a jukebox in the restaurant and everybody would come round.

My brother-in-law was a very good businessman. He wanted to specialize in fish and chips. There was more money in it than in hamburgers. But business wasn't that good and I wasn't very happy. So I wrote to my closest relative in Toronto—he had a fruit store on Mount Pleasant—and told him I was unhappy and could I come back to Toronto with my sister Dorothy. He wrote my parents and they said it would be okay. So I came back in 1936, '37. It wasn't for very much money, $50 a month or something. But things worked out.

Business got better. So we decided to open another store at Bathurst and St. Clair. Wong Brothers. It was February or March of 1937 and very cold. Business was good and I thought why not bring my brother and sister from Vancouver? My parents were getting on, why not? And then a letter came from my parents and said I was to help support my brother through school. I said I would.

How did you feel about all this supporting of family?

We all helped each other. When we opened the fruit store my cousin and uncle lent me $200 for my share, to be one-third owner of the fruit store. I told them they could take it out of my wages and in due time I would pay for it. But, for the time being, I needed my wages to help support my brother through school. So my older brother came and I told him I could manage $100 a month to support him to go to Parks Air College. And I told my mother that now that the other sisters are working, I won't have to send money any more. They'll support the family and I'll support my brother. And the business grew and things got better, so finally we thought to bring the whole family in from Vancouver, whoever was left.

In 1937 we went house hunting. Even though we didn't feel there was discrimination, there was still the feeling of not wanting the Chinese people to live in certain areas. There were a lot of empty places at that time. We found a place on Davenport. We were so excited, it was our first home. I'll always remember that the first month's rent was $19.50. To us it was wild—all that money! At that time we were earning better money than $50 a month. I think maybe easy $20 a week.

How did you meet your husband?

That's another story. My mother came to Toronto about 1937. In the spring of 1938 she said, "Jean, you're nineteen years old, you know. Girls around that age should get married." She said to me, "Do you have a friend yet?" "What do you mean a friend? I have lots of friends." "No, someone that you'd like to get married to." I said, "No, no, no. I don't have anybody I want to get married to." She said, "Well I'm going to find a matchmaker and find you a nice boy." My mother, after about three months or so said, "Jean, we found someone . . . a very nice boy . . . he's a Lumb, and we are going to bring him to tea today and I want you to dress nice and properly and be nice. And if you don't like him, tell us."

I'll always remember the first time I saw him, he was such a good looking boy.

Between sixteen and nineteen you always have these dreams of Clark Gable and good looking boys . . . and he was. The funniest thing was that he had spats and a long black coat with a band in the back and a fedora . . . big round hat. He was a very good looking man. I said "Wow." When he came for tea he had his uncle with him. For about six weeks he came up to the house every Sunday to tea. We'd go out for a walk and my brothers and sisters would come along, so if he bought me an ice cream he had to buy them one too! And we went to a few shows together and had a good time.

When did you realize you wanted to marry him?

My mother asked if I liked him. She said if I didn't like him I didn't have to see him anymore. I said, "Yes, he's nice. We get along very well." She said, "Well, you're always with your brothers and sisters. Do you feel that you can go out with him by yourself?" I said no.

I was scared. But I continued to see him and finally I said, "Yes, I like him." My mother said that in that case we'll set an engagement date. We've checked him through and this is what we've found. She had gone to the Lumb family organisation and checked him out. He was involved in the dramatic society and was in a show that was coming up to raise money for the war orphans. They said you know he's very quiet and my mother said. "That's fine, Jean talks a lot." And he's got a business. He was also in the fruit and grocery business way out in the west end . . . Eng's Fruit Market. . . . He was in partnership with five others.

Was he older than you?

Ten years older. When he came to Canada he had to lie about his age. He said he was twelve but he was really about seventeen. He had to say he was twelve because if he'd been older they wouldn't have let him in. But my mother said it was okay because my father was ten years older than her. I think my mother really liked him and she really wanted me to be happy.

What was your wedding like?

We had the best wedding of the year. We got married at Knox Church. We got engaged in February 1938 and married in April 1939. When we were officially engaged I finally went out with him, just the two of us. He took me to Basil's on Yonge Street and then to a show. I can't remember what show it was, but that was our first outing alone together. . . .

I remember very well that I was going to Sunday School at Knox Church at that time with a bunch of girlfriends and all my girlfriends wanted to be in my wedding. They'd never been in a wedding . . . ever. All of them were ready to buy their own long dress. They all wanted to be a bridesmaid, but I couldn't have so many bridesmaids. So I think we had twelve girls as usherettes and my sisters lined up to be my bridesmaids and my cousin and my brother as best man. My mother had said that Chinese people get married in halls. I should go to the Lumb Association and get married in there. I said I want a white gown. I want a wedding. I want a flower girl and all that stuff. . . .

I worked until Saturday. The wedding was on Sunday. My mother said, "All your friends are in the fruit business, so if you get married any other day, they can't come . . . they can't leave their work." Well, Knox Church was Presbyterian, and Dr. Ingster was there at the time and he said, "Oh, we don't marry people on Sundays." So I told him my mother said if I didn't get married on a Sunday here, I'd have to get married at a hall. He bent the rules for me and we were allowed to marry in the church. No confetti and no noise, no blowing of horns, and we had to have it after the Sunday School was finished. We had two hundred people and I remember it was $1.10 per person for the catering. After the wedding the close family went to Chinatown for dinner, three tables, $10 a table which was quite a lot of money, and my father paid for it. . . .

Jean Lumb with her mother and husband–to–be shopping for a wedding ring.

In the meantime—this is funny—they had checked up on my husband. They checked his bank account and found he had $1,000 in the bank, that he had a business and didn't gamble, and that he didn't play around with girls, so he's a good boy. The matchmaker told us all this. I found out later that he had borrowed some money from a friend to make it that much. So my mother had said, "I'm not going to give my daughter away for nothing. I want to ask for a $500 dowry." A girl's supposed to be worth $1,000 (like 1,000 gold pieces). So she told the matchmaker "I'm not asking for 1,000 gold pieces, but I would like to have $500 for my daughter." And then my mother helped me to choose a ring. We went to Ostranders out in the west end where he lived and the three of us chose my ring. The ring was $200 and he had to give $500 to my mother for the dowry and so that's $700, right?

He was ruined. . . .

That was all the money he had. The other few hundred he had were borrowed. And then my mother said, "Jean, he has to buy the bed, that's the Chinese custom." If he hasn't got enough money to buy the bed, they claim that he shouldn't get married. By then he was really broke. Well my mother didn't want me to have to just make do. She insisted we find a place of our own, not sharing with others. And then she took me down to Yolles and spent the $500 on all the furniture for our place, a beautiful dining room suite, sofa, everything. . . .

So then on the day of our wedding, in the morning—now we were going to go to Niagara Falls for our honeymoon—but in the morning, a friend of my husband's came to him and said "You better not go to Niagara Falls, there's going to be a showdown at the business." His partners wanted to buy him out because they thought now that he was married he'd bring me in there and there wouldn't be enough to go around.

Well, he was broke. He had no money to buy the others out. The one who came to warn him said "I don't want to be bought out, don't worry about me." So somehow we had to come up with enough money to buy four of them out of the business. I called my father and I said, "Father, we're in terrible trouble here. There's five of them. That's $1,000 total. Only four of them are willing to sell. The other doesn't want to sell, so I need $800 to buy these people out." I said, "What shall we do?" He said, "Oh Jean, don't do anything. I'm coming right over." He came over with a $1,000 bearer bond and said, "I'll take you to the bank. We'll go and cash it and you can buy those goddamn people out!" That's what he said to me. He said, "That's a lot of nerve, trying to put him out on his wedding day." Boy, were they surprised. He just bought them out—the four of them—and that was it. And the fifth remained, the one who warned us, he stayed, and later on got involved in the restaurant with us.

When did you open Kwong Chow?

In 1959, after twenty years in the fruit store. We raised the six children in the fruit store.

Was the restaurant a success from the beginning?

It was hard. It wasn't easy in the beginning but we were very successful. Three different people had owned the restaurant before we took it over. We just took it over through a bankruptcy. We bought it from the landlord for $60,000 and formed a company. I think it was $500 a share and my husband was the biggest shareholder—he had ten shares. Mostly people had one or two shares, but it was all the people in the family. We sold it in 1985. . . .

In the meantime I got a call from the editor of the *Sing Wah Daily News* and he said, "Jean, we're looking for a home for a young boy, sixteen years old. I know you have three sons who would be wonderful company for him. His grandfather passed away unexpectedly. It's only been two months since he's been here from China and he's very much alone. . . . He needs a family."

So we took him in. He was the best thing that happened to me. When we went to pick him up and bring him home he was a pale, lost boy. So thin and skinny. . . and here were my robust and fat children! I said, "Oh my gosh, they're going to think that I'm treating him wrong." But he was the best example for my kids. He was such a role for my son to follow. He took the garbage out. He helped me with everything. So, later on, we got him to be a partner in the restaurant.

What's his name?

Leonard Chong. He's the one we sold the restaurant to with his brother-in-law. . . . I left the restaurant in 1982, when I was sixty-two. I said to my children I've worked since I was twelve. The only holidays I had were having children.

How did you get involved in community work?

Well, I had been working with others in the community lobbying to get the immigration changes. Roland Michener was the MP for Chinatown and he was instrumental in getting the hearings arranged when the Diefenbaker government came in. We couldn't get anywhere earlier because it was the Liberal Party that put this law in and they weren't about to undo something, as much as they knew it was wrong. I had been the president of the Women's Association in the Chinese community since 1940.

In 1957 they had chosen representatives from Vancouver, Toronto and

Montreal to go with Mr. Michener to present the brief. So Mr. Michener came in and he said, "You know, the Immigration Minister is Ellen Fairclough, and you people are going to ask her about family re-unification, you better send a woman along; you better send Jean. If the Immigration Minister was a man, it would be different, but this is a woman and she may have more sympathy if Jean's along. . . ."

So the night before they decided I should go. Roly Michener in the meantime had gone to Ottawa to make arrangements. The guy from Vancouver was a dear old friend of my father's from way back. He was supposed to be the spokesperson, Fun Sing Wong. When he saw me he said, "Jean, I need some help with my brief, my pronunciation and that, could you help me?" I said sure, so he came up to Kwong Chow and we sat down and went through his brief. I had memorized it by heart, then we went through it phrase by phrase. We got to Ottawa and sat down at this big long table at the Commons. Mr. Diefenbaker walks in and says, "Who's the spokesman?" So he sits Fun Sing Wong on one side and then asks me to sit at his other side. There was nothing anybody could do about it.

So then it was time for Mr. Wong to talk. He got very nervous and whatever he said Mr. Diefenbaker couldn't hear him properly. He kept saying, "What did he say?" Of course I knew the brief by heart. I spoke the whole thing through and afterward Mr. Wong said, "You saved the day, Jean." That's when I became the unofficial spokesperson. . . . I only found out later that Mr. Wong had been sitting at Mr. Diefenbaker's bad ear and I was sitting at his good ear.

Tell us about getting the Order of Canada.

JEAN LUMB SITTING AT DIEFENBAKER'S GOOD EAR; DOCK YIP STANDING BEHIND WITH HIS HANDS ON THE PRIME MINISTER'S CHAIR. ROLAND MICHENER STANDING TO THE RIGHT.

First let me tell you about being presented to the Queen in 1967. She was coming for July 1st. I had started a Chinese dance group with my six children, called The Chinese Community Dancers of Ontario. It wasn't for money; we were known to do it for charitable work. They were looking for some dance groups to go to Ottawa. We auditioned for it but I didn't think anything about it. They chose twelve groups, and lo and behold, we were chosen. It so happened my son was getting married June 30th. This was the time we were supposed to be in Ottawa. I was to be presented to the Queen, but I couldn't go because of the wedding. So they said you have to do it, Jean, because it's a command performance. To make it happen, they arranged to have a plane to pick me up and take us back to Toronto. But the funny thing is the next day they had to take us back to do the performance. Imagine!

What happened when you got the telegram telling you you'd received the Order of Canada?

I was pretty excited.

The first thing was what was I going to wear! Thank goodness I had this Hong Kong jacket. I had it made in 1965 and I got the Order of Canada in 1976 and I'm still wearing that gown for all my weddings and that.

I went to Ottawa with my husband. They sent me a letter telling the particulars about which hotel to stay in, the Chateau Laurier, and they also allowed so much for travelling expenses. The night before we had a little party and my friends gave me a corsage to wear. You know they're very strict about protocol, so I asked them if I could wear my corsage during the ceremony. Nobody else had a corsage. I was the only one with a corsage. It was quite thrilling. I thought I was going to have weak knees when I was standing there waiting. You know you have to stand there and they tell you what you're nominated for. The two things mentioned were the immigration changes to allow families to be reunited, which is the most important one, and the other was the saving of Chinatown. I feel very strongly that a lot of people were responsible for it besides myself. It just happened that they chose me, just like the way I was chosen to speak up in Ottawa.

How difficult has it been to hold onto Chinese traditions and language?

I think deep down we know that we'll lose a lot of it. A lot of people think that if you don't speak your language and retain your writing and reading in Chinese, slowly you will lose it. I gave my children the opportunity, I sent them to Chinese school, but it's hard. But because I tried, they do retain a certain amount of it.

What do you think of the language question in the country?

I think the only people that are having problems are the French. The other multicultural groups are not involved with that type of a thing, but once again, it's a fight for survival, right? The harder you try to keep your children holding on to a culture, the easier it is for them to reject it.

Do you think what they're doing is futile?

No. I think they have to hold on to what they have. The Chinese people feel the same way. What's going to become of my children? They don't even speak Chinese. People think in another generation the Chinese culture will be completely wiped out, the traditions and culture. And then there's the question of interracial marriages; some accept it, some don't.

Your children have married other than Chinese. What happened the first time one of them brought home a Caucasian?

One of my daughters was scared to bring a non-Chinese boy home, because she thought mommy wouldn't like it.

Was it mommy she was frightened of . . . or daddy?

No, I think mommy was the one. Her father was very easy going. He was Chinese, but he would accept a westerner faster than I would because he was that type of man. The thing is, I was firm with them when they were twelve years old . . . about going out on dates with any boys, not necessarily a white boy or whatever colour. You'll have to realize that at that time no Chinese boy would take a teenager out. They just didn't date. That's how the families were brought up. . . . They wouldn't date until they were ready to talk about marriage. I told them they could go out as a group, to a function, but not out alone with a boy. I said maybe when you're older, past sixteen, I would allow you to have serious dates. It's not because I don't want you to marry them, it's just that it's too soon . . . you don't know what you want yet.

What kind of discussions did you have about interracial marriage?

We talked about it because we had talked about it with our parents. My parents said that it would be a second-class citizen who would marry a Chinese man because that man probably already had a wife in China. This was due to the Exclusion Act of 1923. The husbands were stuck here with their wives back in China. There were very few Chinese women in Canada at the time so if a man would marry it was probably going to be a Caucasian. So the ones that could afford it would start living with a woman, or marry here and sometimes even have a family. The Chinese people termed them as halfbreeds, and if you're a halfbreed you're really not accepted into the Chinese community.

And was the assumption that the white community wouldn't accept them either?

I don't think they thought much about that. There was so much discrimination earlier on. You have to remember that the Chinese restaurateurs were not allow to hire white girls to work in their restaurants, so you would feel that if we can't even hire the whites to work, how can we let our son or grandchildren marry one?

What happened if the children brought home a white date?

Some people would drive the children out of the house, they wouldn't accept it.

But in your family?

In my family? No. Never. I would just want them to be sure about their feelings, that's all. I remember one of my daughters would take the side street in the hope that I wouldn't see the boy walking her home. One time I looked out of my kitchen window and saw her walking along with a boy. She said, "Oh, did you see him?" I said, "Yes, why didn't you bring him in?" She thought I wouldn't approve. I said, "Listen, children, I'm not that hard on you. It was only when you were young and I wanted you to wait."

Did the children ever have problems with the parents of the boys or girls they went out with?

There have been some. Problems like the girl would be outcast. Even as late as today there are still some families that will not accept it. It is better now. I think with education, if the parents are educated it'll be easily accepted. I was always for it if they were happy. They used to say, "Just you wait Jean, when it happens to you you won't feel the same." I said "Oh no, I can't see how I could. If you love your children, you just want them to be happy." I did say to my children, "Don't you just show up one day with a stranger and say we're married, I don't want that." I said, "Bring them home. I'd like to see them and if I like them, I'll say I like them, but if I see some faults with them, I'll tell you. And then if you still want to marry them then that's your business. . . ."

You once said that if you were to marry again you wouldn't marry a Chinese man. Why?

Yes, I said that. I don't know. I've always felt very comfortable with non-Chinese.

Why? What's the difference?

Well, I never had a date until I was matchmated to my husband, but it was as much what my parents wanted in a husband as anything I wanted. . . . But it was a very happy and a family-raising type of a marriage. And I was lucky because I had a man who was willing to do different things along the way. But then, I've seen some very, very unhappy marriages—Chinese marriages—because of the difference in thinking.

The way the man wants the woman to be?

Yes, that's right. My mother was right. She said, "You marry a Chinese man, you live in a 2 x 4 and you'll stay in a 2 x 4. You won't have anything more." That's the way they are, you see. I felt if I let my husband do as he pleased, he'd possibly wear the same jacket every single day. I knew that so if I wanted him to change his shirt, I had to take it away at night and replace it with a clean one. If I wanted his pants changed, I had to steal them from him at night and put fresh ones out. My husband was an amazing man. He became the best dressed man and he let Studio 267 clothiers look after all his needs. Mother taught me a lot and I really think I'm like my mom, but I married my husband because he was a lot like my father.

What do you think of the new wave of immigration from Hong Kong?

They're much more affluent. They have a lot of money to spend. It's been good for Canada to have all these newcomers, but I'm afraid there might be a backlash. There's going to be too much money put into areas where possibly it's going to affect people's jobs or positions. I don't know . . . I'm a little scared of it being too powerful. . . . It used to be said that my children would walk on the street and everyone would know who they are because they look like me. That's the way it was. But today, if we go into a restaurant, we don't see a familiar face. I think earlier my main concern was to be accepted into this Canada . . . being a Canadian. And I feel we succeeded without really pushing to get where we are. But today all of a sudden, we have these new people who are ready to push. They say they'll push for everything they want. They don't care. They'll speak up and there's not that same type of getting along. I think if we were in that situation earlier, I don't think we would have been able to go to Ottawa and appeal peacefully for the changes. We didn't even have to carry placards—not until we were trying to save Chinatown did we do that.

Is it a question of style?

They want every bit of their Canadian rights to do what they want to do and yet they're newcomers to me. And it all takes time, that's what I say.

What do you think of the future, the future for your family, yourself?

For myself . . . my days are numbered, but I can visualize the future very, very well. I can see Canada as continuing to be the best place in the world to live. We have many young people with good educations and opportunities. There's always a tomorrow and we should not lose faith or trust in it. . . . I would like to travel, but there's nothing like home. . . . Even when I went to China, I thought I was going to find my roots. I'll go back to Canton and walk into my father's village and find my roots . . . and by gosh, there's no feeling of roots . . . just amazement exists . . . and my father's home. And when I came back, when I arrived in San Francisco, I was glad to put my feet down on my old ground. My roots are in North America. We're very compatible with Americans, our lifestyles are very much the same, so we have to learn to get along with them . . . no matter what happens.

Do you see the future as being positive?

Yes. You bring up your children and you think you've done the right thing and later on you think "I should have done this, or I should have done that." My father used to say our parents have to be good parents before we have good children. I have three sons and three daughters and they are wonderful and we are a very happy family, just like my parents.

You always mention your father with great affection.

Yes, and also because my husband was very much like him.

And your mother?

My mother was so busy raising twelve children. Later, after I was married, we became very, very close and she was a great influence for my happy married life. I learned a lot from her and I think now how very much I'm like her. I love them very much that they made me what I am.

Do you still miss them?

Yes. My father died in 1950 and my mother died in 1971 and I still miss them. I always go visit them, at the cemetery, we have their pictures there, mother and father. . . . I always taught my children to go there at Easter . . . no matter what the weather or whatever . . . Christmas and Easter we go. We each carry a flower and put it on the grave. My husband died when he was eighty. He had worked hard and we enjoyed a good ten years of travelling and spent some wonderful times with the family. . . . My children have worked hard. I don't have to worry about them sitting back and letting someone else do it, because that's the way they were brought up. Now it's their turn. I'm very proud of them. I have nine grandchildren, and they are my life and my joy every day. It's up to the mothers, isn't it . . . to be a good mother . . . and you've got to be a good father. . . . Yes, it's true, isn't it? . . .

Jean Lumb was awarded the Order of Canada in recognition of the work she did to change Canada's immigration policy. She is also recognized as a central force in the preservation of Toronto's Chinatown and for her Chinese Dance Group which led her to be presented to Queen Elizabeth II.

Bob Lee

Like his father, Lee Bick, Bob Lee is a businessman of conspicuous achievement. Lee Bick began to build the Lee family fortune before the Chinese were able to vote, practise law or even own property in certain sections of Vancouver—a great irony in that both father and son have had their greatest successes in real estate. Upon the firm foundation established by his father, Bob Lee has built an impressive edifice, a thriving real estate empire, in which he is now being joined, to his great satisfaction, by his children. For our interview, Bob Lee was open and friendly and remarkably accommodating to us, considering the pressures and demands of his many interests, and his many contributions to the community.

子曰道千乘之國
敬事而信節用
而愛人使民以時

In guiding a state of a thousand chariots, approach your duties with seriousness of purpose and sincerity, love those around you, be prudent and employ only those necessary to complete the work at hand.

I was born in Vancouver in 1933. We lived in Chinatown, and we spoke Chinese at home and English when we were outside the house. By the time I reached school age, we'd moved to 7th and Cambie Street, near False Creek. I went to school next to the city hall, where City Square is today. My dad thought it would be a better environment there.

Did you experience culture shock of any kind moving out of Chinatown?

No, the area we moved into wasn't the most high class area. It was a blue collar area so we fit in quite well.

What do you remember of school?

Oh, school. . . . I went to elementary school, then I went to high school—King Edward High—and I'm probably one of the few who continued on to university. My father felt we had to be well educated. He wasn't, so naturally, he wanted the children to be, especially the boys. But today, everybody goes to school regardless of whether it's a boy or a girl.

What did you study at university?

Well, my dad was in real estate and also in commerce, so I thought the most logical thing for me was to take a Bachelor of Commerce degree. Of course, I had worked for my father since I was very young—after school and Saturdays and whenever the store was open.

What were the drawbacks to that?

We didn't get a chance to participate in sports or anything like that. It wasn't easy working for Dad because he was very demanding, as most fathers are. We didn't get paid and you had to be conscientious and be there. That was part of life.

What do you remember about your father's business?

My father opened his store in 1920, the company he had until he retired. The business thrived and became one of the six largest importing companies in

BOB LEE AND FAMILY

Vancouver. The Foo Hung Company. We had about thirty employees. But during all this time, he dabbled in real estate. Agents would always be coming by the store and telling him about different opportunities. I was always very interested in that, so I would listen in. One thing that he did: he bought a greenhouse that was under bankruptcy in 1933, the year I was born. As it turned out, that piece of property was zoned industrial and my dad sold it after the war—actually in the late 1950s—for a handsome profit.

British Columbia was a particularly racist province at that time. What would you hear about that in the home?

Dad really never. . . well, he'd say a few things but nothing that we wouldn't hear about today. . . . I think each generation looks forward and is always improving. . . . When I graduated in 1956 I had one job offer. . . . Out of a class of maybe a hundred, I had only one offer, whereas my fellow students received many, many offers for jobs. I guess even at that time they didn't want to hire Chinese people for executive positions.

What was Vancouver like in 1956?

It wasn't bad. It was . . . I never experienced any recessions because Dad supported us. . . . When I left college, I thought I'd go out and set the world on fire. I got a job and got paid as much as anyone else did, but my expectations were a lot higher. I wanted to do better. When I was in school they said if you didn't make it by the time you were forty you'd never make it. I thought that didn't give me many years and so I'd better hustle and make sure it happened.

What about your brothers and sisters?

My sisters didn't go to university but my three brothers did.

Are they as ambitious as you?

Yes, in different areas. My youngest brother, Bill, is a physicist and has been a professor at a university in Taiwan for years. My oldest brother, Jack, is a lawyer and my other brother, George, is in the furniture and restaurant business.

What sort of religious training did you have?

My parents were Buddhists so we were brought up in that atmosphere. I would go once or twice a year to the Buddhist temple to pray.

Have you visited the village where your father was born?

I've been to Canton, but his village was just too far for me to visit at that time. Hopefully, I'll get there soon.

Your ancestors are all buried there?

Yes. And the house where my father was born is still there. He's very devoted to the area, so he gives money for building schools and so on.

Were you always involved in real estate?

Well, at the beginning I was involved with my dad, which was in importing; I started my real estate career in 1959 when I joined a company called H. A. Roberts on a strictly commission basis, which was kind of hard to take after you're used to a salary, but at that time no company in Vancouver was paying salaries to real estate salesmen.

When did it start to really become an exciting, charged atmosphere for real estate in Vancouver?

I would say in the 1960s. . . . I remember before I started on my own, when I was still working for my dad, we had a drapery business and I was installing some drapes in a house in the British Properties. You know that Chinese people weren't allowed to live there because of certain covenants on the properties. Well, I was installing these drapes and I looked out the windows and this place had such a great view and I said to myself, one of these days I'd like to live on this block. In 1973 I bought a house there and have lived there ever since.

You said it was difficult in the beginning working on straight commission. Was it the real estate market or the economy generally?

No, it was a good market. It was just tough. I've been through five recessions. You have to plan for them if you're going to survive.

I worked for H. A. Roberts until 1967. Then I met a fellow named Peter Wall, and I gave him an offer without any subjects on a property he was selling. He was impressed and wanted to meet me. . . . Normally, you make an offer with a subject period. In this case we purchased without any condition. Peter Wall was impressed with the way the transaction was negotiated. Because of this, he wanted to form a new company and have me as a partner. They were primarily developers so it complemented what I was doing. I was more on the real estate brokerage and financing end of the business. I stayed there for ten or twelve years and the company is still doing very, very well. I still own part of the company.

Did you ever consider going to your father for some money to start on your own?

It would have been quite easy. My father would have been receptive if I had gone to him and asked him for some money. But when you have three brothers and three sisters . . . well, my brothers and sisters might feel that it wasn't really my success because I'd used Dad's money. So I raised my own money. I also continued to look after the family's assets and investments.

What lucky breaks did you have that helped you along the way?

In the mid-'60s I was very fortunate to have been put in contact with some gentlemen from Hong Kong who were interested in investing in Canada. My banker came to me and said this gentleman in Hong Kong is looking for real estate. As it turned out, he bought $50 million worth of real estate from me in the 1960s. That gave me a jump in the business and my name became well known. I eventually had about a half dozen who brought me enough business to keep me very busy. You would know them; a lot of them are Canadians today.... At the time they were investing here as a kind of insurance policy; their principal interests remained in Hong Kong. In the 1960s there weren't that many, but a few were thinking further ahead for the future of their families.

They came to me through referrals and also through the publicity I was getting for some of the major deals I did at the time. I negotiated a building that belonged to our former mayor, Tom Campbell, in 1964 for about $2.5 million—residential. It was quite steady until the 1970s—then I started to get younger people coming to me. It was getting closer to 1997 and their fathers were encouraging them to come here. Quite a few of them were educated here.

How has it changed?

Well, today you've got a lot of younger people who are very knowledgeable, so my role is not as important as it was, say twenty-five years ago when it first began and they were unfamiliar with the country and the business. Now I'm sort of a conduit to sort of help them get established here.

What was it about you that drew them to you?

Well, there were others they could have gone to, but maybe I was one of the few Chinese in the business at that time.

How did you hook up with David Lam?

In 1967 I met Dr. Chan Shun, who was good friends with David Lam, and he said, "I want you to meet a gentleman, a very good friend of mine, David Lam." So I met with him and Dr. Chan encouraged David to join our firm. He became a partner and we were together for eleven years, from 1967 to 1978. He would have the clients and I would have the product.

Was he as skilled with people as he is today?

Very much so. He had all the makings to be a successful person no matter what he did, but particularly at real estate. The only thing lacking was that he didn't know the local people at that time, and that's where I came in. It worked out really well. We negotiated a lot of buildings together. I would say ninety-odd percent of the people I've done business with are friends of mine or partners.

Is that typical of the real estate business?

No, it's not typical. The reason why it's so for me is that I've been fortunate to have been able to accumulate some cash to be partners with some of these people. Normally, that's a pretty difficult thing to do. These people are wealthy because they pay seventeen percent tax and we pay fifty percent here.

How would you and David Lam handle a client?

I would sit down and talk to the client and get a good feel of what he wanted; I also had the product. Then we would negotiate. David would do the negotiating with a bit of my help. In fact, the building he's living in now in Vancouver I negotiated. He only owned half of it because the gentleman that I knew from way back, who was in the construction business, wouldn't sell it to me. So finally I talked him into selling half of it, and when he died his wife sold the other half. It took him a while, but David eventually owned the whole building.

How aware are the Hong Kong Chinese with which you do business of the negative press they've received in B.C., and how has it affected your relations with them?

They are quite aware of it, but I think it's exaggerated by the press. . . . The thing is this: when my father came over he was a houseboy and a labourer, so the average person would say oh, he doesn't bother us; we need that kind of people. Now we're attracting very wealthy Chinese and when they come into town they buy the most expensive home, or two and three expensive cars, and if you're a local person you take a look and say, why can't I have that? It's a two-way street. It's up to the people who are coming here not to overdo it, and I think it's up to us as Canadians to slowly understand what's happening.

Do you address this question with your clients?

Yes, I said to David Lam that hopefully they'll make a tape for all the new immigrants and even show it in Hong Kong and the Far East to show how Canadians live, to try and soften the blow for each side.

Has it frightened away investment?

I would say it has. We were going to do a condominium project, a very large one in Burnaby, and we had everything signed and ready to go, but the principal in Hong Kong heard about this backlash against the Hong Kong Chinese and he backed out of the deal. It was a couple of hundred units. We were going to market it here first—he was just one of our partners. . . . He like the project, but he didn't like the publicity that would happen if they were involved.

What do you think the new Hong Kong immigrants could do to help alleviate the backlash?

I think that we have to encourage them to participate in the community, like universities and charitable organisations.

How and when did you come to be involved in the community?

Well, when you're in business in your thirties, that's all you think about–trying to complete projects and sales. When I was in my forties, I thought it over and said, well, I think I've done maybe eighty percent of what I'd like to do, but there's so much more I'd like to accomplish. When David Lam retired he said to me, "Bob, I'm retiring. I'm going to set up a foundation. I'm going to give things away while I'm alive." I thought it was a great idea, but I thought I was too young to do that. . . .

I was asked to be a Governor at UBC. I said no and then I thought it over and I said to myself, there's a recession on—it was 1981—and I probably won't do much real estate anyway. So I accepted the job and I really enjoyed it because it was working with people I didn't usually come in contact with—academics and so forth. I couldn't help them academically. The only area I could be of help was with real estate. I saw a thousand acres on the campus and I said well, maybe I could develop part of it and help generate some income for UBC. I was the head of the property division and the finance division and it took me two or three years to convince the Board that it was a good way to raise money. To make a long story short, we divided twenty-eight acres into ten sites and we sold two sites for approximately $15 million on a ninety-nine-year lease. In ninety-nine years, UBC will still own the land. Hopefully, by the end of four or five years, if the economy keeps on going up the way we project, we will generate $5 million plus to the university annually.

You said earlier that in university they said that if you hadn't made it by the time you were forty you wouldn't make it. Did you have a time, when you were forty or so, when you asked yourself, what have I done this all for?

I think business has to be fun, and I think I was fortunate enough to be in a field where I met a lot of people and we had a lot of fun. Unless you have that, business is boring. And by the time I was forty we were doing business all over North America. We did a lot of large buildings—one in San Francisco called Watergate. It was a $70 million deal.

What drives a businessman to go after more interesting deals and more money?

It gets to a point where money is only one part of it. I could probably retire and live off what I have and have nothing to worry about. But I need a challenge, so it becomes more a question of the challenge after a while. In the last three or four years I've decided to start working more in the community.

Members of the Chinese community are becoming more and more involved in high profile philanthropy and community participation. Why now?

Well, there just weren't many wealthy Chinese families. I mean, they all came over as farmers and so it took them a while to accumulate. If they did give money it was usually within the Chinese community or to the village in China where they're from. Their contacts and circle of friends was more limited, whereas for me, probably sixty percent of my business is with Caucasians.

How many children do you have?

Four—they're aged twenty-seven to thirty-two.

Are they involved in the business?

Three of them are.

How did they come to be involved?

When they were growing up we always said "You have to go to college and that's it," so they all went to college and graduated in urban land economics, which is a real estate option at UBC. I mentioned accounting to all of them but it was only my youngest who took me up on it. They all liked real estate because of the exposure they had to it in the 1960s and '70s; they were excited by it and all really looked forward to going into the business. I was very happy about that, but I always liked them to go out and get their own experience first, and then maybe after five years come into the family business.

My eldest son, Derek, didn't want to do that. He came into the business in 1981. My daughter graduated and worked for the company and then worked for Daon before deciding to go back for her MBA. She got her MBA at Harvard and worked for an American company for three years. She decided to come back last year. . . . My eldest son started from the bottom up. I sent him to Houston, Texas. We had a building that of nine hundred units, four hundred were vacant, and I told him to fill them up. So he went down there and stayed for six months and every other phone call he would say, "Dad, when can I come home?" I said, "Not yet." He really learned the trade. He's doing very well. He's a broker in the company and he does very well. My second daughter, my third child, Leslie, worked for me for two years, but she didn't like the business very much; she prefers the fashion business. She works for Holt Renfrew in Toronto as a buyer. My youngest son graduated in accounting and when he came out of school he wanted to start something on his own, so he started an immigration fund. He did all the research, all the work, put everything together. I help him with the directors and the type of investments because he doesn't really have the experience yet. We started that two years ago and we've invested sixty percent of the money. I am very proud of him.

What's the secret? How do you avoid destructive conflicts?

I come from a big family—I have three brothers and three sisters. I know exactly how my children would feel and I'm sensitive to that, so I try to see things from their point of view. Maybe sometimes I'm a little short with them compared to an employee, but I try not to be that way.

Your company is wholly owned by the family?

Yes, the family, my own family—my children, my wife, myself—whereas my father's assets are owned by my brothers and sisters, too. So we separate it all.

When you retire, if you do, do you see your children continuing in this business?

Yes. I'm trying to steer each one in his or her own line of business within the framework of the family company.

Are you a grandfather yet?

Yes, I'm a grandfather—two granddaughters.

What do you see happening in 1997? What will happen in Vancouver?

If interest rates stabilize, I would say in 1994 or '95 there will be so much activity in Vancouver and Canada from the Pacific Rim that it will blow your mind. Right now, people in Hong Kong are still making fairly good income and they're taxed at a very low rate, so the marginal players are still waiting. When the deadline comes, they're going to move. I think it will be a flood.

You're quite pessimistic about Hong Kong.

Not as much today because they've decided to build the airport. But I would say if I lived in Hong Kong I would definitely move. They've allowed for it to continue for fifty years, but I think what you have to do is think of your family and the future. If you're going to make a move you might as well make the move. You can still have interests in Hong Kong, it's just that it's wise to have some outside of Hong Kong, too.

Your father came to Canada at the time of the head tax and became successful; you've built on that success and become a leading member of the community. What is it to you to be a Canadian?

I was born here, so I'm a Canadian first. Secondly I'm Chinese, and if I want to follow traditions, fine. But I have to be a Canadian first.

What is a Canadian?

A Canadian—you have to adopt the Canadian lifestyle and also the Canadian way of life. It's hard to explain . . . I'm proud to be Chinese, but prouder to be a Canadian. . . .

Of all of Bob Lee's achievements, he is most proud of the creation of the U.B.C. Real Estate Corporation. The University of British Columbia had 28 acres of vacant land that it could not sell, did not have any money to develop and did not want to take any risk. Under Bob Lee's direction, the land was sold on a prepaid lease basis for 99 years. The acreage should now generate 5 million dollars income per year for the university.

I n 1988 the Honourable David See-Chai Lam was appointed British Columbia's twenty-fifth Lieutenant-Governor, an honour far beyond his modest dreams when he immigrated to Canada two decades earlier. Dr. Lam left an established career in banking in Hong Kong and came to Vancouver in 1967 with his wife and three young daughters to begin a new career, embarking on a life that would lead to unimaginable financial success and social distinction. Discipline, openness of mind and a trenchant understanding of human nature are perhaps the key ingredients to his success. David Lam has risen to one of the highest offices in Canada, a position formerly reserved for members of the Anglo-Saxon establishment. He brings to this position a deep attachment to his Chinese heritage, a subtle blend of Christian and Confucian philosophies and the firm support of his cherished wife Dorothy.*

When you meet someone superior try to equal him; when you meet someone inferior look inwards and examine yourself.

I was born September 2nd, 1923 in Hong Kong. But actually, that's not my birthday; my birthday is July 25th. My father's secretary forgot to register my birth, and when he got around to it they said no, you cannot—too much time has passed. So without telling my parents he said, "Okay, just put down the day's date—September 2nd." He came back with the certificate and handed it to my father sealed in an envelope. My dad and mom never said anything about it until I applied for my passport. My mother said, "Wait a minute—it wasn't September 2nd, it was July 25th." And then the story came out about the secretary, the absent-minded secretary. . . . My father had come to Hong Kong from a place called Shantou which is I think one hundred eighty-odd miles to the east of Hong Kong along the coast. He had married my mother in Shantou, China, and had moved to Hong Kong to get a job and to start a family.

Why did they leave China?

They left because things were extremely poor around the Shantou area and my grandfather, being a minister, a pastor, of a small Baptist church, really could not support a big family. So my father wanted to try his luck and come to Hong Kong.

How did your grandfather become a Baptist minister?

My grandfather started his career as a village school teacher. At that time, missionaries were considered to be rich and powerful, and it was decided by the village elders that someone from the village had to join them. It was decided at a village meeting by the elders: "So and so, you will become a Christian tomorrow." That's how they chose my grandfather. He attended the meeting, raised his hand and said, "Hallelujah," but that failed to bring good fortune to the village. The elders told him to try harder. The missionary suggested that he go to the seminary which was, oh, about twenty miles from the village, and so he went. It was in the seminary that he became converted and became a Christian. So, my grandfather became a Baptist minister; my father was a layman, but a very strong layman, a volunteer.

What are your memories of growing up in Hong Kong?

I remember my father working very hard. He left home very early and came home very late. On Sundays we went to church, and to Sunday school. Every day we had to swim for our exercise and three times a week an elderly gentleman, a true Chinese scholar, would come and teach us Chinese philosophy and Mandarin. Mandarin is the proper Chinese, not Cantonese.

What school did you attend?

The first was a kindergarten called Ying Wa, a missionary school. Then I went to the YMCA for primary school and then to Pui Ying School, which is a very well known Baptist school.

How did you reconcile these very different philosophies, the Baptist faith and the classic Chinese philosophers?

I never thought about it. As a youngster you are like blotting paper, soaking up whatever is given to you. It was much, much later—I would say only in the last twenty years or so—that I've had an opportunity to reflect on so many things that I've started to think about how the two philosophies, the Chinese teachings and the Christian faith, could really get together and work together.

Was there an incident that caused you to see that or was it something that had been cooking away inside?

Oh, no—not cooking away. The incident, if any, would have been in the early 1950s when I started my working career. I had kept largely to myself, very much to myself, not at all outgoing. I soon decided that's no way to go through life. I started sort of breaking out, going to be with people; so I joined a Rotary Club. I had good training in the Rotary Club; it gave me the opportunity to meet many, many people. The theme of the Rotary Club has always been Service above Self, to serve others.

How did you come to choose banking as a career?

I didn't actually choose banking; my love has always been agriculture. Horticulture to be exact. If I'd have had free will to choose what I would study, I probably would not have gone into economics or business administration. I would have gone straight into horticulture.

How did this love of horticulture develop?

When I was in high school, I happened by some old book store—actually a junk store—where they sold old newspapers and magazines from abroad. For a couple of pennies I was able to pick up some seed catalogues. I had not seen in my life anything more beautiful than those flowers. I would read the catalogues and enjoy the flowers.

Is that also how you picked up or polished your English?

Not really. I learned about colours and how to describe a flower. But, language is a living thing. Unless one gets a chance to use it one could never fully develop it. In Hong Kong there was little opportunity to develop the living language as there was little need for speaking English.

When one studies English, or any language for that matter, the system has always been that first you learn the grammar. In my case I was drilled in the grammar according to Nesfield. Everybody used the Nesfield English grammar textbook in those days. It's torture because it's a dead thing: 'I do, you do, he does'—you know, that kind of thing. So this is the dead way; the living way is to use the language to communicate with people, everyday language, street language—and we had no opportunity to do that. Not until I left Hong Kong.

You said that you would have chosen horticulture if you'd had the free will or opportunity. How did you come to find yourself in banking?

I needed a job—let's put it that way. I needed a job and it was available, and so I said to myself, I will do a good job at it. Let me just do it.

But it was not as fulfilling as one would hope one's job to be?

Sometimes in life you're given a task not of your own design. Then you start learning about the job, finding out, and then it's a matter of 'adopt, adapt and improve', I guess. You adopt something, maybe not of your own free will; you adapt to it—you say okay, I got this job; and then you say how can I improve it so that I will enjoy it and so that I can do a better job? That has always been my philosophy.

That attitude requires a certain amount of maturity—to profit from what is delivered to one in life.

I have never thought of it as maturity; it is just a natural thing. I either take on the job or I don't. And if I take it on, do I go to work and drag my feet through the day looking at work as some sort of a chore and a torture, or do I try to enjoy it?

You were a banker for seventeen years; what made you decide to retire from it?

To begin with, I love horticulture and in dating my wife I found out that she also loved it. After we were married we spent most of our leisure times in the country, mostly hiking in the hills in the New Territories of Hong Kong. There is a big belt of dikes to catch all the rainwater and channel the water to the reservoir. It's a good area to walk and we spent a lot of time doing that. One day the Anglican Bishop of Hong Kong, Bishop Hall, invited my wife Dorothy and me to his home for afternoon tea. His home was on the top of a mountain. It was quite high, several hills up. When we arrived at his home we found it to be a Chinese-style cottage with a beautiful garden and a small swimming pool, sixty goats, thirty turkeys, a lot of chickens and a few dogs. . . .

A paradise. And we said, "Bishop Hall, Mrs. Hall, this is paradise. We haven't found anything in Hong Kong that we like better." Then he said, "We are going to England on furlough for one year. If you like, you can come stay here while we're away and if you pay a nominal rent to the church you can have it." We actually spent about fifteen, sixteen months up there in heavenly bliss. Every day we took lots of flowers from the garden. We even had goat's milk for the children. It was just totally, totally, totally heaven.

So, we said we could not go back to the city and started looking for and bought a small, small lot—very small—around that area, and we built a small house there with a big garden. We enjoyed that; we loved it until the city started to grow and we saw the fields of flowers and the market gardeners that we had gotten to know so well—that we visited almost every other day—one by one they were gobbled up by the growth of the city. People would buy the gardens and turn them into storage yards for gasoline drums–can you imagine? It was totally appalling. Then, before you know it, the whole garden, the whole valley—it was so beautiful and so green–it turned into a huge open storage of junk steel and drums and wood piles, and so we said we've got to go, we've got to move away. . . .

But then we looked around and asked ourselves, how long will it be before it's all taken over? We had to either change our thinking or move away. Well, I had just finished a very difficult project of building a bank building and when it was done I said, okay, we'll take three months off and travel. We went to Australia, New Zealand, Tahiti, and then came over to Seattle and British Columbia—to Victoria and to Vancouver. That was 1961. After we came to British Columbia we said let's look no further—this is it!

It's so impressive. . . . We continued with our trip around the world and when we got back to Hong Kong, luck would have it that we got to meet the Canadian High Commissioner and I told him, "I love your country. When I retire, I'll go there." He said, "When will that be?" I said, "Well, I'm forty; in another twenty years or so." He said, "Ah, that's not the right way, that's not the right attitude. One shouldn't retire to a new, completely new environment. One should go and make friends and get to know the place. And then retire." It made a lot of sense.

By then a path near our garden had turned into a truck route—all day long trucks coming up and down; it was just killing us. We used to not even have locks on our gate to the garden. And the people by that time would help themselves to flowers from our garden and would drop garbage all over the place—it was just murderous. We said okay, that's it. So I went to the Commissioner and said, "It makes sense, I want to go to your country, but I'm not sure I can make a go of it." He said, "It doesn't matter. You can always come back to Hong Kong." "But," I said, "I cannot go to your immigration office to stand in line and be seen applying for a visa. There will be a run on the bank if I'm seen standing in line to get a visa." He said, "I understand." So he sent an application to our home and we filled it out and sent it back. That was in 1965 or '66.

How much did the other changes going on in Hong Kong at the time, the political changes and riots, affect your decision to leave?

It was more a question of our lifestyle. How did we want to live for the rest of our lives?

Was there concern for the future of your three children?

Only in the sense of wanting them to learn as much of their Chinese heritage and culture as possible before we left. Instead of preparing them for English, we fed them more Chinese. Looking back—this is almost sad . . . sad in the sense that you're going to be starved for your Chinese, so let's feed you more now.

How did you meet your wife?

We had known each other from an early age. You see, our fathers were schoolmates. I remember when I was a youngster in high school I used to grow a lot of flowers and when they were in harvest I would send bunches of flowers to all my friends, and then my parents' friends, and I remember having sent, on more than one occasion, flowers to Dorothy's family because they were my parent's friends. But then she's seven years my junior. . . . The gap was too great. Only when a person is sixty-seven and she's sixty—as it is now—do you catch up. Nothing happened between us until 1952. Her Royal Highness the Duchess of Kent came to Hong Kong and the Hong Kong Governor gave a ball at Government House. The Duchess of Kent is the mother of Her Royal Highness, Princess Alexandra. Princess Alexandra came to Government House last year and stayed with us for five days and I told her that I had met my wife at a ball in 1952 in honour of her mother's visit to Hong Kong.

It was at the ball that the romance began?

Yes. And I told the Governor that last year when we were there for dinner. Right after dinner the Governor, Sir David Wilson, asked everybody to go to the ballroom and they turned on the lights for us to see. . . . We were surprised that the ballroom seemed so much smaller than our memory of it.

What role has your wife played in the major decisions in your life?

She plays an important role. I do not believe in the old Chinese way where the man is the head of the household and the woman follows. In my talks to women's groups, I say, "Paul, in his letter to the Romans, may have said that the man is the head of the household, but don't forget, you ladies, you are the neck. When the neck turns, the head turns." I believe in teamwork—it's always a partnership.

You have built a management research centre and library. How do you see the changing role of women in management?

Gender doesn't come to my mind at all when it comes to business. . . . I used to be very conscious of the differences in people and I found that that was counterproductive—to be noticing differences. I was conditioned; I was brought up to notice differences in Hong Kong. Everyone is conditioned by their family, by their parents, to notice differences, to identify the differences between people. Language differences. Everything. When I was growing up in Hong Kong I was conscious of the differences between people. It was a sort of discrimination that was so finely tuned it was just terrible. I found it very alienating. Why should I keep looking for differences between you and me, for instance? Why not start looking at those things we share? When I started doing that it helped me tremendously, in my business, everything.

What caused the change?

I don't know. I guess my experience in the Rotary Club has a lot to do with it. In Hong Kong I used to have names for people outside of Hong Kong, for instance, and I used racial slurs to describe others depending on where they were from—it's terrible. I've changed a lot.

Did Confucius emphasize these differences in the Chinese society?

Yes. And you must understand also that the business class of China was always considered the lowest class—the lowest according to Confucius. From this they developed a sense of inferiority complex. The scholar comes first, then the farmer, then tradesman and then merchant. The merchant or business class never really prospered inside China; it was always under the control of the government. Most Chinese businessmen prosper when they are outside of China, in places such as North America, South America, England, Europe and of course Southeast Asia. It's extraordinary. So what's the difference? Why are they prospering once outside of China? I believe it is because finally they are given a fair chance and protection under the law, and can live in a society with a high degree of order.

What made it possible for you to combine both Confucian and Christian beliefs and benefit from it?

I think it is very important to combine Christian and Confucian beliefs. Christianity gave me peace of mind, confidence and a certain value system. Yes, I want to make money and yet my aim is not solely to make money. John Wellesley said something like, "You've got to try to make as much, to save as much, and to give as much." . . . The Christian work ethic says there is no limit to the amount of money you can make or how hard you want to work to achieve your goals. But Confucius says there is a limit; you've got to have a balance. . . . It's so important to strike a harmonious balance in our thinking. To combine the best of both cultures puts a tremendously powerful tool in your hand.

This is how you can address it personally, but how do you apply this to a whole population?

I said to myself, when I finish my work, I want to become a missionary. I don't mean a missionary like Billy Graham who talks to thousands of people. I would like to be a missionary to the smaller group of the intellectuals and the highly educated few. I believe I can relate to those people. They need it as much as the masses of people.

How would you propose doing that?

I don't know yet. But if I am to embark on that I will adopt, adapt and improve, and try to make it so.

I would think that these people would be the most difficult people to approach.

Exactly, but because of my position in the past, by that time, because of my record, I can open doors that ordinary people couldn't. I don't know. I mean, that will come. That may come. I don't know yet.

THE HONOURABLE DAVID C. LAM AND MRS. LAM 1988.

If we can step back a few years, what was your first impression of Vancouver, when you first arrived?

We lived only a few blocks from where we are now; we were staying at the English Bay Motel. It was called the Cove Motel back then. We stayed there for a month and a half and most of the time I was out trying to land a job. I remember I would want to stay away from this area when I did my walking because there were so many beautiful and huge apartment buildings and I couldn't imagine having enough to pay the kind of rent to live here. It seemed so unreachable, an impossible-to-attain kind of high standard of living accommodation. Never did I imagine that I could come to own the whole building, especially one as beautiful as the one we're living in now.

How did you find that first job in Canada?

The first job I was offered I turned down because it was working for a bank and they wanted to send me back to Hong Kong. I said to myself, I must try my luck in Vancouver. But one thing quite interesting about newcomers like myself, I think part of our strength is in what we do not know. Our ignorance sometimes becomes our blessing. I met a number of people who were very knowledgeable about real estate, but I soon found out that while they were very knowledgeable, knew historic values, the various pitfalls, and why I shouldn't do certain things, their knowledge became a negative element that affected me rather then helped me. I wanted to retain a bit of my naive enthusiasm and was more interested in finding people who were prepared to help me make deals.

What was the most difficult thing for your children in coming to Canada?

Oh, the language. Also, the eldest one went to junior high school and, you know, kids can be cruel. When they see something different they point it out. Our eldest one had a really tough time.

What did you tell her when she came home upset?

Unfortunately, I have not been the best kind of father. I was always so worried about my own survival—worried is not quite the word—I was so wrapped up, absorbed, and spent too little time to truly understand the problems they faced. So it was left to my wife, really, to advise, console and guide them.

What advice would you give newcomers?

I think the biggest problem comes when they keep to themselves, they create a walled city which I think often becomes a jail . . . a ghetto. This is the sad part: a secure walled city can be temporarily comfortable, but in the long run, it's not helping them. I say, keep your culture, fine, but learn to be a Canadian, learn the Canadian culture. The Canadian culture, basically is Anglo-Saxon, it's white

Anglo-Saxon. To me, multiculturalism doesn't mean one can just stay in one's own ethnic group. Multiculturalism to me is love—love for your country—and the desire to contribute the best of your culture to make Canada better. What is the point of hundreds of different minorities living together in isolation, ignoring each other?

Multiculturalism is not totally understood. People think that it is my shield, my wall, my protection. Leave me alone to speak my own language, follow my own culture and do my own thing. If it is so, then I would ask in what way are you contributing to your country? . . . When I speak to various groups a lot of my message is that the best way the country will improve is for everyone to contribute his or her best. Participate, I say. Coming to Canada is like being invited to a pot-luck dinner; if everyone brings leftovers, we'll have a leftover dinner. But if one spends some of one's time, picks one's best recipe, and is prepared to give one's best, we will have a feast.

What is it to be a Canadian?

I think some Canadians are still searching for an identity. It seems that some of us always know what we are not. For instance, we are not Americans. Some can always say what we are not but have difficulty in saying what we are.

Canada is on the verge of a new wave of immigration from Hong Kong because of the 1997 situation. What advice would you have for those immigrants?

It takes both sides. We shouldn't be looking at a person for his or her differences. We should look at this newcomer as a potential partner. A partnership is a win-win situation. With a slight change in attitude we can build a common ground with people. From a common ground we can find a higher ground. . . . We should learn to celebrate the differences rather than merely tolerating the differences. We can turn diversity into enrichment and perplexities into strength.

For the newcomer I would say don't come here and always compare it to what you left. Say, if every time you go for dim sum you say, "Hong Kong is much better." If you do that you're still mentally living in Hong Kong although physically you're here. You've got one foot on the dock and one on the boat; you're going to be torn apart, you're going to go down the drain. Burn your bridges. Burn them. And walk away.

What do you think will happen in 1997?

In 1997 I think nothing drastic is going to happen. Hong Kong will still be there. There may even be a boom before that and there could be a boom right after the turnover. Nobody can pressure China. We think they can only survive and have prosperity through democracy and free enterprise, but China says no. They think they can have prosperity through a controlled market system. Maybe they can do it . . . I don't think so, but maybe they can do it.

And what will be the impact on Canada of this immigration from Hong Kong?

It's one of the best things that will ever happen to Canada. We get talent. Those talents, education and experience represent billions of dollars of time and investment. We get all that plus the entrepreneurial spirit and the capital. What more could you want?

What's in the future for you and your wife?

I think we will continue to enjoy this job. So often, I work seven days a week and on many days I receive from six to eighteen invitations. We send out five hundred letters and mail items a month. Every month I entertain, on an average, a thousand people at Government House, and meet about five hundred outside. When things slow down a bit in the months of January and August, those times are used for catching up and for routine maintenance on the House and grounds. There are often functions that the Governments of Canada, B.C. and Hong Kong want me to attend in Hong Kong, so my wife and I have been to Hong Kong three times since I took office. Don't get me wrong—I'm very busy, but I'm enjoying it.

And after?

And after, I will want to be a missionary. . . .

Among those things of which David Lam is most proud is his involvement with the Dr. Sun Yat-Sen Classical Chinese Garden in Vancouver. When this ambitious project was first conceived, the obstacles—availability of land, funding and a lack of local expertise—seemed insurmountable. Miraculously, all of the seemingly impossible hurdles were overcome, and the garden now brings enjoyment to many thousands of visitors.

VANCOUVER, 1968
THE LAM FAMILY: DAVID, DOROTHY, DEBBIE, DAPHNE, DOREEN.

Roy Mah

Suicide squads, the Pacific Unit and Force 136 came up frequently during the course of our research for this project. When we contacted Roy Mah to arrange an interview he told us that he was a veteran of these Second World War fighting units. We were understandably excited to have found a participant and have the opportunity to include his stories in this book. We interviewed Roy Mah in his office at his newspaper Chinatown News *in the heart of Vancouver's Chinatown. It was difficult not to begin the interview with questions relating to his experiences during the war. Roy Mah unfolded carefully—and with modesty—the events of his life leading up to his involvement. Always a passionate fighter, especially for causes concerning the Chinese Canadian community, Roy Mah has led a very full, rich life and continues to make his voice heard through his newspaper.*

子曰君子病無能焉不病人之不己知也

It is not lack of recognition that disturbs me but my own limitations.

I was born in Edmonton, Alberta. My father was a merchant and a part-time court interpreter. He had learned English at church. My father had come to Canada at the turn of the century. China at that time was an impoverished country, particularly in the Guangdong province where he came from. Many people wanted to emigrate to where there were opportunities for them to grow and to blossom, so they came either to Canada or the United States. He travelled over from China on the Blue Funnel Line which took about two months to get here.

Did he pay the head tax?

Yes.

How did he end up in Edmonton?

The Chinese by nature are a gregarious people. There were a lot of Mahs in Edmonton who had settled there ahead of him, so he thought, "Oh, lots of clansmen—we can help each other out."

What do you remember of Edmonton?

Very little, because I left at the age of four. At the age of four my father took the whole family back to his village in China. At that time it was a very racist society in Canada. Even if you did acquire a university education you'd still end up in the bread line because the Chinese were restricted as to what kind of profession they could practise. Those who were lucky enough to do well moved back to China to pursue careers. Many thought Canada was a dead end street. That was the prevailing thought for those who could afford it—I'd say ten percent of the population.

When did you return to Canada?

Well, my father had to return because of the immigration law. At that time the immigration law specified that a resident of Canada could only be away from Canada for two years. So he left the family in China and came back to Canada to seek a living.

How did the Exclusion Act affect him?

People couldn't do very much about it. They knew it was a racist society, they knew the law was unjust and discriminatory, but what could they do? They had to submit. The Chinese were a very, very submissive race of people in those days.

Why do you think that was?

It was a sort of worker-master mentality. Today we call it "Canada our home and native land"—we sing the glory of Canada, but not in those days. In those days, Chinese were classified as aliens.

What do you remember of your time in China?

I went to school there. The village was called Pak Sa in Taishan county. I stayed there for about eight years before coming back.

Did the whole family return together?

No, not the whole family. We came back individually. My mother never did come back. She stayed in China and is buried there. When I returned, I went to a little town called Lamont which is about thirty miles outside of Edmonton. My father had lost his business. It had gone broke after he'd given it to his brother to manage when he returned to China. I stayed with my uncle in Lamont where he had a restaurant called the Royal Cafe. I worked for him and went to school there. It was a very small town. My family was the only Chinese family there. The population was about seven hundred and there was only one school. I stayed for a couple of years.

My father had moved to Victoria to find work. The climate suited him better—warm, moderate climate. He worked but he never entered business again. He worked as a cook. I joined him in Victoria when I was about fifteen. He helped me out a little bit—he gave me $2 every month, and then I found a job working as a waiter waiting on tables.

And your education?

I attended two years of college at Victoria College following my graduation from Victoria High School. It's a university now. Then the war came and I enlisted.

At the time we had a big debate. In the Chinese community there were two opposing points of view. One said the country treated us as second-class citizens. The argument went like this: "If you're a full-fledged citizen you have duties as well as rights. In times of dire need you should answer the call to duty. But we're second-class citizens, so why should we help the government?" I led the faction opposing this point of view. I argued: "If we refuse to go to war when the country calls, we'll never get any rights. We'll never be able to improve our status in Canada." So I said, "This is our opportunity. Let's go and serve. Let's put on His Majesty's uniform, put on the Canadian Army uniform. When we return, we'll have solid credentials to demand our rights."

Our side won out.

Was your side composed of younger people?

The older people didn't take sides. They cared about the war and they supported the war effort, but they were seniors. We were the youth so it concerned us more. The young ones were single, they were bachelors. They didn't have any family or children. After the debate, everyone became united and everyone enlisted. But at that time don't forget that the total Chinese population in Canada was about 27,000. All together there were only about five hundred Chinese who served in the Canadian Armed Forces.

What were your experiences during the war?

I was in the army. Japan had occupied practically all of Asia, all the way from China to the South Pacific: Singapore, Malaysia, Borneo, nearly to Australia. Douglas MacArthur was the commander-in-chief of the Pacific theatre of war at the time. When the war was over in Europe, the Allied forces had to figure out a strategy to defeat the Japanese. I was in England at this time. They sent us to England for training. What they had in mind was to recruit us for special duty behind enemy lines. We learned demolition and wireless—the Morse code. They recruited a group of us to fight on the Burma front under the command of Lord Louis Mountbatten. We belonged to Force 136. That's the force that carried out those exploits which gave rise to the film *The Bridge on the River Kwai.*

Why did they select you?

Burma, Malaysia, Singapore and Borneo were heavily populated by Chinese, so Chinese Canadians could pass as natives and could perform their duties more effectively behind enemy lines. After we did our basic training in England, we went to India for parachute training. Normally parachute training took six months; we had only six weeks. The commander gave us an option as to whether we wanted to join the communications unit and learn to become a wireless operator so we could communicate with the outside from enemy-occupied territory, or we could join a demolition unit. We were to liaise with the guerilla groups and send information back to headquarters. From India they shipped us to Ceylon—it's now called Sri Lanka. We were posted to a dispatching centre, waiting for our assignment.

How did you feel about being dropped behind enemy lines?

To tell you the truth, I was scared! . . . I had been selected to go into operation. We had to be ready to leave at a moment's notice. The procedure was at midnight they would drop us in, so they started issuing us with supplies and equipment. They gave me a fish hook, a mosquito net, a revolver and a cyanide pill in case we were caught. It was only issued to those selected to go behind enemy lines. In case you were caught and tortured, use it. That was the instruction.

So you were all set to leave?

Yes. . . . About a dozen of us were ready. They only flew in one group a week.

My turn had come and I was ready with my equipment and everything. Just five days before my scheduled mission, the Americans dropped the atomic bomb on Hiroshima. Hiroshima and Nagasaki. Right away the Japanese sued for peace and my mission was cancelled. . . . So I wasn't dropped in. I was involved all the way up to that point. All the preparation had been done. At that point, after the Japanese surrendered we didn't have anything to do. The war was over so we had ourselves a grand time.

How many of the Chinese Canadians who were part of Force 146 are still alive today?

I'd say eighty percent. There were more than two hundred. I don't know the exact figure; more likely it was twice that number. All of them came back.

What did you do when you returned from the war?

When I came back I got a job with the International Woodworkers of America—a union in the woodworking industry. I was an organizer for them. At that time there was a wage differential in the industry. I think the Chinese were getting about 25 cents to 45 cents an hour, while the whites were getting 65 cents, 75 cents, even $1.00, so they needed a Chinese-speaking person to organize the Chinese labourers. I stayed with them for a couple of years and then I started a paper.

I started the *New Citizen* in the late 1940s. It was a tabloid in English. It went belly-up after three years. I switched to a job with a company called the Chinese Publicity Bureau. The firm was printing directories at the time. I took over that business eventually and launched the publication *Chinatown News.*

What led you to a career in the media?

I was involved with a publication put out by the woodworking industry called *The Lumber Worker.* I had a hand in some editorial work there.

What was it about newspapers that attracted you?

When I was a boy attending school in Victoria, I got a job as a waiter and a second job as a newspaper delivery boy. I worked at the newspaper. The editor asked me to try out on a couple of reporting assignments. He read the stories and said "Hey, you're pretty good." That's when I got printer's ink infused into my blood. Moreover, I was always involved in fighting for causes. When Japan invaded China I took a leading role in a youth club to fight against the export of scrap iron to Japan and led the movement to boycott the importing of Japanese goods to Canada. In the army I was one of three non-commissioned officers who led the Chinese contingent overseas. I joined the woodworking industry because I thought the wages paid to Chinese workers were discriminatory. The Chinese labourers were getting a raw deal. Our slogan at that time was "equal pay for equal work."

Were you involved in the repeal of the Exclusion Act?

Yes, I was involved in that. After I came back from the war, I fought for civil rights for Chinese Canadians. I fought for the improvement of our political and economic status in Canada. We submitted briefs often and sent delegations to lobby the government. I've used this publication as a vehicle to articulate the aspirations and hopes of Chinese Canadians.

How much did the Chinese Canadian soldiers' role during the war help?

It made a big difference. At that time the sentiment was still pretty strong against the Chinese. Ninety percent of the population in B.C. was Anglo, the national anthem was "God Save the King," Canada's national flag was the British Union Jack and Canada's constitution rested in Westminster, in London. There was fierce resistance to granting rights to minority groups, but we tried to make alliances and enlisted the support of church groups, some trade unions, as well as individual organizations that were sympathetic to our cause.

Did you ever go to Ottawa?

Yes. Ottawa was not as bad as B.C. Whenever there was a large concentration of a particular ethnic group like the Chinese in B.C., it aroused fear in the local population. They viewed us as a threat to their economic security. A lot of the discriminatory laws only applied in B.C. For instance, the Chinese couldn't practise law here and couldn't work for the government or own property in certain areas of the city. A lot of professions were barred to them.

On immigration we went through different stages of appeal. At first we asked for family reunions. In those days we had a bachelor society here. The men had been separated from their wives and children. Step by step the government granted family reunion. The next step was the extended family—cousins, brothers, grandfathers and so on. Ottawa gradually opened the immigration door a little wider in stages.

In B.C., we didn't get the vote until 1949. It also took a long time to remove the other restrictions against Orientals—the economic barriers. At one time we even had school segregation in Victoria. When I came back from China in the 1930s, the schools were segregated just like the situation in the southern U.S.

What would you say was the most significant event that turned the tide?

It wasn't one event that came dramatically on the scene. It was a very, very slow process that took place over a period of time.

What's your position on the head tax question?

On the head tax issues, I say no. We don't have the legal nor the moral right to demand redress. I'll tell you why: No court in the land would convict a grandson for the misdeed, the wrong or crime committed by his grandparents. No court in the land would do that. Of course the tax was unfair. Of course it was racist. Of course it was discriminatory, but the Chinese had a choice. They didn't have to come. They came here because they considered Canada a land of opportunity. In their own words they called it *Kam san*—the land of the golden mountain. They knew it was a racist society. They walked in with their eyes wide open; they weren't bamboozled. Even though it was a racist society, it was still better than staying behind in China.

This is a controversial position.

Controversial to the young people. They don't understand Canadian history. Canada did make a proposal to China at one time. Ottawa said, alright, if you voluntarily restrict the flow of immigrants into Canada we'll remove the head tax. At that time China was ruled by the Manchu Dynasty. The B.C. population viewed the influx of Chinese as a threat to their jobs. The B.C. government of the time had to react to the people's wishes. If the government hadn't acted, it would have been booted out of office at the next election. The most popular party at the time was the one that adopted the strongest anti-Oriental platform. "Down with the Chinese" was the most popular rallying cry. That was the time when people would say, "Oh, you haven't got a Chinaman's chance."

The situation in B.C. was terrible. One of my schoolmates from Lamont, Alberta, moved out here. His name was Latowski. He couldn't get a job because he wasn't of Anglo stock. He had to change his name to Nelson. Such was the political climate of the time.

Part of the activities of the Victoria Chinese Youth Association of which Roy Mah was the founding president.

To the people who demand redress, head tax payers are called "victims." I attended a conference at which a delegate pointed out that the term is a misnomer. "I'm a son of a head tax payer and I'm not a victim," he said. In the olden days, immigrants who returned to China from Canada for a visit were regarded by the villagers as élites, the cream of society, because they were the only ones who had money.

Do you think it's only the young people who want the money back?

Yes, it's the young people. Absolutely.

What are their reasons?

I'd say they're misguided. They don't realize that once they set a precedent in getting redress, all the other ethnic groups will line up and demand the same, for they have grievances, too. There'll be no end to this. Don't forget that besides racial discrimination the country had gender discrimination as well. In the course of 125 years of nation-building there have been all kinds of injustices perpetuated by different governments. How can you right the wrong by asking for money? "Give me some money and everything will be okay, hunky-dory." That's just not the right way to go about righting a wrong.

What do you think is going to happen?

I don't think they'll get what they demand. Far more realistic is that they ask only for a token compensation—a token of $1 million to fund an education program or to establish a commemorative project. For if they give it to the Chinese I can guarantee other groups will demand the same. The Italians will be next, the Indo-Canadians, then the Germans, then the Doukhobors, and all the other ethnic groups will be lining up.

Is this issue going to split the community?

No, I think not. After everything has been explained to the head tax redress campaigners, they'll know that on this issue, they are off target. They don't have a very strong case to convince the government.

What advice would you give to the new immigrant to Canada?

I'd tell them that they're very, very fortunate to become new Canadians because Canada today is a multicultural society. Chinese Canadians are moving into the mainstream now. There's still a little bit of discrimination in some areas of national life, but nothing like what it was in the olden days. But we have to be vigilant at all times to safeguard our rights. I refer to the Reform Party. This party seems to believe that multiculturalism is bunk, that the government shouldn't devote so much money to fund this type of program. Reformers are wrong. We've got to encourage this kind of program. Besides, the amount of money devoted to promoting multiculturalism is peanuts—a drop in the bucket in relation to Canada's overall budget. Respect for diversity is a concept we must preserve.

What does it mean to you—multiculturalism? How would you define it?

Canada in the olden days was a homogenous society. The Anglos constituted as high as seventy percent of the population and the French, thirty percent. Today, we have one-third Anglo, one-third French, one-third ethnic. The world has changed. Today we have communications breakthroughs. People and ideas are flowing into the country as never before. The old guard wants to fight against this tide. They try to preserve the country as it was. Multiculturalism will encourage the flow of people and ideas. It will help us preserve our identity. This is a fact we can't hide. In nine more years we'll enter a new century. By that time, the demographers project the Chinese alone will constitute forty percent of the population of the city of Vancouver. Moreover, by the end of the century seventy percent of Canada's gross national product, her economic activities, will stem from her ties with Pacific Rim countries. The world is being drawn closer with each passing day.

Vancouver is the favoured destination of most of the new Hong Kong immigrants. What do you think of the new Hong Kong immigrant?

Hong Kong immigrants have drawn a certain amount of backlash from the local populace. There's a lot of resentment over soaring house prices, the shortage of school facilities needed to handle the influx of students, extra budgetary considerations to provide English as a second language classes, and so on. But the local population has to understand that the world is changing. It's not a trend that they can stop. By the year 2000 half of the world's economic activities will have shifted to the Asia Pacific region. The world is moving closer together all the time. The global village concept is here.

Roy Mah's Chinatown News *has been at the forefront of the fight for the enfrachisement and the civil rights of Chinese Canadians. Roy worked hard toward the liberalisation of immigration policy and the re-unification of families, organizing the first national conference of Chinese Canadians in the early 1970s.*

Bob Wong

On September 29, 1987, Bob Wong became the first Chinese Canadian appointed a minister in either a provincial or a federal government when Premier David Peterson appointed him Minister of Energy for Ontario. His hard work and dedication in that post were typical of the life of selfless service to community and country which he has led, and continues to lead. It is surprising that a man who held such a high profile public position should be camera shy, but without the encouragement of his charming wife Alice and the comfortable surroundings of his own back yard we might not have succeeded so well with the photograph reproduced here.

子路問政子曰先之勞之請益曰無倦

TSZE-LÛ ASKED ABOUT GOVERNMENT.
THE MASTER SAID, "WORK HARD
AND INSPIRE THOSE AROUND YOU
WITH YOUR EXAMPLE." HE ASKED FOR
ELABORATION AND WAS TOLD,
"BE TENACIOUS."

My father came to Canada in 1923, several months before the Exclusion Act was passed and implemented. He came from southern China, Guangdong province, from Taishan. In Canada, he arrived on the west coast, then travelled by train to Welland, Ontario, where his older brother was living. Eventually he settled in Fort Erie and started a restaurant there called the Paradise Grill.

Can you tell us some of the family history prior to their arrival in Canada?

When I went to China in 1988 I visited my father's village, Pak Sa. An elderly gentleman gave me a copy of our family tree. It was written on very delicate paper tied together by string and there were some worm holes in it, but it traced the family history back twenty-eight generations to the Ming Dynasty. It was difficult to translate because it was written in classical Chinese characters. But I understand that at the beginning of the family tree the family was in Fujian province, and then they moved south into the eastern side of Guangdong province, and finally moved westward to Taishan.

BOB WONG, ON RIGHT, WITH SISTER

Was that the first time you had been back to China?

I had been there previously with my wife in 1985.

What was your first impression of the country?

I think I had a sense of how large the country was and how advanced it had become. It was still a long way from the state of western countries like those in Europe or Canada, but it was making progress. The first visit was just to Guongdong province; the second time, in 1988, we were in four of the major cities of China: Beijing, Nanjing, Hangzhou and Guangzhou. So we had an opportunity to see the diversity of China, and I think something else that came through was the sense of culture and history, the sense of 5,000 years of civilization.

When did your mother come to Canada?

My mother was of Chinese origin but was born in Canada, in Hamilton, Ontario. Her parents had emigrated from China in 1910.

What was it like growing up in Fort Erie?

It was a nice place for a young person to grow up. It's still a very nice community; the people are very friendly. It's very scenic. You're also on the border with the United States, so there's that perspective, too.

How important was education in the family?

Education was a high priority. I remember that my father was extremely happy when I was accepted for university, and then later when I graduated.

And the other children in the family?

I have one sister who lives in Toronto and is in the real estate business and I have a younger brother who is an M.D.–Ph.D. at Johns Hopkins University in Baltimore, specializing in PET, which is Positron Emission Tomography.

Can you give us some background on the choices you made in your education?

Through high school I found that I liked mathematics and the sciences very much. When I went to the University of Toronto I studied mathematics and physics and graduated with a bachelor's degree. I then taught mathematics and physics at a collegiate in North York. At the same time, since I also had an interest in business, I focused in on the new MBA program that was starting at York University. Halfway through the MBA I was offered a job working as a political assistant to a cabinet minister in Ottawa. That in itself was a special opportunity and education, especially at the tender age of twenty-seven and for a Canadian of Chinese origin. I returned to Toronto after two years to complete my MBA in the evenings and to start into business in the world of finance and investment on Bay Street.

Before we go on to the business, you said that this experience in Ottawa was an education in itself. Can you tell us what kind of an experience that was?

You learn how government works. You understand the dynamics of people and relationships, how laws get changed, how things get done, how the impossible can become the possible, how dreams and aspirations can be shaped by ordinary Canadians and ultimately consummated in the Parliament of Canada.

It sounds like it was an energizing experience.

Absolutely. It was energizing to the point where I probably would have stayed there forever, but I realized a priority at that time was the completion of the MBA.

Was your experience in Ottawa what led you into politics?

In part, but I think it was a combination of factors. It may have had a lot to do with my upbringing and my experiences when growing up. When you live in a community like Fort Erie or Hamilton, where I had relatives, you see both the good and the bad in society. You see people living in less fortunate circumstances, lacking opportunity. And early on I asked myself, how can it be that there are people in Canada living in such conditions? I thought, if one day I'm lucky enough to be in a position in my life where I can help, I'd like to do something about those injustices. That's probably about as far as it went in my mind. At that time there was no serious thought of running for elected office; it was really more a sense of wanting to give something back to the community which had treated me so well compared to the hardships of my parents' generation. And then I think it's fair to say that during the early 1960s, when I was going to university, that President Kennedy was a great inspiration, especially to the younger generation. He set out many challenges and ideals that generated an emotional interest in me in the political arena.

But you entered into the world of finance first?

Right. After finishing my MBA I started a small brokerage company with a friend. It grew from being a small firm to a medium-sized one by Toronto Stock Exchange standards. It was called Goulding, Rose & Turner Ltd., and we had a dozen offices and a staff of 175 across Canada, from coast to coast. In the mid-1980s we sold it to Walwyn Stodgell and this merger moved the combined firm up into the top ten in size in the country.

Did you remain politically active during your business career?

Yes. Actually, in the mid-'70s I was elected the president of the Toronto and District Liberal Association. In those days it was both a federal and a provincial association. It included thirty-six provincial ridings and twenty-five federal ridings, from Burlington east to Scarborough, and from the waterfront right up to Aurora. To me it was a challenge and a contribution I could make. Why the Liberal Party? Well, fundamentally because I believe that it places a stronger emphasis on the individual—the interests and the aspirations of the individual.

Was there a desire on your part to build a strong financial and professional base before launching your career in politics?

It was a choice I made in the early '70s. There are two traditional routes to take to get into politics: The first is to jump right in, get elected and take your chances on whether you stay on the back benches or move to the front benches. The alternative, of course, is to have a successful career first, establish your credentials in another field. Mitchell Sharp was a very successful civil servant. Robert Winters of the same era was very successful in business. I think it crossed my mind that it was more rational to follow the second path because you'd have potentially more experience to offer later, and also you'd have a more responsible family life.

Besides business and politics you've also become a prominent and active member of the Chinese community. Was that by accident or were you drafted into it?

Keep in mind that through the 1960s and 1970s the Chinese community was relatively small. Everyone knew everyone else. From time to time issues or problems would arise in the Chinese community and whoever was able to contribute would step forward to help. Several years after my political time in Ottawa, the Chinese community across Canada had a problem with the federal and provincial health departments. The community was largely involved in the restaurant business at that time, so a national lobby was established. Here in Toronto, the Chinese community felt that because of my experience in Ottawa I might know how to get things accomplished. It was a natural thing to participate in and to help. But this was part of my upbringing. I can still see, in my mind, my father and my aunt in Hamilton, who later became a citizenship court judge, helping individuals who had relatives who wanted to immigrate to Canada. There was always an atmosphere at home, an environment, where I saw my family members offering to help. So it was a natural thing to participate.

How did you come to be elected to the provincial legislature?

In 1986 both the Liberal Party and leaders in the Chinese community wanted to set up a Liberal Association in the Chinese community. The Ontario Chinese Liberal Association was formed and I was elected as its first president. I think the Chinese community had matured to the point where it felt it should be more involved in the political arena, because as Canadians we wanted to help shape the direction of the country. Meanwhile, the Liberal Party had been wondering how to reach out to the various ethno-cultural communities, and in particular the visible minority communities. And so both were on a parallel path. I think everyone in the province realized that there was a potential election on the horizon. Some members of the Chinese community and the community at large posed the question, would I run? I thought that I had enough to do, not only in business, but also in my volunteer activities with the OCLA. But after discussions with friends and listening to the different viewpoints I made the decision. I felt that maybe this was the time that I could make a contribution. I entered the nomination race which had six candidates. In three and half months the six of us signed up about 8,000 memberships. The organizers had to move the nomination meeting from the local school to the Metro Convention Centre. I think it became the largest nomination meeting ever held in the province of Ontario. The nomination meeting started at 2:00 on a Sunday afternoon and it went for four ballots and finished fifteen hours later at 5:00 on Monday morning.

What was the most exciting or satisfying moment in this process? Winning the nomination or the riding?

Well, a very difficult question because so much of it was exhilarating and satisfying. But I think receiving a phone call from the premier asking me to join Cabinet was probably the highest point. The election was on September 10, 1987, and I was appointed Minister of Energy for Ontario on September 29th.

Had it been a hard campaign?

Yes, it was. I was going to say that sometimes people comment on how lucky I was, winning the nomination in July, elected in September and minister a few weeks later—what's the secret? The real answer is hard work. It probably goes back twenty years to the door knocking that took place in the late '60s and early '70s. If I have a message for young people interested in getting involved in the community or public life, it would be to just commit yourself to it. That experience of commitment in itself is very meaningful.

How did your parents feel about this?

Well, keep in mind that my father was an immigrant to Canada. He was very happy that I got accepted to university and completed a degree. When I was entering the teaching profession, again that was an important milestone that also made him very happy. And later, when I started in business, I'm sure he had his concerns, but was pleased at yet another successful career. He's still living, he's in his eighties, and I guess he had seen enough, either surprises or developments in the careers of his children, that for me to be elected, to become a cabinet minister, was probably as exciting or satisfying for him as it would be for any parent.

You've had many different careers, you've done a lot of very different things. Was there any one particularly difficult and dark time for you?

No. The way I see it, with every career, as you call it . . . they've all had one common factor: they've been people oriented. Teaching mathematics was very enjoyable. The satisfaction came from talking to and teaching young people. It wasn't just teaching mathematics or physics; it was teaching students a philosophy of life. In the investment business, you advise and counsel individuals about something that is very precious to them—their savings. And in politics, again it's about people. That's been the common factor, I think. It goes back perhaps to that innate and early sense of wanting to help the community and to help people. It's something that affected my life when I was very young. I think the point is not that there was a dark moment or a difficult one; I think I turn the question to what was the most challenging time in all these years of experience? And I would say that it would have to be the last three years in public life as a minister of the government. It is most challenging to be pushed to the limit, physically and mentally. And that to me is exhilarating. There were times when I had a stack of briefing material in front of me and it was midnight, but to do a good job you want to read it and comprehend it, if you're going to be ready for the next day, and so you do it. Physically, being in that position can be exhausting, but ultimately very satisfying.

There was never a time when you felt you'd had enough?

No. I think that the challenge and the adrenalin were the things in my case that made it all very exciting. I remember especially the development of the energy policy for the province. We were dealing with Ontario Hydro, which is the largest electrical utility in North America. At that time, it had an annual budget of over $5 billion. There were tremendous challenges in the issues and problems that faced Ontario, and it was very rewarding for me to be able to apply some of my background to this whole area.

You have a very linear, analytical way of thinking. When we ask a question, you respond in a very orderly fashion, hitting each point with equal force. Is it a result of your background in mathematics or is it a result of realizing that it's the best way to deal with people and complex questions? Are you aware of it?

No, I really hadn't been aware of it. It might be the mathematical background. I think, perhaps, it's a sense of knowing that when people ask me a question I prefer to give them an answer. It's as simple as that, I think.

Will you return to politics?

Well, I'd like to, if the people and the constituents said they'd like to elect Bob Wong again.

What do you think are the significant political questions facing Canada today?

Well, federally, I think the most important questions are about the kind of country we want in the future. I think that the economy is another very important issue. We have a huge deficit and if we don't make the correct decisions we could move into the status of, and I hate to say this, a third-world kind of economy. In provincial terms, I think the economy is crucial to Ontario, a province which historically has always had a strong industrial base. I think we have to think about a long range economic strategy and the kind of education our people should have. We should think about the kind of labour adjustment strategies our workers should have because we're in a world of rapid change. When companies and industries close down, the workers should be helped and retrained. We also have to consider the other support services, whether it's health care or transportation.

I think the other important issue facing us is the reason I became a Liberal, and I'll phrase it differently than I did before: How can we express ourselves and help the people in our society who need help? You need economic growth and prosperity to support "a caring society." It's an important issue for Ontario in the 1990s: How do we help the poor and disadvantaged? How can we help the single parents, and the single mothers in particular? These are examples of typical people in Ontario and the ones who are experiencing and will experience greater hardship in the 1990s, and we have to find ways to help them.

What about cultural questions, the language question, and the French-English question?

I think we have to recognize that we live in a very diverse society and, as a result, there are inequities—inequity in terms of employment, job entry and promotion. It can only help us as a people, especially in economic terms, if we can learn to recognize each other's potential.

What about the language question?

Language? Personally, I'm comfortable with what the Fathers of Confederation and what succeeding governments have done in recognizing that French and English would be the two official languages of Canada. In the province of Ontario our government was not for official bilingualism, but certainly was sensitive to the needs of Francophone Ontarians in offering government services in French to those who wished it where numbers warranted.

What do you see happening for you in the future, personally and professionally?

Well, obviously I've been very lucky. I'm comfortable working with people in public life and equally comfortable in the business world. I think what I'll do at this stage is to continue to offer my assistance not only in the Chinese community but in the community at large, and if there's a place I can help out, I'd like to.

After teaching mathematics and physics, Bob Wong began a successful career as a securities analyst, eventually becoming the chairman and director of Goulding, Rose & Turner Ltd. As a founding director of Toronto's Channel 47, he helped to launch Canada's first multilingual television station. Today, he remains active in community and political affairs and is currently deputy chairman of The Glen Ardith-Frazer Corporation, a company which manages investment portfolios for individual and corporate clients.

The Wong family

SUSAN ENG

When we did the first part of this interview with Susan Eng, she was pursuing a career in law with a high profile Toronto legal firm and was active both in the Chinese community and with her duties as a member of the Metropolitan Toronto Police Services Board. Three months after our interview Susan Eng was appointed Chair of the Police Services Board. The significance of this appointment can only be appreciated by the civilian if we use its former title, Police Commissioner of the City of Toronto. Shortly after her appointment she contacted us and expressed a desire to speak out on issues she hadn't covered in her first interview, as well as comment on her new position. Conscious of the prominence of her role, as a public servant, as a woman, and as a Chinese Canadian, her words reveal a deep concern with making the most of the opportunities she has earned to benefit the public good.

子曰君子之於天下也無適也無莫也義之與比

THE SUPERIOR ONE DOES NOT FIGHT FOR OR AGAINST ANYTHING; THAT WHICH IS MORAL IS WHAT IS IMPORTANT.

My father came to Canada in 1919 as a sixteen-year-old. He came as an immigrant and paid the $500 head tax. My grandfather was already here and had also paid the head tax. He was a bit of a gambler and after having borrowed the money to pay for my father's head tax, proceeded to run up gambling debts, so in the first few years that my father was here, he was working not only to pay back the money borrowed for his head tax—which was about two years' salary—but was also working to pay back my grandfather's gambling debts. He worked in the usual types of jobs that were available to the Chinese at that time—laundry, restaurant, that sort of thing. In fact, he ended up buying one of the restaurants he worked in. That was around 1930.

Then he was ready to get married, but that was during the exclusion of the Chinese, so he had to wait until after 1947, when he could return to seek a bride. He inspected a number of candidates and chose my mother, who was the middle daughter of five daughters. My parents came from neighbouring villages in Taishan. They got married in Hong Kong and returned to Canada in 1951. Because he had to wait so long before returning to China for his bride, my father was forty-nine when he married my mother, who was nineteen.

There's a thirty-year difference between your mother and your father. What sort of problems did that create for you growing up?

I didn't notice it one iota when I was growing up. It's only now, after his death that I reflect upon it as being important in our family's life. But in terms of how we regarded him as a father? I only have that single experience so I can't compare it to another. We certainly were not mindful of that age difference.

SUSAN ENG, SECOND FROM LEFT, WITH FAMILY.

What did your father think of the success you've had?

He never lived to see it. He died in 1970. I was the eldest and I was just about to enter university . . . my mother hasn't remarried. In Chinese society you don't marry out of your widowhood unless you are destitute. She's a very proud woman. . . . It was not easy for us; we did not have very much money. We didn't know about movies. We didn't travel. My parents were not educated. . . . They would never have come to parent-teacher night. We brought our report cards home and they signed them and that was it. They were not involved in our education. We didn't expect them to be. They just expected us to come home with A's and be done with it.

Did they always live in Toronto?

Yes. There is a difference between being in Toronto versus Vancouver because there was not as large a Chinese population here. When my mother first came, they thought she was Canadian-born because there was nobody her age here in Toronto. It was still largely a bachelor society in the 1960s. When I was growing up many of my babysitters were single men who worked in the restaurant or hung around the restaurant because they were at loose ends. They were labourers, many without families.

You learned Chinese from your parents?

Oh yes, because my parents didn't speak English. I learned what English I spoke at the restaurant, and of course at school. . . . In fact, I found a report card of mine that said that I had a reading problem. That was in grade three, and in fact, I was accelerated from grade three in every other subject but reading. I had to go back to catch up on reading.

School was fascinating for me. These days I think students tend to question, "Why am I learning this and why do I have to do that?" I never had that. I knew precisely what I was there for. I was there to learn and I did what I was told and I got very good marks. All of us did. We had few distractions. We didn't have a lot of toys at home. We didn't spend a lot of time with friends and neighbours. We lived in downtown Toronto—not a residential area but on top of my father's restaurant. So we didn't have movie theatres, we didn't have a television, we didn't listen to radio. We were always very studious and were always in the top one, two or three in the class.

Do you still speak Chinese?

Oh, yes. Fluency is a matter of judgement. I speak Taishan, which is unusual for a person my age. Taishan is a dialect that's really difficult for Cantonese people to understand. The idiom and the pronunciation are really quite different. It's difficult to cross over between the two, so if you speak both you are really speaking two languages.

Our parents tried to help us keep our language by sending us to Chinese school. Every Canadian-born Chinese kid can tell you about Chinese school. It's a real aggravation because it was something you had to do over and above everything else.

Chinese is your first language and English is your second. What do you think of the language question in this country?

For the Chinese, language is not a source of defending our culture, but it is a source of access to our culture. I think for French Canadians, it is what distinguishes them. It's a way of hiding your culture from somebody else, of protecting its integrity. In some respects we used Chinese in the same way when we were growing up. Between our brothers and sisters and our friends, we would speak in Chinese when we wanted to hide something from the people we were dealing with. But we would speak in English to hide something from our parents. So language became a source of secrecy, a means of confidentiality.

But language also became a sore point with Hong Kong Chinese. As we were growing up there were many more people emigrating from Hong Kong, many our age who spoke Cantonese exceedingly well. Our parents would draw our attention to how well they spoke Chinese. We would sit there and bristle because we figured these kids can't find the washroom unless we point it out to them, and the only thing they can do better than us is something they've done all their lives. Our parents didn't understand all the other problems we were going through on account of them being Chinese, and yet they wanted to keep pushing this in our faces—that we didn't speak Chinese as well as these new immigrants? That became a real source of tension and, interestingly enough, it still affected my sister and me as recently as five years ago.

We were at a wedding where some Hong Kong people sat down at our table and proceeded to mock my sister and our family, saying obviously we were Canadian-born and wouldn't enjoy this food so maybe we should order some hamburgers for you. We were stunned. My sister was very upset and I just said these people are peasants and who cares what they think. But my sister was upset because here was this person treating her in that old hurtful, shabby way. That was part of our upbringing, too. As Canadian-born Chinese, we always had that feeling of not belonging and having to find some source of pride for ourselves. It was an awkward time for us and some people, other Canadian-born Chinese, went native. Some of the girls actually dyed their hair red.

You've been talking about a kind of racism from within the Chinese community. We haven't yet approached the subject of racism from without. When was the first time you experienced that?

I would say that it was always around us. When I was growing up there didn't seem to be a stigma attached to being a racist. People were quite blatant in their racism and it was accepted that 'they' would always treat us like that. At home our parents always had a way of saying these people really haven't got much to say for themselves. What they say is valueless because look at how they live their lives: "Look at that guy spitting. Look at that guy smoking. Look at that guy drunk. That's what these white people are all about." . . . There was a certain amount of acceptance, of thinking that there were certain things you were just not going to get or have a right to. . . . They would say, "Well, it's time to vote. Now what does Chan in the community say about who we should vote for?" Instead of realizing that they had a much broader responsibility to understand the voting process, they simply cut themselves off from that. I don't know if they felt that they were actually denied access to things, but there was always a sense that there were certain things you could never expect to have because they belonged to a whole different group of people. But there wasn't a bitterness about that. There was a sense of . . . that's the ways things are. . . .

Finally, it was always a question of looking at our own values and seeing how 'they' failed by those standards. It was more important to judge ourselves according to our own values than to be judged by other people's values. I think our environment helped us to learn this. We lived upstairs above the restaurant and it was in a very difficult part of town, so we had all kinds of people coming through. You had drunks and workers, you had pimps and prostitutes, you had very rough petty criminal types. Transvestite prostitutes when the gay community first moved into town. It was a very rough kind of life.

Most parents today from "Scarberia," as we would call Scarborough, would not let their children see this for fear that they would get 'turned' or something. Well, we were living among that and none of us ever explored or experimented with any of that lifestyle whatever. We also didn't judge people. We got very offended when the Scarberians would come down on Easter Sunday when the transvestites would have their Easter parade and scoff at them. Who are these people to come down and mock these people? Who do they think they are? These people are people and have a right to their own lifestyle. My parents didn't have the Dr. Spock type of education to do anything about childhood responses to these kinds of influences. They simply had their own set of values and approach to the situation, and that was that.

You are a lawyer. How much did your parents influence that choice of profession?

My choice to become a lawyer had nothing to do with my parents. I had finished second year in commerce and finance, and a friend of mine, who was going into law, suggested I go as well. I applied and got in. It was as simple as that.

But were they anxious you have a profession?

Yes. I find that endemic to the Chinese population. As a professional I think people felt it would give you access to the system, it would give you access to getting things done, and to knowledge that would help when you needed it. No matter what profession I might have chosen, as long as I was a professional, they would still ask me what immigration advice I could give. That kind of thing.

You're considered a prominent member of the Chinese community. Was that by choice or by accident?

Around the time I began practising law I was invited to become a member of the Federation of Chinese Community Professionals. Then in 1979 there was the *W5* protest. *W5* was a CTV program that alleged that university places were being taken by foreign students. To show who the foreign students were, they showed Chinese faces and to show who Canadian students were, they showed a white girl. People in the Chinese community protested and, as an apology was not forthcoming from CTV, a national protest was set up. I was a member of the initial protest. After CTV capitulated and apologized, we formed the Chinese Community National Council, which is now a federation of local chapters across Canada. That's how I got involved in public protest.

And politics?

I went into a by-election for the Chinatown seat. It was for an alderman's seat that John Sewell had vacated. The NDP candidate had been grooming himself for that position and they figured it was a shoe-in. The Chinese community felt it shouldn't go down without a fight. They drafted me for it. The reason why the people in the community thought that I ought to do this was because they felt I should take my community activism to the next logical stage, to the public platform. I dove into it without knowing anything about the political process whatsoever, and what I learned has been very interesting.

What did you learn?

Oh, lots of things.

Are you disillusioned?

No. I think it opened my eyes. It makes me very cynical about things. It makes me watchful. It opened my eyes on many, many fronts. It told me about the power links between the backroom boys and the politicians in power. I saw who those people were and I know now how they work. The backroom boys, or gatekeepers, in the Chinese community delivered the votes of the Chinese community to a candidate, who was usually white. The people never really knew who the candidate was. And I thought to myself, that has to be the history of our community. We get delivered to people, those people who do the delivering get all the kudos, but the community never gets anything from this because when the election is over, that's it—thanks guys, see you around next time.

That little clique of people tried to infect our campaign but couldn't because we had no use for them. They helped sometimes, but they got in the way of other people who were family—family who belonged to the Eng Association and those people who came in and were interested in helping because I could reach them personally. They didn't have to go through the gatekeepers to talk to me. And I could talk to the voters directly, not only in Chinese, but in Taishan, which most of them were.

What do you think are the most relevant political questions right now, locally or nationally?

I think that all Canadians, but particularly groups that feel disenfranchised, must come to understand how much power they have and then proceed to use it responsibly. Research tells us that ten percent of the voting population in any riding can carry the riding. It doesn't take much to get ten percent of the votes. All you have to do is spend ten minutes and vote and you can change the course of that election. That is a scientific fact, but people won't believe it.

You're a professional, you're very politically active, and you're also deeply involved in the Chinese community. What are the personal costs?

Well, I think the personal costs are heavy. Each time I look at that balance sheet I think, was it worth it? In many respects, because I've paid the cost personally, I don't feel I owe anybody any excuses or explanations, nor do I feel that I have to accept their values or standards. That attitude breeds a certain arrogance. I can be difficult to work with—I've paid for my independence. With that independence comes a sense of isolation, a sense of not being able to just take some system off the shelf, fit myself into it and go on automatic pilot. I tend to challenge everything and guard viciously my ability to come to an independent conclusion. The price for that is that you bear all the blame when people start handing out blame. But at the end of the day you realize that you're happy with what you're doing and you're happy with having the freedom to make your own judgements and not having to apologize to anybody for them.

You explain very clearly how you deal with your public life, how you operate, but you only touch upon the personal side?

The relationships that I've had have very little to do with anything I do publicly, but they have been affected by the lack of time I have. . . . To not have children is not a choice . . . so far. I haven't ruled it out. It's an important thing, I just haven't measured how important it is in my life. My sister gives me lots of access to her kids, her two little ones, and that takes the edge off of not having my own. I think the importance to me in kids, seeing kids, is to have an influence on their future. . . . But there are times . . . when you talk about that isolation and independence, that I'd like to have somebody to share that with me, take the edge off, and share the challenges.

How do you see the next ten years, the next twenty years and the roles you might play in the community?

It's not clear to me what I'll do next. I think what I'm doing now in my own life is arranging my priorities, what things I value and what things I don't, and that will, I think, help to define for me what I want to do next.

What do you think of the current wave of Hong Kong immigrants?

Canadians have decided that there's an 'invasion' of people from Hong Kong. The economic jump-start that this new immigration has brought on has been very important for the economy. But rather than look at it positively, they try to find something negative about it. Controversies, for example, about monster homes. Why call them monster homes? That is a planning decision made by, by the way, white planners to allow these homes. They didn't sprout out of the ground. They didn't come in the suitcases of Hong Kong immigrants. They were planned for and permitted and allowed to be built. . . . There's also the issue of an unstated pattern of behaviour that says well, it's okay coming to our country to serve our food and wash our clothes, but when you start doing the same things that we're doing, then we have to draw the line. It's okay for us to own property in Toronto, but not for you to start buying up some of the prestige property. It's okay if you buy the slums or if you buy in Chinatown, but when you start buying our downtown office buildings or properties in Forest Hill, then you've crossed the line. . . .

I think what we have to do as Canadians is to recognize that our population has many different value sets, none of them better than the others, some of them more entrenched than others perhaps, but that doesn't make them any more right. If we truly mean to build a multicultural country, we have to find some way of equalizing the expression of all those cultures, not by singing and dancing on Canada Day, but in how we approach each other and how our governmental and political systems work. If we want to participate in this wonderful country, then we participate at all levels of it, all the way up and all the way down. . . .

We have become very passive, we let the media tell us what we think, we don't try to figure it out for ourselves. We don't read that much, don't come to our own conclusions much. We've abdicated our responsibility for defining what our culture is. We've only fought. We've never compromised.

It could be said that you belong to two visible minorities. You are Chinese Canadian and you are a woman in a profession that until recently has been male-dominated.

Yes, and together they make sure no one forgets me. It means that everything I do is under great scrutiny. Frankly, for a couple of the positions I have been appointed to, I was picked on account of being both of those things. They could solve two minority problems in one blow.

How does it make you feel—always conscious of the fact that this might be happening?

Well, you know what happens. It goes right back to my childhood and the story I told, "That's their problem, not mine." They are the weaker for being trapped in that stereotype. It's not my problem. If that's all they see of me, then that makes them really easy opponents, if opponents they be. And if they seek to be a comrade, then they'd better unlock their minds.

You seem to have a lot of experience dealing with people who are looking to find the cracks in your armour. . . . You prepare yourself by seeing yourself as they do; 'I'm a woman, a professional, and I'm Chinese, therefore this is going to happen to me.' Most people don't have that observer sitting on their shoulder watching. They react without reflection. Is that perspective something that's been honed over years and years of being exposed to this kind of treatment?

I think you're right. I hadn't thought of it that way but it rings very true to me. I think that I can see many instances in my life where I might have honed that skill. At the restaurant where I would sit and observe others and watch my own reaction to it, find my way to deal with those things. And at school, where I wasn't part of the common flow, but outside of it. And even today, among the much more polite crowds I deal with, the words they use and the approaches they use differ and get more and more sophisticated, but ultimately, the message is the same. The message is: you are extremely different from anything I've ever had to deal with before.

You have to assess the person you're dealing with, deal with this thrust that they've made and deliver it into the path that you think this situation and this conversation should go. In that respect, in new encounters, quite often I'm 'on'.

It's not sort of a relaxed, flowing way—let what happens happen. If it's not a casual situation with friends and people I care to be with where I can relax, it is always a matter of, where is this going?

People have a tendency to become very self-conscious when they're dealing with a different culture, someone or something different from themselves. That's because they're not treating the person they're dealing with as an equal. That's part of the colonial attitude of conquering a race and then 'civilizing' it.

It's the arrogance humans have that will destroy our planet. You know, first I think you have to be forced to believe that the other person is your equal and then you will take the lock off your brain and see that you are one and the same.

How has your life changed since your appointment as chair of the Police Services Board?

The experience has sharpened my focus as to what needs to be done and where racial and ethnic minorities fit in the broader political climate. We were running around thinking that everything was fine here, so long as everybody was nice to everybody else. Most of us, through our business lives and professional lives, have never really had to concern ourselves with whether or not racism would affect *us* directly. What we saw at the time of the announcement of my appointment was a lot of cries of anger and betrayal that must have had some racist underpinnings.

What really brought it to a head was the fact that I hadn't taken the oath of allegiance to the Queen. The government, around the time of my appointment, changed the wording of the oath so that it would read the way that I would have preferred it, but everybody suggests that I had the government change its laws to suit me. That's utterly ludicrous, utterly inconceivable. Nonetheless, the two things are tied together and so the whole issue of the oath heated up again. I think what then became an issue was the dominant culture's loss of the primacy of its symbols and that I, a visible minority, was going to be taking on a position which, without trying to flatter myself, is a very significant position in the city. I don't think that people recognized how important a position it was until such a position went to a Chinese female.

The chair of the Police Services Board and the board itself have the ultimate authority for setting the policy, priorities and budget of the police force. It is the ultimate decision-making authority in terms of how money is spent, how matters of discipline are resolved and how contracts are negotiated—all of these things are within the purview of the board. The chair sets the agenda for the board, and although it cannot control the board, nonetheless it has a very strong role to play. Judge Charles Bigg, who was the first chair, paid me a very great compliment by saying that I was the first, since his retirement, who tried to bring back the relevance of the commission itself. I think that also spurred on some of the criticism.

You're being very diplomatic.

Well, experience teaches that. People seem to hang on every word, trying to dissect the sentences to find something that is offensive. The negative is that somehow I've been intimidated by an environment that requires me to watch my words. My hope, on the positive side, is that perhaps I've become more professional at how I present myself. I don't know and actually I bristle at the thought that I can't be as free-thinking and free-speaking as I was in the past. I think that's unhealthy; that's an unhealthy state of affairs. To not be free. I think that it's very important for a wide range of debate to occur and I'm struggling as I carry on my duties to . . . at least if I don't cover the full range of the debate in my own way, to try to make sure that those points of view are represented.

But you have to be a manager. A manager really can't . . .

Take sides. That's very true. In the past the people coming forward to speak on policing issues were very, very radical on both sides of the issue—radically conservative or radically progressive. In order to get my view into the debate, all I have to do is make sure that part of the spectrum is also represented. In that respect, perhaps I'm still being a bit of an advocate, still being an activist.

How has your role in the Chinese community changed?

Well, I realize that public perceptions and public issues tend to focus on the end zones, but the real work and the real energy is spent in the forty-five yard zone. That's where you have to remain because that's where the critical mass of activity occurs. That's where you have an impact on making change, or in trying to influence public opinion. Yet all of the attention, media attention and public attention, is in the end zones which is where the points are scored. But when you're talking about fundamental change for society you should be looking at where the critical mass of the population actually plays out their lives.

Does the Chinese community accept that or do they say you have sold out?

I think that they are going to have many different opinions about what I'm doing. I think it's important for the community not to continue to allow itself to be talked about as having a single voice, that it be allowed to mature and hold a variety of opinions. My only hope is that this variety of opinions is brought out in an open and honest way rather than subjected to some of the manipulations that occur easily in a population isolated from the mainstream.

What is your position on the head tax issue? Do you think that there should be government recompense?

I think it's really an important statement for this government to make about how this country will treat its various racial and cultural minorities. To make an apology for past misdeeds, yes, but more importantly, to show how it intends to treat these parts of the population in the future. I think there has to be a recognition about the depth and breadth of discriminatory acts. What this meant for a lot of families was not only the payment of $500, which in those years was tantamount to two years' salary, but in addition to that the Exclusion Act caused the separation of families. My own family was touched by this. Not only did my father pay the head tax, but because of the Exclusion Act, he wasn't able to marry a Chinese person until after the Exclusion Act was lifted in 1947 when he returned to China to marry my mother who was thirty years younger. He didn't live to see his children grow up.

I think the government should put some money where its mouth is. It keeps talking about how we're one big, happy family—well, let them show it. How much money is a detail. I think an apology has to come first and compensation in some tangible form for seniors is a necessity.

What about those people who say this is just a bunch of young Toronto lawyers trying to make a name for themselves?

Well, they have to look at the fact that between 1905 and 1914 approximately 27,000 individuals paid the head tax. They're the people to whom we have to look. Also, we must look at ourselves in the mirror and decide what it is we want to do as Canadians.

National magazines have covered the explosion of crime from the Chinese gangs and the Vietnamese gangs. What do you feel about the way that's being treated?

I think the most important thing to remember is that crime is not a one-dimensional thing, that it is the result of various and complex social and economic factors. I think that you have to beware of leaders who give you simple-minded solutions for complex problems. So you're going to hear the cry "bigger jails, stiffer sentences, more Chinese cops, more cops generally." Well, it just won't work. Those aren't the answers.

The answers are broader, concerned with, generally, the decay and deterioration in the social and moral fabric of our society. There's a certain level of heartlessness that is developing, particularly in these bad economic times. The issue of organized crime is quite a separate issue, and that, too, doesn't have a simple solution. If organized crime has an international network, then police forces must be less parochial and more internationally focused, more technologically advanced. If there is either a language or cultural barrier that they have to cross, they will only cross that with training and with recruiting from that community, as well as developing better community liaison than they have in the past.

Will it be up to you to decide how to treat this particular wave of crime in Chinatown?

I think that the board, technically, has the responsibility for developing policy. But in the real world you have to work with the police force and the expertise that's there, together with the expertise that we can glean from other police forces also dealing with this problem. We're not going to be able to provide all the answers, but I think that we can organize ourselves to actually start asking the right questions in the search for those answers.

The issue of organized crime has been with us for many, many years. I think the danger lies in seeing all people of Chinese origin become tied to organized crime in the public's imagination.

What are your immediate goals?

I want to start building a consensus around the table and give the board and its functions some real meaning.

Do you mean meaning or power?

I think that you govern through leadership rather than authority.

That's very diplomatic.

Well, I think it's also realistic because you have to convince people to follow. I think the days of strong-arm control are over, whether at the board level or at the chief's level. I think it's really important to get away from the images of manipulating or controlling.

What would your father have thought of your appointment?

What would he have thought? . . . [long pause] . . . I think he would have delighted in it. He knew he was excluded from access to power and politics but he had made his peace with it; he was never angry. He was a very forgiving individual. To see me now, perhaps having a real impact on changing things, would have made him feel as though it was worth the sacrifices he made.

Susan Eng has had a high profile within the Chinese community for over ten years. Her new role as an important public official working at the heart of the mainstream has led her to see herself as something of a pioneer: a woman and a Chinese Canadian, her success will inevitably make access easier for those who follow.

Doris Lau

Doris Lau began this interview by grilling us for thirty minutes about the purpose of this project, its financial viability and possible marketing strategies. She allowed us to begin our questions not because she was satisfied with our answers but because the time was fast approaching when she'd have to leave us for yet another engagement in her very busy schedule. She is a woman of dizzying vitality and charm. She can lead a complicated conversation while calling up facts, figures and currency shifts on a computer at her desk in a corner office of the Sun Life Tower, or pose for a photograph on the floor of the Toronto Stock Exchange while discussing the subtle pleasures of ballroom dancing.

If you want to do your work well you must first sharpen the tools of your trade.
To do this you must make the acquaintance and seek the advice and assistance of the most distinguished members of the community.

子貢問為仁子曰工欲善其事必
先利其器居是邦也事其大夫之
賢者友其士之仁者

I immigrated to Canada in 1975. Hong Kong is too small, too crowded, and too polluted. It's not a pleasant place to live. Everyone in my family had always been sent abroad to study. My parents felt there was no future in Hong Kong. They encouraged all of us—my brothers and sisters and myself—to emigrate. At the time the choice was between Australia and Canada. I chose Canada because it seemed closer to the rest of the world, the United States and Europe. I went to London, England, first. I didn't like England; it's not for immigrants. So I returned to Hong Kong and applied for a visa to Canada.

As soon as I arrived, I said this is my place. I knew it. I came in February, the beginning of February, and it was about thirty below. It didn't bother me. I was all geared up. I thought it would be very, very cold, but I really had no idea what very, very cold was. So I bought my first fur coat before I took off. When I arrived and left the airport, I didn't think thirty below was so bad. And then everything is heated. When I was living in London, I found many places were unheated. You have to put in a coin for heat. I thought the cold was refreshing, so fresh compared to Hong Kong, which is so polluted. Canada is quiet compared to Hong Kong, but there's lots of life.

My first goal was to get a job and I found one in a week. I didn't have much working experience so I started at entry level at a life insurance company. After about a month they gave me an aptitude test to be a computer analyst or programmer. I passed the test and they trained me. After about a year, I was managing people and had my own office. I worked so hard—you cannot believe how hard I worked. I didn't feel that I was a foreigner; I felt that people accepted me and I felt at home.

Of course, there is no such thing as equality. I have always believed that there is no fairness in the world, so why should I expect it in Canada? I think the reason immigrants are sometimes treated badly is because they lack the necessary communication skills. In Hong Kong I was thought to have very good English, but as soon as I arrived in Canada I realized that I had a long way to go. What I did was listen to people, observe the way they spoke and how they expressed themselves, how people put things together, even how to do a presentation. In Hong Kong things were done more abruptly; here it is gentler. It took me a long time to know how to communicate. If you can communicate effectively, you can make your way up, along with hard work, of course.

Why do you think you're so driven to work hard?

I've always been driven to work hard. When I came to Canada I felt this was such a big new country with so much opportunity and so much to offer. When I was in London I saw that there were few opportunities for young people. It's so established, and in Hong Kong at that time, women weren't treated well. But in Canada everything seemed possible. Even in Canada, back then, it was not easy for a minority person to be in a managerial position in a huge insurance company. I'm realistic; I've always admitted what was a fact of life. And I always believe you have to work hard for what you get. If you want to achieve, super achieve, there are lots of opportunities for you here. Nobody will stop you from that—nobody.

Do you think there are as many opportunities now as there were in 1975 when you came here?

Oh, yes. I think now it's better. Back in 1975 nobody talked about multiculturalism. You were penalized for being a minority. There was no such thing as multiculturalism. The word did not exist.

What do you know about the history of the Chinese in Canada, the exclusion policy and the head tax?

Okay, history is history. That's how I look at it. I'm a very progressive person. I always look ahead. In the past, many different minority groups were penalized in one way or another, not just the Chinese. There's a lot of debate now about the head tax, and the community is pretty divided on the issue. In my experience, when I've talked to older Chinese who paid the head tax, they say, "We wanted to come to Canada and that was the price tag. As simple as that. We didn't have to come." They don't want the money back. Certainly, there's a point to be made about the fact that it was only Chinese who had to pay it, and I think it was discrimination. I can't compare that to today's Hong Kong entrepreneurs who have to pay millions to get in.

It's certainly similar to a head tax . . .

Yes, I agree. The difference is that it applies to all entrepreneurs, not just Chinese. I don't think the head tax should be paid back, in the same way that I don't think the entrepreneur who comes with his millions and loses it all should be paid back. At one point in time Canada needed farmers; now we want entrepreneurs. People with business experience and cash. Lots of cash. I think for the last twenty years the Hong Kong immigrants coming to Canada have been coming with money, education, wealth, skills and entrepreneurial experience. And I think it's a category of immigrant any country in the world would be happy to have. I think Hong Kong immigrants are among the best of the lot.

What do you think of the current wave of immigration, those fearing for the changes coming in 1997?

People, and immigrants in particular, leave their homes because of political reasons or economic reasons. Most people are leaving Hong Kong for political reasons. Now, I think every single immigrant group has some bad eggs. I mean bad people. And in this respect the Hong Kong people are no exception. I can tell you, based on my experience, that most young people who come to Canada are determined to live here for good and want to make it, and they are about the best immigrants. I'll tell you why: they never become a social burden. This is a big plus. Now there are some big businessmen who send their families here, but they mostly stay in Hong Kong temporarily. They have huge businesses. They apply for an immigrant visa and get it three months later. Do you think they can close down their businesses in three months? It takes maybe ten years to gradually slow down and close a business like that. So the family comes first and waits. It's a sad thing.

When you were a citizen court judge, did you ever refuse anyone citizenship, and why?

When I was a citizenship court judge I sincerely and seriously believed it was important for all those applying to understand some basic truths and general knowledge about this country, as well as a basic understanding of English and/or French, and if they didn't I failed them. I felt that not knowing those basic things was showing disrespect for this country. And I think that's unacceptable.

What sort of questions did you ask?

Oh, from history, politics, the formation of government, geography and basic English. The schedule was packed. We could not afford to stick with one candidate for one hour. On average, I'd give about twenty minutes per person.... I used to go to citizenship classes and speak to different immigrant groups on my own time, not during office hours, to tell people why it was important that they at least know basic English and something about Canada before becoming a citizen. I tried to help the underprivileged, needy and elderly people to go through the citizenship process. It is meaningless to live in a country without knowing anything about it.

In the Chinese community there were some who expected me to pass them because I was Chinese too. But they soon found out I wasn't going to do that. When I first started, they didn't like the way I preached, but later they appreciated it because they could read the newspaper and understand the Constitution, Parliament, the three levels of government and different political issues, all because they had learned the basics. They enjoyed more success when they gained confidence in English. The citizenship classes renewed their desire to learn more.

How much of your Chinese background, your heritage, do you maintain?

I am so Chinese you cannot believe it. I eat Chinese food and I speak Chinese at home; I'm very Chinese. But when I'm out in the work force, I'm completely Canadian. We are in Canada, so we should accept the culture. We shouldn't look back and say, "Oh, this is not how it's done in Hong Kong. This is not what it's like in China, so why should I do it?" That's not the way, it's the wrong attitude, because we have so many benefits here: the freedom, democracy, *everything*. We should try to adopt the Canadian way of life. If you don't enjoy it, you may as well go home or go back to wherever you came from. No one forced you to be here. As an immigrant myself, I think it is the best country I can think of, anyone can think of, for immigrants. However, I think it is a two-way street. We cannot just take; we have to contribute to the country, give back because of all that has been given, all the opportunity.

Are your parents still in Hong Kong?

My father lives in Hong Kong. He's in his eighties now and likes to live in Hong Kong because of the weather, but my mother has immigrated to Canada. She just loves the cold and the snow. She's in her sixties.

Presenting Citizenship Certificate and congratulations.

And your brothers and sister?

Half the family is in Australia, the other half in Canada. My sister came for a visit from Australia and she said that all the Chinese here walk with pride, with their heads up. She said in Australia they are miserable, they walk with their heads down. She said everyone here has so much life in them. They walk with their heads up, with pride, always smiling.

You're recognized as a prominent member of the Chinese community. Is that something you have aspired to be?

When I was seventeen, after finishing high school, I applied for a job as a junior reporter for an English newspaper in Hong Kong. I was a columnist; I had my picture there; I was well known. It was a tremendous experience for me. I was the youngest reporter ever in the whole organization, so I was well known even back then. In college, I was always the prefect or head girl. I was used to succeeding and to being recognized. So when I came to Canada I did nothing but concentrate on developing myself and helping others, going to all kinds of night schools, taking all kinds of courses.

In 1980, I decided I didn't want to work for anybody. I knew that I would have no further promotions for maybe the next twenty years. Back then, for a woman and a minority to become a manager in a big firm was impossible. I always liked investments. I became a stockbroker because all the stockbrokers I used were lousy—lousy and lazy. I said to myself, I can do better. I wrote all the exams and was accepted. Since then I've never looked back. I started in the industry in 1982 and on the day I got my licence the bull market started. It lasted five years, from August 1982 to August 1987 until the crash. And now, the bull market is back.

What do you see yourself doing in the future?

I want to be a very successful role model in this male-dominated industry with professionalism and integrity at all times. At present, I am the only woman managing a branch of very experienced and professional male investment advisors. I would like to be a role model in the business world and in Nesbitt Thomson. They say the drop-out rate for women is high due to the unusually high stress level in this business. That's why there are so few women, women who are successful and stay long. At present, I am handling multi-million-dollar portfolios for serious business clients. Eventually, I would like to be a giant portfolio fund manager. I also have an investment column in the Chinese newspaper and I host an investment show on national Chinese pay T.V. I give timely investment analysis and advise on how to invest in the North American market, as it is very different from the Asian market. I think this is a very good way to educate the public on how to invest in Canada, and I think this is very good for the country economically.

Are most of your clients Chinese Canadians?

At the present moment, yes. There are so many new immigrants from different parts of the world who want to invest in Canada and need professional and timely advice. By helping people to invest, I think I'm doing the community a bigger service than being a judge or a community worker. It think it is even beneficial for the country.

What would you like to be doing ten or twenty years from now?

I'd like to do some good things for the community and for the betterment of Canada. For example, I would like to contribute my limited time and money to charities and to the promotion of the arts and culture. And, of course, I would like to see myself as one of the top women in money management, and hopefully, make life happy for many people.

Have you ever considered politics?

I do not think I am the right type of person to be in politics; it takes a certain personality type to succeed in this area. One type is genuine and wants to serve people and work towards the betterment of the country. The other type is in politics for the betterment of their own egos, profile, whatever. I have every respect for the former and I usually contribute and support excellent individual politicians regardless of their flag.

Do you support any one particular party?

Well, I'm a business person, so of course I firmly believe in a party that is concerned with the country's economics first, then social welfare. Many people say the Progressive Conservatives are only for rich people. How can a party, how can any party, afford just to support the rich people? Only five percent of the whole nation makes more than $50,000. Do you think any party is stupid enough to only support that five percent? I vote for the party that promotes a sound economy. A country without a good and sound economy cannot support a rich social welfare program. You have to build your economy first. I don't believe in a party that cares for social welfare only but doesn't care about the economy; it doesn't make sense. I'm a very realistic person. In fact, I support any party that is brave enough to have policies that can improve the country's economy and unemployment.

You have so much energy and such a positive attitude. Was there ever a time when you doubted yourself, when you despaired?

The way I look at life, there's never an end. There's never a problem that comes to me that I can't solve. Sure, I've had bad days, but I always look ahead. I manage many people's money. If I have a bad day, I think what's next? What strategy? I recover. I have to. So I always look ahead. For every problem, there's a solution. And I find it.

How does it make you feel when people refer to you as a role model?

I am conscious of that. I make sure that whatever I do, I do with lots of integrity. Integrity and professionalism. Always genuinely caring for others' feelings, and being compassionate.

Is your husband's life as busy as yours?

Oh, yes. He's a gynaecologist-obstetrician. I think in order for a woman to be successful, the most important thing is to have your husband's support. Just imagine if every day you go home and your husband complains about you working so hard. It's too much pressure. My husband is very supportive, and whatever I do he thinks is great. He thinks I should expand myself to whatever I want to do. And he respects me.

PRESIDING OVER A SPECIAL CANADIAN CITIZENSHIP COURT WITH THE PRIME MINISTER, THE RT. HONOURABLE BRIAN MULRONEY.

What do you think of the language question in this country?

I think everyone should speak more than one language. It's an asset. I think it's a sharing process. When I was appointed to the bench I didn't know a word of French. But I believe in bilingualism. I didn't know any French, so they gave me classes with other judges. On the third lesson I started to speak and they almost flipped. I was so proud I could speak French. Everyone looked at me, expecting an Oriental to speak only Chinese. And believe it or not, I don't know how well I spoke, but everyone said I spoke French well.

What was the high point of your term as a citizenship court judge?

I initiated a project to help all the needy Chinese to become citizens. It was in the third year of my term. It turned out to be the largest court ever held in the history of Canada. Why did I do it? Because there had been a Greek court, an Italian court, and I said why not a Chinese court? I worked with all the agencies helping immigrants and I appealed to all those immigrants who had been here more than ten years but hadn't got their citizenship because of language problems, or other problems, to come forward and enrol in the programs to become a citizen.

There were eight hundred. The Toronto Board of Education held special classes for them. I gave them a year to learn. And when I held the court, it was so big we had to have it at the Metro Convention Centre. Prime Minister Mulroney and then-Finance Minister Michael Wilson came and participated in the court. It was the largest court ever held in history.

Being a judge gave me the chance to see and understand all the different cultures. I am very much a people person. When I was given the appointment I never, even one day, felt I was superior or more privileged. Even the dishwasher would come up from the kitchen and ask me questions. "Judge Lau, what do you think I should do? I cannot speak English." I answered all the questions, every single one. There are lots of people who put on airs when they get an appointment. I never did that. I believe life is a merry-go-round. Today you are here, tomorrow you are there. Why bother? I think all human beings should be respected as long as they are good human beings. They should be respected and well taken care of no matter if they are a dishwasher, a labourer or a business person.

Formerly a Canadian Citizenship Court judge, Doris Lau is a vice-president and branch manager of Nesbitt Thomson Inc. In addition to managing a dynamic and professional team of investment advisors she effectively handles multi-million dollar portfolios for a diverse range of clients.

JOSEPH WONG

We conducted the interview with Dr. Wong at his office on a Thursday afternoon. Thursday is the day he reserves for his community activities, on this particular day committed to his role as chairman of The United Way. Near the end of the interview we noticed that his wrist watch was running one hour fast. He explained that it was thirteen hours fast—the difference between Toronto time and Hong Kong time—and that he had just returned from a trip to Hong Kong. When asked how a man on such a tight schedule could manage with a watch set to the wrong time he laughed and explained that out of homesickness he had kept his watch at Hong Kong time for the first five years he lived in Canada. It was only the day after his graduation from McGill University, which was the day he married his wife, that he realized Canada was home and the place he would raise his children.

子曰君子恥其言而過其行

I AM ONLY CONCERNED THAT MY WORDS MAY EXCEED MY ACTIONS.

I came to Canada in 1968 on a student visa. I was advised by almost everybody that I should stay in science and not apply for medicine because 'Canadian medical schools did not accept foreign students'. I was unhappy. I switched to engineering and got my Bachelor of Engineering in electrical engineering in 1973. I came to understand the system and I realized that even though it was difficult it would not be impossible to study medicine if that's what I really wanted, so in my third, fourth and fifth years at McGill I carried perhaps sixty percent more work than a regular student—the extra courses I would need to get me into medical school. It was very difficult. During the academic year I worked as a porter in the residence, a telephone operator and other odd jobs on weekends and holidays. But I earned most of my money during the summer.

Why did you choose to go to medical school in the United States?

Well, first of all, Albert Einstein is one of the best medical schools in the States. Secondly, they made me an offer I couldn't refuse, so to speak. It was a very generous grant and a large loan to help support my wife and me. I was in New York for three years; I graduated in 1976.

What made you decide to come back to Canada?

I chose to practise in a public system rather than a private one. I think we have to go back to the reason why I wanted to study medicine in the first place. I grew up in a very poor neighbourhood in Hong Kong. There was no welfare. We always said Hong Kong was the heaven of the rich and the hell of the poor. . . . Before 1965, I had never heard of a strike or demonstration in Hong Kong. You could not organize a protest or march to express your opinion. In 1965 something drastic happened. A ferry company raised fares from 10 to 15 cents and a number of young people came out to protest the increase because they thought it unfair to the poor. That was the first time I had heard of something like a protest in Hong Kong. I wanted to be part of it but my mother was terrified; she locked me in my room so I wouldn't go. It was a very peaceful demonstration, no violence at all. In western countries it would have been accepted but it was unprecedented for Hong Kong. If you protested against the government it was close to committing suicide.

Economic suicide or physical suicide?

Both. One of the organizers died mysteriously a few years later. He was arrested and jailed and sometime later was found hanging in his cell. That was the official story. People died every day in Hong Kong and nobody gave a damn. I was extremely unhappy with the way people were treated, particularly poor people in the areas of medicine and education. . . .

My family was very poor. My parents came from China. They went to Hong Kong during the Japanese invasion of China. My father was a mechanic. He was very skilled and yet he was paid perhaps $200-$300 Hong Kong a month, just barely enough to raise a family of four or five. He worked seven days a week from seven in the morning until about eight or nine at night. He would eat his dinner alone because the rest of the family had already eaten and the children were in bed. . . .

I was outraged at the unfairness of the society, at the corruption of the government and the injustice the poor must suffer. There was absolutely no protection for the labourer in Hong Kong at that time. If you got injured at work it was simply your bad luck. I was about ten or twelve when I came to realize what was going on.

What sustained you? What kept you from despair?

I lived in a very poor neighbourhood, but I was extremely happy in childhood. The neighbourhood was close; we all played together. Life was really very good; I mean, it was always happy. I had clothes to wear and food to eat. We didn't have many material things. We didn't have a car. We bought new clothes once a year. We bought our new clothes the day before the Chinese New Year. It's a very vivid memory for me because that was the day I was always happiest. We would go shopping along a street lined with small booths, hundreds of them. Rows and rows of booths with different types of merchandise. So every year on Chinese New Year's Eve we would buy new clothes because that was the only day my parents had some extra money to spend. I still remember, thirty years later, my parents buying me a little red tie. It cost my parents 50 cents, Hong Kong cents. Wow! I was on top of the world. Eventually I got a blue jacket to go with it.

How did you come to see that there was another world out there, a world for the rich?

I read newspapers. There were some who wrote about how the rich lived. Gossip columns. It seemed like a different world. But in Hong Kong at that time there was quite a bit of oppression from the government on freedom of the press. Even the newspaper owners would not want to offend the government. For example, in the mid-1960s, they might be able to say a little bit more, they might be able to report on the protests, but they would not cause an uproar in the editorials saying this is unfair and make a big thing of it. . . . I never saw that kind of editorial except maybe in the smaller newspapers. Of course things have improved a great deal since that time.

But I was not so much concerned with the lavish lifestyle of the rich. If they had money, if they could afford it, I didn't have any problem with it. I'm someone who can tolerate all types of people. All I'm saying is that the ones at the bottom, the disadvantaged, should be given some share of the resources that society has.

How did you direct your energies to get yourself out of that environment?

Actually, thinking back, it was a dream. It was a dream that had very little chance of becoming a reality. In my childhood, from the time that I could remember to the time I came to Canada, I had only two things in mind that I wanted to do. I wanted to be a doctor or a teacher. I saw poor people die in front of my eyes because they did not have the money to seek medical attention before the final stages of their illnesses set in. I always had the idea that if I grew up to be a doctor, I would be able to help these people. And I wanted to be a teacher because I had been deprived of an early education; I didn't start school until I was about ten. Thinking back, I see it was very naïve of me, or for any child from that kind of neighbourhood, to think of going through school and then university. It was a dream.

How did it become reality?

When I was twelve or thirteen, a businessman came to my father and asked him to work for his company on a contract basis, so that my father would be his own boss, operating his own business. My father thought about it for a long, long time. The family's livelihood rested on my father's income. He agonized over it and finally decided he should strike out on his own and try to build something better for himself and his family. So he went to his boss and told him he wanted to resign because of this contract he'd been offered. My father's salary was immediately doubled to $600 and then increased again to $900 a month. That meant that my father was being paid $300 a month but he was really worth $900 a month to that company.

It made him angry, made me angry, made all of us very, very angry. But my father had made up his mind and he refused the $900 and left the company. So all of a sudden our standard of living got better. My father was able to send me to school instead of making me an apprentice. Up till then my schooling hadn't been in regular schools. I went to night schools, some schools organized by the unions, a school organized by some other group, but nothing that was recognized by the government. So at age fifteen I entered regular grammar school in the equivalent of grade eight. I had done very little studying in my first fourteen years but, surprisingly, I did extremely well and never scored worse than number two in the whole class. In Hong Kong a class is two hundred or three hundred people. Something clicked. I learned very well. I was very happy and because of my interest and background, mathematics, science and biology were easy, easy subjects for me.

And the move from Hong Kong to Canada?

After grade eleven, we had to write an examination. It is called the middle school examination, and the best, the cream of the crop, would be chosen by the best schools in Hong Kong. It's very competitive. Studying in Hong Kong is not fun. The exams are difficult as are the pressures exerted by the family and by the society. I was among the top and I was admitted to one of the best schools for grade twelve. If you graduated from this school you had a good chance of entering the University of Hong Kong. Anybody who graduated from the University of Hong Kong twenty or twenty-five years ago was guaranteed the best jobs the colony had to offer. Eighty percent of those graduating from this school went on to take medicine. Medicine at the University of Hong Kong is again the cream of the crop. Hong Kong doctors make more money than you can believe. The equivalent of $400,000 or $500,000 Canadian. Plus they pay only seventeen percent tax. Added to the buying power of the money in Hong Kong, it's like making $2 million here. So there's a lot of temptation to stay. But my desire to go into medicine had nothing to do with money.

How did your family feel about that, considering the hardships they had suffered?

I have to give them credit. They gave me a free hand and I think that's unusual for Chinese parents. Chinese parents, particularly those from Hong Kong, almost carve a path for their children to follow: You have to go into engineering, you have to be a lawyer, you have to be a doctor, you have to be this, you have to do that. Although my family is quite traditional in many ways, I was allowed to choose my own destiny.

Joseph Wong with parents (his grandfather stands at right rear) just before his departure for Canada July, 1968.

Why are they that way?

I'm not sure. As I said, they are very traditional in other ways but in this, I chose my career, I chose my destiny, and they didn't interfere.

But you decided not to go to the University of Hong Kong; you decided to leave. Why?

Several reasons. The most important was my girlfriend. My girlfriend at the time, and now my wife. I've only ever had one girlfriend and one wife. She emigrated to Canada in 1968, March 1968. Until March 10, 1968, I had intended to go to the University of Hong Kong. I saw her off at the airport and then went directly to the Canadian High Commission to find out how I could go to Canada to study. I applied to three universities in Canada. I was accepted in all three and chose McGill. McGill had a very good reputation.

And your girlfriend?

She was in Calgary. We saw each other once or twice a year, for five years.

Why did you return to Canada after you finished your studies at Albert Einstein?

I think it had something to do with the experience I had one summer in Toronto. I came to Toronto to work during the summer of 1972, in my fourth year. I worked for a professor at the Faculty of Medicine at the University of Toronto doing medical research. I had a wonderful time. So when I was at Einstein I wrote to the professor saying I wished to return to Toronto. He helped me find a position at Toronto Western Hospital to do my postgraduate studies. So I did my internship in medicine, my residency in internal medicine, and then my fellowship, which is a further specialization, in chest medicine.

How did you come to practise family medicine?

I came back to Canada in 1976 and started my volunteer work at Mount Sinai in 1977. I was a volunteer helping the hospital reach the Chinese community. There was a large Chinese neighbourhood surrounding Mount Sinai Hospital. It was felt that the Chinese community was not using the hospital. There were several reasons. The first was language. Secondly, the hospital was perceived as a Jewish hospital, rather than a general hospital for everybody. To help resolve the language problem, I helped start the Chinese community clinic in 1978. And they organized a blood pressure clinic, health screening clinic and breast screening clinic to make the neighbourhood aware of the facilities.

How did you get involved in community projects that were not related to medicine?

The crisis of the boat people began in 1977–78 and peaked in 1979. I remember every day after work buying the Toronto Star and seeing the photographs and reading the horror stories of the boat people from Vietnam and Indo-China. I kept waiting to hear that somebody was doing something to stop it, to help them. But the world reaction wasn't very strong, nor did Canadians at the time seem to be very interested. There wasn't even very much interest in the Chinese community. I waited for something to happen from February until sometime in June 1979. I had never organized anything, but I was prepared to help.

I had dinner with a friend in June and said that I couldn't understand why no one in the Chinese community had organized to help the boat people. Out of that conversation we put together a list of fifteen or twenty friends, contacted them, and arranged for our first meeting. We organized ourselves into a committee called the Action Committee for Refugees from Southeast Asia. I was the one who yelled the most, who felt the most, who talked the loudest, so I became the chairman. We appealed to Ottawa to allow more refugees to enter Canada and we organized to help them once they arrived. We raised about $300,000, which was no small thing. At the time, I was a resident earning $15,000 a year. I had a family. It was tough, but we did it. Everybody chipped in and went out on the streets asking for donations. We went to street corners, put up a table with posters and information about the refugees, and brought in a few thousand dollars a day. I also joined up with Howard Adelman. He is a professor of philosophy at York University and also the director of the Centre for Refugee Studies at York. Two days before we had organized our group, Howard had founded Operation Lifeline. We met and became very good friends. Howard invited me to go into Operation Lifeline, which I did. So I was working in several organizations for refugee relief in 1979–80.

Joseph Wong with fellow students at McGill.

Can you think of an incident or an individual that made you think all this work was truly worthwhile, something that sustained you?

There have been many. I really don't need an emotional story to convince me because it is what I believe in. I've been drawn to other projects, too. In the latter part of 1979 I was involved in the protest against *W5* for their program called "Campus Giveaway." It was a documentary that portrayed foreign students as being Asian. Whenever they spoke of foreign students, they showed a shot of an Asian student without knowing anything about his citizenship. It was clear stereotyping. And of course the Canadian students were always shown as being white.

How much did you know about the history of the Chinese in Canada?

Not very much, but it made me want to find out. I was extremely shocked when I read about the riots on the west coast in the nineteenth century and that a head tax was established to try to limit the immigration of the Chinese, and of course the Exclusion Act from 1923 to 1947—all terrible things. I was even shocked to learn that Chinese people in Canada did not have the right to vote until 1948. In a strange way it was the *W5* episode that made me learn more about the history of the Chinese in Canada. I was very angry with the *W5* episode. I was vice-chairman of the committee and I carried the tapes to a lot of other cities across Canada. My wife and I had bought tickets to go to Calgary at Christmastime, so I thought why not take advantage of the trip and show the tape to some of the communities out west. My wife's relatives organized a meeting with the Calgary Chinese. I helped them organize a committee and I went to Edmonton and Vancouver. I went to Windsor, Waterloo, London and Ottawa.

What do you think of the situation now?

Unfortunately, there has been a lot of stereotyping in this country. We have to correct the image. In the old days, Chinese were seen only as laundry or restaurant workers, not professionals. Now everybody from Hong Kong is seen as a tycoon with tons of money, driving a big Mercedes or Rolls Royce. I do admit that there are some of those very wealthy people coming from Hong Kong, but there are far more ordinary people, struggling to find a job, struggling to find something compatible with their skills and experience.

How do you rectify or challenge the stereotyping?

We try to be a little more high profile, in the sense that we work for the society, for a cause. I was organizing the first walk-a-thon for The United Way in the Chinese community and I was interviewed about it. The interviewer said to me that it was about time the Chinese community got involved because so much money had been directed to the Chinese community from The United Way. I stopped him right there. I told him that there were a lot of workers of Chinese origin at Ontario Hydro, at The Bank of Nova Scotia and other big banks. All these people donated to The United Way through payroll deduction plans and employee deduction plans. Unfortunately, donations coming from Hydro and the banks are regarded always as white deductions. This interviewer was not stupid but he suffered from the kind of bias or stereotyping we're talking about. It's very dangerous.

What are your principal concerns today?

I am involved in two things outside of my medical practise. I am presently Chairman of the Board of The United Way, and I am helping to build the first geriatric care complex for Chinese Canadians in Scarborough. It's a place where Chinese seniors can enjoy a lifestyle that caters to their culture and language. It is being constructed on about four acres of land with a total construction budget of about $30 million.

Do you see yourself going into politics someday?

I have been asked that question since 1979. I don't think I'm really suited to go into politics. Sometimes you have to say things you don't mean. Sometimes you have to say things you don't think are right. I don't want to do that. I always want to be able to say what I think is right, to live by my conscience. I am very happy with the kind of work I am doing. I would not give up my work as a medical doctor and as a community activist or advocate for politics.

Have you met politicians you have admired?

Pierre Trudeau. He's very arrogant, but I like him. Trudeau is one of the few politicians who speaks his mind. Rightly or wrongly, he speaks his mind. That is why I admire him. I have a very close friendship with Bob Rae. I admire him and I think he is a very conscientious person.

What do you hope for your children?

My wife and I are raising them by the example of our own lives. We encourage them to volunteer their time to the community. They are still very young. One is ten years old; the other is fourteen. They volunteer their time. They participate as they can. We are very proud of them.

Dr. Joseph Wong is Chairman of the United Way and Chairman of the Chinese Community Nursing Home for Greater Toronto. He was also deeply involved in the search for a bone marrow donor for Elizabeth Lue which led to the establishment of the largest Chinese bone marrow data bank in the world.

Victor Ling

The three scientists in this book, Dr. Tak Mak, Dr. Lap-Chee Tsui and Dr. Victor Ling, occupy similarly small offices, crowded with books and journals, filing cabinets and desks disappearing under stacks of documents and computer equipment. Their offices are not affixed with name plates and are typically hidden away in a far corner of their research laboratories. Their doors are always open and in each case our interviews were regularly interrupted by colleagues, research assistants and graduate students seeking advice. When we sat down to do this interview and shut the door for some privacy, Dr. Ling began apologizing for the stuffiness of his office. He explained that there were birds nesting in the air conditioning duct and until they were finished he would not be turning it on. Dr. Victor Ling is a warm, friendly man with an engaging sense of humour. He was very curious about our project and posed almost as many questions to us as we did him.

子曰不患人之不己知
患不知人也

I AM NOT DISTURBED THAT PEOPLE DO NOT RECOGNIZE MY ABILITIES;
I AM ONLY TROUBLED THAT I DO NOT RECOGNIZE THEIRS.

I was born in Shanghai in 1943. We left in 1948. My ancestral family was from southern China, from a small port city called Swatow [Shantou]. I remember that my father was in Canada when we left Shanghai. He was a delegate representing the Shanghai Chamber of Commerce at an international trade fair in Canada. I remember, or maybe I was told, that when the Communist army was coming into Shanghai one of the family friends came to our home and insisted that my mother take us to Hong Kong. Since my father was away this friend felt it was his responsibility to look after my mother and the family.

Word came in the morning and we left that afternoon. My mother was very reluctant to leave. She felt that we'd lived through the Second World War and this was just another one of those things that would blow over. My father was unaware—he might have been aware, there may have been a phone call—but I don't think he knew exactly what was going on.

I suspect he thought that eventually we'd return to China. He really loved China; he instilled a sense of pride about China in us. We were never ashamed of being Chinese. Maybe ashamed is too strong. We were never shy about being Chinese, although I've observed that some of the Canadian-born kids wished they weren't coloured; they wished they were white.

Did the family speak English?

No. In fact, I didn't know any English, although I was given an English name when I was born and so were my brothers and sisters. My father and his brother had established a business in Australia, an import-export business, importing Chinese goods to Australia and exporting wood and Australian goods to China. He was in Australia about ten years; my brother and a sister were born there.

Did you come directly to Canada from Shanghai?

We were in Hong Kong for two years before emigrating to Canada. We weren't wealthy but we had a little bit of money. We also had relatives in Hong Kong, and my father, being in business, had contacts in Hong Kong and Australia. So he was able to provide for us and we lived in a small apartment.

My father wasn't sure Canada would accept us and I don't think that my parents were sure that we wanted to come here. I think we stayed in Hong Kong hoping that things in China would change and we could go back. We had a house in China that we left. It's still there, I understand.

Have you been back?

No.

Why did you settle in Toronto, as opposed to Vancouver?

My father's business sense told him that Toronto was a better city to operate from, so he began his business in Toronto in 1950. He had a little store on Yonge Street. I remember that it was just a little place upstairs at 237½ Yonge Street, across from the old Eaton's. It had a little narrow doorway to go upstairs. He sold wholesale, again importing from Hong Kong and Australia.

I think it must have been difficult. He was fortunate in that he knew English. He taught himself English when he was in Australia. He sold to Eaton's and to gift shops around Ontario. My mother was very active in the business; they worked side by side—the kids, too.

How much of your sense of identity comes from those early years spent in China and Hong Kong?

My father always had this feeling that China was our home but Canada was our foreign home, so to speak. I don't really feel that way anymore. I feel I'm Canadian. I happen to have a Chinese genetic origin. I'm very happy to have that background, but which country do I feel I identify with more? Well, surely it's Canada; it's not China. I don't know China, I don't have any roots there, I don't have any relations there that I know personally. So I think that in one generation the feeling about China has changed for us. My father has lived in many countries but he's always Chinese wherever he is and he's always very interested to be in contact with Chinese no matter what country he's in.

You have a very strong sense of your father.

Yes, definitely. Or family. I haven't spoken of my mother, but she's very important. . . . We have a very closely knit family—a lot of it is due to my mother. However, I think if you want to analyze it, it's probably because, even though we were Chinese emigrating to Canada, we weren't Cantonese and we weren't Mandarin. We came from an area of China with a unique dialect. The family supported itself because there was no one else. Perhaps it also has something to do with the family travelling a lot, the family relying on each other for support; the only people you could really trust were those in your own family.

What was it like growing up in Toronto in the 1950s?

I can't say that it was hard. I would say that it was interesting. For example, it's different now, but in the '50s my brother and I were the only Chinese in the public school we went to. . . . But kids being kids, they liked to tease us because we were different. I think we got into our fair share of fights.

Were there other minorities at the school?

There were. But I don't remember any Black kids, for example. I'd sort of identify with the kids who might not know English very well, and certainly I didn't know any English at all when I came. It was a little tough.

What did your parents tell you when you experienced these difficulties?

They'd say, "Well, you're Chinese, of course you can't expect to be treated exactly like the other kids, but the only thing that you can do is your best." They instilled a sense of pride in being Chinese. They didn't say well, it's too bad you're not white. They said to be proud. The only way to get back at those kids is to show that you're better.

Success is the best revenge?

That's right. That must have sunk in at some point, I don't know.

Did your father's business do well through the 1950s?

I think that it was comfortable. It was enough to raise a family of five children and send them to school.

Were your parents anxious that you go to university?

Well, it's interesting. My parents never told us what we should do or be. They never said you should be a lawyer or a doctor, anything like that. The only thing they've ever said to us is "We want you to do well." My parents are Christians, they have very high moral principles about right and wrong, and they taught that to us. I'm very clear myself about being a Christian. It was through my mother, who is a very strong Christian, that we were taught Christian principles. . . . How can I put it, if you were very 'Chinese' you could be very polite, but you might not be very genuine. But she taught us that, being a Christian, you had to

Victor Ling with mother and siblings in Shanghai.

be very genuine about your feelings and also show respect for the other person.

Did you do well in school?

Yes, but not because my parents were forcing me to do well and not because I felt any competition or anything like that.

Was there anything you weren't very good at?

Oh lots! I wish I could play the piano—I still can't play the piano. I wanted to be an NBA basketball player, but I'll never be one. I love sports; I love to play tennis, and I do play regularly, but I'm never as good as I wish I was. Most things I can pick up quite easily, but I'm never as good as I wish I was.

When did you first become interested in science?

I knew I was going to be a scientist when I was in grade eight. My sister introduced me to the library. She felt it was time I got a library card. I didn't even know what that was. So we went to the library together to get me a card and that's when I discovered reading. In fact, I think I read as many books as I could get my hands on.

I read the biography of Isaac Newton and was fascinated by the way he thought about things, reasoned. I thought it was very creative. I don't know if it really happened or not, but we've all heard the story of the apple falling and hitting him on the head and how that led to the discovery of gravity. I think this is extraordinary—to take something that everybody sees all the time and to put a twist to it. And then everybody says, 'my gosh, that's obvious' . . . I think it's just the sense of natural curiosity. It's something that I felt that I wanted to do; I never seriously thought about being a doctor or an engineer or anything like that. I wanted to be a scientist.

What kind of science?

I didn't know. In fact, when I went to the University of Toronto, I thought maybe I would go into engineering physics, and maybe more quantitative science because in those days when you went through high school, biology wasn't considered to be a very serious subject, but if you took chemistry or physics, well it was a different thing. It's a kind of snobbish approach, I guess. Biology was for people who did home economics. So I didn't know very much about biology. I thought I should do something more general so I went for honours science, and then went on to do my Ph.D. at UBC.

By that time I really enjoyed biochemistry and biology. So I asked around trying to find out who was the best biochemist in Canada. There were different opinions, but one of the people a few had mentioned was Gordon Dixon in Vancouver. I hadn't just limited myself to Canada—I had been accepted at

Berkeley, but the Vietnam War was on. I was offered a scholarship, but if you read the fine print it said that you would become a state resident and would be eligible for the draft, so I said forget it! They said it was unlikely I'd ever be drafted but I disagreed with the whole thing. I mean, I was going to do science, I wasn't interested in being involved in the war. So I decided not to go to the United States. The second choice was to do it in Canada. While I was at UBC, Fred Sanger, who at that time had the first of his two Nobel Prizes, came to UBC to give a lecture on RNA structure. I didn't know much about it but was fascinated. I wrote to Sanger and asked him if I could come to Cambridge to do my post-graduate studies with him.

What was Cambridge like?

I was a little scared because here I was going to an institution where almost every second staff member was a Nobel Prize winner. I wasn't sure I was going to be able to make it. But it was a very exciting environment. Initially, I expected everybody to be more brilliant than I was. I genuinely thought that would happen. But after day one I knew that it wasn't going to happen.

People are people; they could be very smart or have achieved great things, but essentially—as we are doing now—I could talk to them one to one. I wasn't going to be blown out of the water. It gave me an enormous sense of confidence. What I realized at Cambridge is that if you're artificial, if you try to impress, or speak with authority on something you don't really know much about, people pick it up just like that. But if you're genuine, no matter how brilliant these people were, they take the time to listen. Definitely a sense of community. Also, I got the feeling that they respected the kind of thing I was trying to do.

What were you trying to do?

By that time DNA had already been discovered, but we did not know the actual sequence of the nucleotides that make up DNA, which is the code for the genes. Fred Sanger was working on that at the time. When I entered his lab he asked if I knew anything about nucleic acids. I said no. He said nobody knew how to do DNA sequencing, how to sequence nucleotides. Since you don't know anything anyway, why don't you start working on it. Other people in the lab were doing other things: RNA structure work. I really appreciated the fact that Sanger—this was his own pet project—chose somebody like myself, who had no experience at all in this area to work on it. . . . Of course you have to have the background, but often what a lot of people don't appreciate is that when you're discovering something new, you have to go with your instincts. You can't go to a book to read about it. Sanger liked to say that research was like being parachuted into the middle of a jungle—you have to find your way out. Now, how do you prepare for that? You have to use your wit, your sense about what is going on; being loaded down with a lot of equipment won't help you.

How did your research for Sanger go?

For about a year and a half, nothing. Everybody around me seemed to be enormously successful with whatever they were doing. It was hard going into the lab knowing you weren't getting anywhere while everybody else was publishing and making discoveries. In fact, at one point I went into Sanger's office and said, "Fred, this DNA sequencing business is going to take at least fifty years. I mean, there's no way." He said, "It's going to take that long? Huh! Well, somebody's got to start." That was really encouraging. Somebody's got to start. . . .

I put aside my DNA sequencing project because I had lost a lot of self-confidence and decided to work on another project, also to do with nucleic acids and RNA. I published a paper on it. But it took me three or four months to do. Fred kept telling me not to waste my time. But I knew that I needed to prove to myself that it wasn't me, it was the problem. I think that was very important for me. I realized that if things aren't working it's not always to do with me. It's okay to work on problems that may not have easy solutions. . . .

I stayed at Cambridge for a little over two years. It was all very new stuff back then. Sanger went on from there to develop an even better way of sequencing DNA. He developed the technique that is now being used; in fact, he won his second Nobel Prize for that work. I left at the end of 1971. I was invited to join the faculty at Rockefeller University, but I turned it down. I wanted to stay in Canada. Canada had given my family a home and me my education. So, I approached Jim Till, who was director of Bio-Research here at the hospital. It was very strange how I got this job. We were at a meeting and I bumped into him. I asked him, "Are there any jobs at the Ontario Cancer Institute?" He said, "Yup." I looked at him and said, "I want one." I don't think we ever signed a contract or anything like that. He just asked, "When do you want to start?" And I've been here since.

When I came back and, not being immodest, I had done some of the real pioneering work on the techniques of DNA sequencing, many people thought I would continue with that work. But I didn't want to. The reason I came here was because of the work they had been doing here: animal genetics and the manipulation of cells in culture. I thought that was really neat because I felt that's going to be essential work if we're ever going to learn about human genetics. I wanted to come here to do that sort of work. I didn't come here as a student or a trainee; I came as a staff member to work on something I'd never done before in my life. And the researchers here, particularly Larry Thompson and Bud Baker, were really kind. They took time to show me how to manipulate cells in culture—it was a real thrill seeing these things grow!

We're sitting in your lab. What is it about? What are you doing now?

What we're doing now is we're using cells in culture, the same kind of genetic system we started to work on, to identify genes and molecules that are important for drug resistance. We've never had an idea of trying to apply research or anything like that. We had an idea that we wanted to learn something very fundamental about cell genetics.

When you say drug resistance, do you mean its resistance to medication?

Right. It's like the situation when you're given chemotherapy. They hope the drugs you're taking will kill all the cancer cells. Let's say that by the time a tumour is detected in your body, there are at least 100 million cells. There are 100 million cells in the tip of my finger. If one of those cells becomes drug resistant, it could survive the drug treatment and multiply. The cell becomes drug resistant spontaneously, without even knowing that a drug has been applied because a tumour cell is mutating all the time. . . . And if one cell of the 100 million survives the treatment, well it doesn't take very long for it to become another tumour of 100 million cells. . . . A month. . . . You think you've cured a patient, but if one cell, just one cell remains. . . .

Your research is focusing on this drug resistance?

Yes. The genetic changes that give the cell this protection mechanism. Let me give you a two-minute lecture on Paul Erhlich, who was a German physician and chemist in the early 1900s. He was the father of chemotherapy. He had the dream that there could be found a chemical that would wipe out microorganisms and parasites. He was working with dyes. He thought that dyes have affinities for different things so one should be able to find "dyes" or chemicals able to selectively kill parasites. He was absolutely right. However, we also know that microorganisms can mutate and become resistant. That's why if you're given penicillin, the doctor tells you to take the full dose in order to wipe out all the infection. If you only take part of the medication, some resistant bacteria might develop and next time the medication would be ineffective. One of the lessons we've learned is that it's very rare for the same bug to develop resistance to two different medications. It's like the joke about the guy who's afraid to fly because there might be a bomb on the plane. He phones the airline and asks what is the probability of a bomb being on an airplane. They say one in 10,000, may be one in 100,000. So he asks what's the probability of two bombs on board? They say never. So he always carries a bomb when he flies. It's warped but it's the same idea: it's very rare to have two bombs on board; it's impossible. It's also very rare, if not impossible, to have a cell resistant to two different medications. So using a combination of different chemotherapies was the idea that therapists had. In fact, in the last ten or fifteen years combination chemotherapy has had some remarkable success. In cancers like Hodgkin's disease, it was previously considered to be a non-curable disease, but now, with a combination of the appropriate drugs, it's possible to have great success. . . .

Just as a side anecdote, being in a treatment hospital, we see cancer patients, bump into them in the elevator all the time. I remember one wintry day I was in the elevator and hadn't had a haircut for about three months; I just hadn't had the time to do it. One of the women being treated with chemotherapy had lost all of her hair—which is not unusual—and she looked up at me from her wheelchair and said, "You are disgusting!" I said, "What's wrong?" "Look, you have a full head of hair and I've lost all of mine." I got a little impatient with her and I said, "What are you talking about? The fact that you lost all your hair means that the chemotherapy is working! The drug is in your system, it's killing your hair follicles so your hair falls out. It's also probably killing a lot of cancer cells, so stop feeling so sorry for yourself!" I don't know what made me say that. She looked at me and said, "Thank you. You made my day." . . . I wasn't being very patient. But to me the fact that the treatment was killing some normal cells

Victor and older brother Winston in front of 7 Oriole Parkway in Toronto in the early 1950s.

was the clearest sign that it was also killing cancer cells.

Our discovery has to do with the fact that the tumour cell can develop what we call multiple drug resistance. Resistance, not to a single drug, but to a combination of drugs. In tumour cells, there's this mechanism which we've discovered—luckily stumbled on it—that causes these cells to be resistant to a combination of different drugs, which was unexpected. . . . We found that the cells we were working with were resistant to most of the drugs we threw at them. To do a control to see exactly what drugs they were resistant to, we went down to the pharmacy—being in a cancer hospital here—and we said, "Give us some drugs, any drugs." They gave us drugs that they use to treat cancer patients with and the cells we were using were resistant to all the drugs. Then we said, "What's going on here? This is really a lousy cell! We're not interested in this. We're interested in cell division. This is crazy." And then it's just like we were sitting there, chatting and thinking about things and it dawned on me: "My God, this could be important!" Because it's not by chance that these cells happened to be resistant to all these anti-cancer drugs. This was the point where we became very interested in the cell membrane, as to how the cell keeps things out.

We discovered, as it turns out, a protein that acts like a pump. The drug enters the membrane, is recognized, and is then pumped out. The most important discovery was the pump. Secondly, we're discovering many ways that we can inhibit and shut this pump down. We think, if we live long enough, that we can make a real difference in cancer chemotherapy. That's what the excitement in this field is all about, that this could be a really fantastic breakthrough.

That's a remarkable story. It's like crumpling up a piece of paper and throwing it over your shoulder and then saying "wait a minute!" and running to pick it up again.

That's right. But you know, science is like that. By the way, we were not the first to observe this multiple drug resistance; other people had seen it even earlier than us, but they always said well, this is because there are many mechanisms of drug resistance in a tumour cell. But from our genetic analysis, we said no, there's only one mechanism—this pump. We didn't know it was a pump at the time, but from genetics we said there was only one gene involved. If there are a hundred genes involved, then there's no way you can manipulate them all, but if there's only one gene, then there's a chance we can target against it.

Has it had any effect on treatment yet?

Unfortunately, the thing about cancer is that even if it does have an effect, it will be five years before you will know because it takes that long to know whether you're doing any good or not. It had an enormous effect in the sense that many drug companies now are trying to develop drugs that will inhibit this pump. We're starting to put some of these drugs into clinical trials and we think it's going to make a difference.

We've talked about science, we've talked about theory and research. How do you relate that to the human beings attached to these diseases?

I'm not a medical doctor so I don't normally see patients. Patients, when they read about our discovery or the research we're doing, many of them contact me and want to talk. It's not easy; it's very difficult. . . . My sister died of cancer, I guess it was seven or eight years ago. She was a physician, a psychiatrist. She died of breast cancer. She was treated at this hospital. She, like all doctors, ignored it until it was too late. It was traumatic for me because we were very close. . . . Having gone through that experience, I know exactly what the people who call me are going through. It's not always the patients that are feeling bad—it's the relations and close friends who are feeling guilty and feeling bad. . . .

I had a call from someone in Italy. He said, "My mother has ovarian cancer. I know you're a great scientist. I will send her there tomorrow if you promise you'll do something for her." I said that I knew a very good doctor in Milan; she's an expert in this area and she'll talk with you and help you decide whether to send her here or not. So I phoned up this doctor and explained the situation. I said I felt what he needed was to be reassured and asked her to talk it over with him. She called me back and told me that I had been right, what he wanted was assurance that he was doing everything humanly possible for his mother.

You have one young daughter. What do you hope for her?

Well, maybe it's corny . . . I certainly hope that she will enjoy her life, that she will cherish her heritage, and that she will accomplish something. . . . But also that she will be a useful person to whomever she is in contact with. . . . You know, most of us may, if we're lucky, have seventy, eighty years on this earth, but no matter how long we have, I think it's important to know that we made a difference, that we had an impact on life. I think that's important. . . . That's what I hope for, that she will have that sense of accomplishment. . . .

In 1962 Dr. Victor Ling was named an Ontario Scholar. He received an Medical Research Council of Canada Centennial Fellowship to study in Cambridge from 1969–71. In 1988 he received the Milken Family Medical Foundation Cancer Research Award, and in 1990 he received the Gairdner Foundation International Award and was made a Fellow of the Royal Society of Canada.

TAK MAK

Dr. Tak Mak is primarily responsible for identifying the T-cell receptor gene—a discovery that is crucial to our understanding of how the immune system works and a development that may lead to the cure or effective treatment of such diseases as multiple sclerosis, juvenile diabetes and rheumatoid arthritis. We interviewed Dr. Mak in the office he uses off his research laboratory at the Princess Margaret Hospital in downtown Toronto. The work he and his colleagues are doing is hugely complex and difficult for the layman to understand. What struck us most were the practical concerns of this research—the struggle for grants and government funding. Dr. Mak told us that he spends roughly three months of every year filling out grant applications and making appeals for government funding. This seems a sad, if necessary, preoccupation for a brilliant mind. He explained that it is a fact of life for most scientists, that years of research, careers and sometimes lives hinge on acceptance or rejection of applications for funding. Philosophically, Dr. Mak accepts this task as part of the personal sacrifices a scientist must make to further the greater goal of his research.

子曰學而不思則罔
思而不學則殆

IT IS CONFUSING TO LEARN WITHOUT THOUGHT; IT IS DANGEROUS TO THINK WITHOUT LEARNING.

I was born in China but moved to Hong Kong at the age of a few months old. My parents divorced when I was nine; my mother brought the children to North America about thirty years ago. We first lived in Wisconsin. In the 1960s the University of Wisconsin was considered one of the ten best universities in the United States. I graduated from the University of Wisconsin and then came to Canada.

I have one sister living in Boston; the rest of the family is now here in Toronto. My mother moved here when I did in the mid-'70s.

How did you come to choose science?

Well, science is an international language, so it's easy to compete with natives, with North Americans. I would have been at a disadvantage if I'd gone into arts because my English was not very strong. Many of us chose to go into science and engineering. It's also the sociological aspects of growing up in Hong Kong. Science and engineering are stressed very strongly in Hong Kong. They are the avenues one takes for a good career.

Was there something specific that directed you toward science as opposed to engineering?

Not really. I was actually enroled at the University of Wisconsin as a chemical engineer but I just didn't like it; it was too regimented for me. Hours and hours of calculating the same thing over and over again. It was just too restrictive in terms of one's thinking. It was not as creative as I would have liked. I'm not very good at crossing all the T's and dotting all the I's—especially first thing in the morning—so that I would be able to complete and submit all these problems. I don't know if you've ever had any engineering courses but some of the professors are totally obsessed with formats and details, for example. The first professor I had stipulated that the whole class use a particular weight of bond paper. The graph papers had to have the same serial number and your name had to be in the upper left corner, one and a half inches from each of the edges, and the page number had to be perfectly placed in the upper right corner. If it wasn't done properly, he just tore it up.

He was totally insane. He hated me; I hated him. We parted. And I switched to biochemistry. And the University of Wisconsin, in the 1960s, the late '60s, was one of the top—if not the top—biochemistry departments in the world. There were a lot of very good professors, though many were kind of aging. For whatever reason, these people were not being replaced by top young professors, which spelled the decline of the institution. Places like Stanford and MIT eventually took its top place.

Biochemistry at Wisconsin grew out of agriculture. In the 1940s there were people there like Karl Paul Link who discovered dicurmarol, a rat poison, and Steenbock who discovered that if you pass milk through an ultraviolet light you can change the 7-dehydro-cholesterol into vitamin D. There was a group of very brilliant chemists there at the time who took advantage of the agricultural environment to put their mark on science. To this day dicurmarol is still used and they still fortify milk by passing it through ultraviolet light. Obviously, it was a very good place to be studying biochemistry.

What did your mother think of this rather esoteric interest?

Most Chinese families push their children to be doctors because of the security. My mother could never understand what kind of a job I could get as a biochemist. I did a bachelor's degree and master's degree at the University of Wisconsin. At the end of that, I felt it was time to get out of the University of Wisconsin. I was still very interested in what I was doing, which was basically working on viruses. Come here, I'll show you. You can see here the AIDS virus. This is a polio virus. The AIDS virus is much bigger than the polio virus.

It seems about twenty or thirty times bigger.

Oh, in diameter, maybe. But in volume, it's a lot smaller. You can see here these sub-units on the photograph of the virus. They are not randomly stuck onto the virus; they are arranged in almost exactly the same design as the geodesic dome by Buckminster Fuller. He did it from a purely architectural and mathematical point of view and it turns out that nature already had it.

My first research project—now this is in the early '70s—was in fact to determine the molecular structure of the Picorna virus, of which the polio virus is one. I really enjoyed doing that, so when I left the University of Wisconsin I found that there was a very well established professor who was working on that same thing here in Canada—Professor John Colter at the University of Alberta; he's now retired. It was one of the things that brought me here.

You mentioned that chemical engineering was very confining and very strict. How is what you're doing now different?

I think basically scientists are very practical people. I consider science as a job. It's not like the old days when science was either for the very rich or the extraordinarily gifted. For most of us, it is a job with a lot of variety and something new and different all the time. You cannot discover something twice. However, we still have to manage our job and our skills and get what we need from granting agencies to support our labs. A very important part of the job is the management of the very diverse groups of people working in the lab. . . . It's a job, and like any job, we're expected to produce so much every so often. In the past—and to some extent this is still true in Europe–scientists were made professors and once you were made a professor it meant never having to say you're sorry. And it was expected that these brilliant ideas would come while you were walking through the meadow. This is not true in Canada or the U.S., unless you are very brilliant, and very few can survive only on their brilliance. The rest of us have to be very aware of how much work we produce. We do our science and we do the best we can, but basically we're trapped into an intense competition with the rest of the world's scientists. Science is very international and you cannot say, "I'm the first to discover this in Canada." That absolutely makes no sense because what if somebody has made the discovery in France or Liechtenstein? It's also impossible to speak of the best scientist in Canada because the measure of worth does not recognize a border; it's always an international perspective that counts with science.

How do you keep up with the rest of the world? How do you share information—through journals?

These periodicals here on my desk are, in fact, mostly outdated, even the one that arrived yesterday can be outdated. For our field, basically we go to meetings, we talk on the phone, and now for the last two years, faxes go back and forth. Just last week we sent two of our doctors to New York. They attended a meeting there and today they're going to tell all of us what they learned from that meeting. People who go to meetings usually think that they are three to six months ahead of what appears in journals. And if we were to miss those meetings, the risk is that you might end up putting your people through months of unnecessary work. . . . It's almost kind of like a maze. You have to make a decision every so many turns because strategies have to be updated.

There are certain fields in science that are moving very fast. It just so happens that the two fields that we are involved in, virology and immunology, are very fast moving fields.

Can you tell us a bit more about your involvement in these two fields?

I was trained as a virologist and I continued to be trained in virology all the way through the 1970s and early '80s. In the early '80s we decided to pick an additional subject to study in the laboratory. There are two major granting agencies that support medical research in Canada. One is the National Cancer Institute, which collects its money through door-to-door donations, and the other is the Medical Research Council, whose money comes directly from the federal budget. The two agencies support research in medical schools across

Canada. They make a very strict stipulation that the work they fund cannot be duplicating—in other words, if we're researching project A, we can only receive funds from *one* of the agencies for project A. So we decided to extend the laboratory and choose another subject and we chose T-cells. Initially, we chose to work with T-cell leukaemia. We began in the late '70s. But the T-cell project was still the smaller and of five or six people in the lab, only one or two would work on T-cells and the rest would work on viruses. . . . Leukaemia happens because the red cells in your blood are arrested in the early stages of development where they are still undergoing a lot of growth; they cannot mature. That's what leukaemia is roughly about. We were interested in finding agents that could induce them to mature and, hopefully, come to understand why they are arrested at these early stages. We were then interested in finding which genes were being turned on and off. To do that we did a simple procedure, called gene subtraction, that molecular biologists use to identify genes.

When we did that procedure here, we ended up with a whole series of genes. One of the genes that is involved in the maturation of our T-cell is the T lymphocyte receptor. When it is immature it does not express the receptor on the cell. But when it is mature, the function of the T-cell is, in fact, to use its cell receptors to identify foreign antigens as they have to alert the B-cells to make antibodies or alert other T-cells to kill cells that are infected with the pathogen. So, on the surface of the T-cell is a receptor called the T-cell receptor. We know it exists but we don't know what it looks like, smells likes, or how it does what it does. But it is what our immune system is all about—identifying foreign pathogens. Until the T-cell starts the process our immune system lies dormant, but once the T-cell identifies a pathogen the system goes into high gear to attack the pathogen in a concerted way. And most of the time, ninety-nine point nine percent of the time, you emerge without the cold, without the headache, and without the need of medication.

So the most crucial thing for the immune system is that identification. It's been called the holy grail of immunology because scientists hadn't been able to find the particular structure that says, "Ah ha! this is foreign—let's kill it!" Now if you only think of it from the point of view of infection then you say it's not very important because we can cover the problem with antibiotics, but antibiotics don't work for viruses. By and large we are still without anti-virus drugs. . . . Another problem facing us is that the immune system is sometimes triggered for no apparent reason to attack our own tissues–this is where we get diseases like multiple sclerosis, rheumatoid arthritis, childhood diabetes and lupus. Our T-cells have mistaken something in us as being foreign. In the case of juvenile diabetes, our T-cells have mistaken something in our pancreas as being foreign.... Anyway, to make a long story short, our lab's contribution to immunology came in 1983 when Dr. Yanagi, a Japanese doctorate working in my lab, was able to clone the gene for the T-cell receptor.

When you say that it sounds very anti-climactic—"he cloned the gene"—and there we are. What does that mean?

With molecular biology, getting hold of the gene is the beginning of understanding many, many things. We have 100,000 genes in our body and we probably know less than 1,000 in terms of their purposes. To identify which one is for *what* is, of course, still a formidable task. By cloning the gene we, in fact, followed up with a whole series of experiments and now we at least have the very superficial knowledge of how it works. This allows us to understand how the immune system identifies foreign substances or structures. If you think about it, it's quite amazing because there's an almost limitless repertoire of foreign viruses and bacteria and plants and insects that we're exposed to. Our immune system can, in almost all situations, identify the foreign substance and win the battle. . . .

Anyway, cloning the gene for the T-cell receptor was our contribution to the study of immunology. . . . Now, let's say before 1983 when Dr. Yanagi had cloned a gene for the receptor, you would be sitting there just guessing at how the immune system worked, when it was obvious that we only have 100,000 genes. You must be wondering how the T-cell receptors end up with billions and billions of combinations. So then our contribution is, number one, that simple understanding. It is an understanding which will hopefully allow us in the future to manipulate this system, to know what receptor sees what pathogens, what sees tumour antigens, pieces of stuff from cancer cells that we can now attack by inducing the immune system, and what is causing juvenile diabetes—maybe we can block that particular shape that will attack the pancreas.

Where does AIDS come from? As I told you before, I was working with these types of viruses—not the AIDS virus but very similar viruses in the same family. It became for us kind of natural that we have the working knowledge on both sides of the fence—immunology and virology—and just putting the two together would give us what we think may be an advantage to study AIDS. We started on AIDS maybe four years ago. Of twenty-five people working here in our lab, probably about four or five are working on AIDS and the rest are doing immunology.

Do you see any progress in AIDS*?*

I wish I could say yes, but I don't think there's very much significant clinical progress at this stage. There's a lot of understanding of the basic nature, but AIDS is very complicated. Even if we understand something at the level of tissue culture or a piece of a virus, when it comes to the whole human being it's tremendously complicated. A lot of cures to diseases could still come in the absence of understanding, but that is the drug company's approach, which is to screen hundreds of thousands of compounds until you get the right one. Vitamin B12 is a perfect example. We still don't know how Vitamin B12 works but it can cure us of some kinds of anaemia.

There is a lot of what you could call suspenders. The immune system, for example, wears many suspenders, so if you break one you will still be safe. What we've been doing now in our lab is mainly engrossed in a very, very new technology of science, which is now going all the way up to the level of the animal. We could, for example take the gene for cystic fibrosis and create a mouse strain with that disease so we can study how to cure it. Lap-Chee Tsui discovered the gene for cystic fibrosis and it's one of the greatest discoveries in medical genetics.

First of all, it's a very high profile disease; one in twenty individuals is a carrier. That's very, very high. So, from the point of view of health, from the humanity point of view, it is a very high profile discovery because it effects a lot of people and causes damage at the level of costs and emotions. Society cannot stand to see children who are sick. So from that point of view it's a very important gene because of its magnitude, both in terms of cost and human suffering. From the second point of view, the scientific point of view, we've often been able to identify mutations in our cells by something that is grossly wrong.... You can look at the chromosomes and you know exactly what's wrong. But when you look at a kid with cystic fibrosis, you look at their chromosomes—absolutely nothing is wrong with them. There's no way; you cannot put your finger on anything. For muscular dystrophy you can see part of the X chromosome is gone, you can see it. So there it is, that's muscular dystrophy. For children with eye tumours if you look at it—wow!—chromosome 13—a whole chunk of it is missing. Or Down's Syndrome, you get an extra chromosome 21, you can see what's going on. Lap-Chee Tsui, through a heroic effort, was able to identify the cystic fibrosis gene as being on chromosome 7.

In fact, what's curious is that it's almost right next door to the T-cell receptor gene. On a gene map, it's next door. And even after you know where it is, it's still like walking from here to Windsor—you know that in between those two points is the cystic fibrosis gene—so the task was not unlike walking to Windsor looking for a house with a broken window on the south side, that was the job. Even after having found that the gene was between Toronto and Windsor, they had to find the house with the broken window. Repairing it—that's still years down the road because you're talking about repairing at the germ-line level.

Tell us more about your cancer research.

I think Victor Ling's work is closer to cancer research. Our work is still only pointing in that direction. If anything, people are criticizing our work as a little bit more geared toward immune diseases. My defence is that, in fact, the immune system also fights cancer.

It's ironic that AIDS should come along at the same time as you're working on the immune system.

Yeah. . . . Let's say that we've been trained as carpenters and also as gardeners and it so happens that the job of dealing with AIDS is like building something in a garden, in the middle of all the trees and plants. We just happened to find ourselves fitting in the groove between two different fields. . . .

Dr. Tak Mak is recognized for the co-discovery of the T–cell receptor in 1983. He has received a number of awards, including the Emil Von Behring Prize of Germany and the Gairdner International Award.

Dr. Tak Mak, his wife, Shirley, and daughters, Jennifer and Julie.

Lap-Chee Tsui

Dr. Lap-Chee Tsui identified the gene responsible for cystic fibrosis. This was not the sort of scientific discovery that sprang from dream-like inspiration but the result of laborious calculation and analysis. We told Dr. Tsui that Dr. Tak Mak had described the task as being similar to the search for a damaged window on a house somewhere between Toronto and Windsor. Dr. Tsui was flattered and delighted by the analogy but added that it was more in the order of finding a burnt light bulb in one of those houses, and to do so one would have to turn on and off every light switch in every room of every house. In the course of our interview, it became clear to us that Dr. Tsui, with his colleagues, is dedicated to turning on many lights, so that the darkness surrounding our knowledge of major diseases may be illuminated.

子曰由誨女知之乎
知之為知之不知
為不知是知也

Knowledge is the ability to identify
the truth when you see it
and to admit it when you do not.

I was born in China. My family moved to Hong Kong when I was three. I got my Masters from the Chinese University of Hong Kong, then I left Hong Kong in 1974 to go to the United States for my graduate work. My father was a salesman and my mother worked at home. We were relatively poor. It was quite difficult but I managed to get some scholarships. I also worked part time to support my years in college.

How did you come to choose science?

I've always liked science, especially biology. As a child I remember going to creeks and picking up all kinds of things. We lived in a village—nature was close by. We could always look and explore.

When you were growing up in the 1960s, were you at all aware of the political changes that were going on in Hong Kong?

Yes. In fact, I was involved in the first student demonstration in Hong Kong, the fight to make Chinese the official language. I didn't play a major part, but I was very active. That was in 1969. I thought it was the right thing to do. The official language had been English. The majority of the people were Chinese; most didn't even understand English.

Were there risks?

Not really. I'm against violence. There were some clashes with the police and a couple of people were put in jail. I was mostly involved in putting up posters and handing out flyers.

LAP–CHEE TSUI WITH MOTHER AND FATHER.

What were your reasons for leaving Hong Kong?

The main thing was to get further training, but even if you get accepted in a foreign university there are financial considerations that make it very difficult. I was accepted by quite a number of schools, but only two offered me a studentship or assistantship. I chose the University of Pittsburgh. The professor who offered me the position had interests very similar to mine.

Molecular biology these days is about trying to understand how the body functions, why it functions the way it does. That information comes from the genetic material and it determines the whole life process. Environmental factors may determine some of your behaviour, but otherwise everything is programmed, including certain diseases. Not infectious diseases; susceptibility is another thing.

You said that the role of the imagination attracted you to molecular biology. Can you explain?

Well, biochemistry is mainly the study of the process. You have a reaction, a biochemical reaction. You have starting material that is affected and changed. You study the pathway between the starting material and the end product. Now, molecular biology is a collection of all fields. You could describe me as a kind of handyman: I do a little bit of everything to try and solve a problem. I may not be the best in one thing, but I know a little bit about everything. I try to piece the puzzle together, and if I have a problem, I rely on collaborators and others who are better in their field to help me. It requires imagination; it is not strictly deductive.

I think nowadays it's very difficult to invent or discover new equations. It's more a question of finding a more efficient solution to the equation. The study of the genes for cystic fibrosis is mainly the orchestration of a large number of equations. It's a complex study. It involves a lot of disciplines. You have to be able to manage them in such a way that everything comes together to make beautiful music. But we haven't invented any new equations or instruments. It's just that it involves many, many parts. It involves genetics, biochemistry, molecular biology, and we've even involved classical genetics, which most people don't know how to do anymore. It just wasn't fashionable. But with the application of new methods to classical genetics it's become powerful again. The first step in our discovery of the location of the cystic fibrosis gene was classical genetics, and then it was hard core molecular biology, and then a combination of disciplines and techniques, and then a return to classical genetics to do the final calculations.

Now, we have the gene but we don't know the basic defect. We have some idea what the basic defect may be. It's like trying to find the meaning of a word in an encyclopedia. . . . We know it's there because when you compare the gene of a CF patient to that of a normal individual, you find there's something missing. You know something is wrong, but what?

How did this discovery affect treatment?

It was a question of addressing the patient's condition. There is a problem with mucus in the lungs. Well, maybe you help dissolve the mucus. A problem with digestion? Give some pills to aid digestion. Infection? Again, antibiotics. It's all treatment based on symptoms. With this discovery there is the possibility of gene therapy. Putting a good copy of the defective gene into the cells that are not functioning properly. For instance, the lungs. Patients have heavy mucus because the lung cannot secrete water and salt properly. It's possible to put the corrected gene back into the lung cells and restore proper functioning. It's theoretical in humans, but it's been done in animals. The process is possible, but to do it in humans is still too early to tell, because there are a lot of unknowns. I mean, you're putting a new gene into a cell.

How do you do that?

You encapsulate the gene in a virus particle. The virus itself has been inactivated so the virus will not be infectious but will still invade the cells. The virus becomes the carrier. The test animal is made to initiate some virus particles that then infect the lung and transfer a healthy gene to the cells in the lung. When the virus enters the cell, the gene inside finds a way to incorporate itself into the human cell. It is human DNA that has been replicated outside a human and we put it back in the cell. It can be done relatively efficiently in a test tube, but we just don't know how well it will work in a human body.

How has this discovery changed CF research?

As a result of our finding, gene research has shifted to genetic analysis. A lot of research has been going on. Every week we hear something new. . . . The reason I went into this is because it is a disease that affects a large number of people. Interestingly, it does not affect non-Caucasian populations. The reason for that is unknown. It is very peculiar; it only affects Caucasians of a certain origin. About five percent of the Caucasian population are carriers for the disease without knowing it, and when two carriers marry, they have one in four chances of having a baby with CF. So it's a major disease.

Why are there so many discoveries of genetic links to disease at this particular time?

Because all the tools and resources have come together. Interestingly, DNA was only discovered fifty or sixty years ago. The ability to manipulate DNA only came about ten to fifteen years ago. Now you have all this information from other fields converging; the information is growing exponentially. The fear is we just can't keep up.

But it sounds like a very exciting time.

Yes. I would say that I'm very lucky.

How did the actual discovery come about?

Actually, I didn't do much of the real work. I was involved in the analysis of the data gathered. There are about thirty people on the team; it's my job to orchestrate. You can really use the analogy of the orchestra. It's very important that each person does their own part and that all the results come together at the same time. We actually worked for about seven years before we had any solid clues, but now it's been about ten years and every piece of information gathered contributed to the solution of the puzzle. So the planning had to be good.

That sort of 'orchestration' between people requires considerable skill. Are they skills that you had to re-learn to be effective in North America?

Even though Hong Kong is a very modern city, there are many old Chinese traditions. For instance, you rarely come out and say "no" directly. If you ask somebody if they want something they'll say, "Well, I don't use it that often," instead of simply saying no. Even now, when talking with some people from Hong Kong, I have trouble understanding them because of that kind of thing.

Are you involved in the Chinese community?

Yes, quite a bit. When I was a student I was in the Students' Union. I was in the Student Society and was president, and when I went to Pittsburgh, I was president of the Chinese Association. Presently, I'm president of the Bio-Medical Section of the Federation of Chinese Canadian Professionals in Ontario.

Why is that important to you?

To be very blunt, I like to associate myself with people of my own kind. I think we can help each other. The federation was formed ten or fifteen years ago because of discrimination. I don't think there's the same degree of discrimination anymore or it's not as obvious. I think now we are able to do something for society, not just ourselves. For example, the federation Education Foundation raises money for scholarships. We give out about forty scholarships each year. Not just for Chinese people but for anybody who is outstanding in their academic studies.

What do you think the Chinese community needs help with?

We have to help ourselves first. I think, though, that there's a reticence with

Chinese people; they don't like to speak out. Confucius teaches that you take care of yourself first, your family second, then your city, your country, the world. Most new immigrants spend their time making money, trying to make a living. So they have very little time to participate in the community. I do what I can. I think it's important to learn how to integrate ourselves into the society. It's good to maintain our heritage, but you mustn't forget that you're in a new society. It's important to communicate and interact with other people.

What does it mean to you to be a Canadian?

Well, first it means I can travel freely. For a long time I didn't have any documents. I was born in China, raised in Hong Kong. To me, the Canadian society respects the idea of multiculturalism. I like that idea very much, as opposed to the U.S. 'melting pot' theory.

Your children are first generation Canadians.

Yes, but we send them to Chinese school to learn Chinese. We speak Chinese at home and we try to pass along as much of the Chinese culture as we can.

What do you think is going to happen in 1997?

That's a very important question. Hong Kong has developed into such an important place in the world, not just in Southeast Asia. I think the Chinese government will probably preserve it after 1997. I hope that China will absorb some of the modernity of Hong Kong. From a scientific side, I think if there's no science or technology in a country, the country will always be poor. I was very optimistic until Tiananmen Square. There had been a lot of exchange of scholars. In science, the returns take a long time to develop. You're happy if you invest $100 and get back $1. I would say they're at least ten years behind and it will be difficult to improve even if they start now.

In the nineteenth century it was possible to read everything that had been published. Today it's impossible. Is it the same for a scientist?

The reason I subscribe to so many journals is because I don't have the time to go to the library. I subscribe to only a fraction of the scientific journals available and even then I'm only able to read the indexes in some of them. There's just so much information coming out, and the information is accumulating so rapidly. I work as a kind of handyman. We let the specialists chase information in their respective fields. My job is to analyze, interpret and collaborate.

So, as you said, it's like a symphony: you provide them with pieces of music which they then play?

Yes, you could say that. I'm the conductor or manager. It's an interesting analogy—the conductor and orchestra—because you have 50,000 genes in the human cell. All the genetic information is there at the moment of conception, in the fertilized egg. The big question is how it is played out, how it knows how to do the job it's supposed to do, at the time it's supposed to do it. That's the question. The mystery. Who is the conductor? All these sets of programmed events have to go on at the right time and the right moment in the right cell.

Does that affect your sense of the mystery of life? Does it inspire belief in a higher being? . . . Do you know what I mean?

I understand . . . I don't know anything anymore . . . I believe in good science.

Dr. Lap–Chee Tsui was made an Officer of the Order of Canada in recognition of his discovery of the gene responsible for cystic fibrosis. He continues his research at Toronto's Hospital for Sick Children.

As a boy in Hong Kong.

Samuel Wong

It is not difficult to use only superlatives to describe Samuel Wong and his achievements. A graduate of Harvard, an M.D. whose specialty is ophthalmology and the assistant conductor under Zubin Mehta of the New York Philharmonic, he is also modest, polite and extremely well spoken. And he is barely thirty years old! Most of the people we have interviewed are at the peak of their powers and success, or nearing the end of long, rich lives. Samuel Wong is at the beginning of what could become a great musical career.

子曰興於詩立
於禮成於樂

THE ODES STIMULATE THE MIND, THE RULES OF PROPRIETY BUILD THE CHARACTER, AND THROUGH MUSIC ONE BECOMES ACCOMPLISHED.

I was born in Hong Kong in 1962. My father was a native of Canton and my mother a native of Shanghai. My brother is five years older and my sisters are eight and nine years older. . . . The entire family came to Toronto in 1971. It was, I think, in response to the 'Red Scare' and the political disturbances in Hong Kong. . . . My father had his own accounting firm and was also an executive with Kodak in Hong Kong. He was able to arrange a transfer to a Kodak branch in North America. At that time he was offered a position in Rochester, New York, which is the head office, and also here in Toronto.

Do you have any personal recollections of the tensions in Hong Kong?

I certainly do. It affected me in a most direct way. I used to enjoy walking my dog every day and I remember at one point not being allowed to go out and walk the dog. There was rioting in the streets. I didn't read newspapers back then, but I saw television clips and I was told never to go out.

It sounds like you had a fairly comfortable life, an upper middle class background.

I would say so.

Were you aware of the great disparity between wealth and poverty in Hong Kong or were you still too young?

I think one can't help but notice social inequalities in Hong Kong because they're so stark and so striking. Even as a child I saw the most appalling poverty and overcrowding and an anguish you can almost hear and feel in the streets. At the time I didn't have a strong feeling about it or a well-formed philosophy, but you can't help but notice that there are abjectly poor kids and there are privileged kids, and one is a little afraid of the disorderly world out there.

What was the first thing you noticed moving from Hong Kong to Toronto?

Really, just space, the expanse. I was very impressed by Highway 401, the major artery in the city. In Hong Kong there are streets you can barely squeeze a cart or a Volkswagen through. It was very impressive to see these twelve-lane highways. That was the first impression I had coming from the airport. And the second one was the greenery, the vegetation, the amount of green instead of concrete. And the colours were different: softer, verdant—friendlier.

What part of Toronto did you settle in?

We moved to northern Scarborough. It was a residential neighbourhood with good public schools. My parents always explained to us that their choice of residence reflected our educational needs. In Hong Kong we lived near St. Paul's Co-Ed School, within walking distance, while my father commuted. In Toronto, all four children could go to a school within walking distance.

Why was education so important?

I think there are three levels of explanation. The first has to do with Chinese tradition, Confucianism and the respect for learning. At the second level, I think there is a long tradition of Chinese going overseas to study and garner for themselves a better life, a life of professionalism, academics or enterprising business. The third answer is that the Chinese see themselves as entering a foreign culture. The best way to assimilate and to make themselves a useful and valuable asset in society is via education in the language of that country, in the culture of that country.

How did Canada start to invade your household? How and when did the new environment start to enter into the way you lived and change it?

First, I went through adolescence in Canada, and that's a very different experience from adolescence in Hong Kong or the Far East. One hears the stereotype of adolescents in North America as rebellious, uncontrollable, intractable, deviant and independent. Perhaps I wasn't all of those, but to a slight degree I was affected by those ideas. So, for example, I travelled across Canada alone, I went all over the city alone, I had American friends, I had all sorts of friends: Caucasian, Indian, Black friends. It was a very cosmopolitan experience. It was truly a melting pot experience. In traditional Chinese upbringing, adolescence takes place in a more sheltered and controlled environment. I don't think you can leave the family house as readily and have as much freedom.

Is it protectionism?

Yes, it's protection and also the Chinese concept of respect for the parents. You know the classic Confucian relationships: the husband and wife; man and society; the son and the father; filial piety. In Hong Kong, adolescence is more an extension of childhood. There's also the Confucian principle of the mean or moderation. Traditionally, Chinese culture stresses harmony, harmonious relationships, getting along rather than sticking out.

Was there great conflict in the household because of the New World adolescence you were experiencing?

I don't think we were that wild. The children were not that rebellious and the parents were not that old-fashioned. Of course, a few sparks were ignited, but they were minor.

What was it like coming from an homogenous environment to the cultural mix of Toronto?

I remember meeting for the first time Indian children, Black children, other Asian children—Koreans, not just Chinese, Japanese, and then Chinese who didn't speak Cantonese, Chinese who were from Taiwan or Hawaii. It was dizzying to see all these people of different races because in Hong Kong, when I went to St. Paul's Co-Ed, it was all nice, Chinese boys and girls, clean cut, uniformed, probably of very similar values. As I say, it was quite dizzying. But, at a very early age those issues of racism and bigotry were already settled in my mind. . . .

I think there are red-necks in every culture and bigotry in every race, so being exposed as a child to all these different cultures and races had a liberal influence on me, creating an openness of mind. . . . I think it is a tremendous stimulus for personal growth for immigrants coming to a different culture. Not only do they see other cultures, but they see their own culture more clearly by comparison because they have a foil to see themselves, a mirror.

Did you experience any kind of racism or abuse that was of a new order and shocking to you?

Well, I think racism is a very loaded word. For me, the word racism has very bad connotations: premeditated actions of hatred, ill preconceptions and ideas about people of different races. I think children are more naïve. They make fun of anything that is different. If you're fat, if your eyes are small, if you have a different skin colour, if you're missing a finger, anything of that sort will be made fun of, but I don't think it's as sinister as an adult kind of racism. Of course I experienced those sorts of jesting, but I wouldn't call that racism. What I mean by racism is at the adult level, when an employer in his own mind has worked out a system of hatred and bigotry that does not show in the handshake or the smile, but nevertheless shows in his ways of dealing in business and the way he hires and places employees. That's racism.

What else was new for you in Canada?

The range of possibility. For example, when I was brought up in Hong Kong, you could be one of three things. You could be a doctor, a lawyer or clergy. To me, the world was very simple: You went to the best schools, you would go to the best universities, then you would go to the best companies or the best medical school and then do your thing. When I came to Canada I was exposed to other possibilities. I came in contact with playwrights, artists, musicians, and of course businessmen, doctors and lawyers as well, and university professors and electricians. I think the social system or class system is not nearly so clear cut in North America. You have plumbers who earn more than doctors. You have electricians who have better houses than engineers. My world was changed by those sorts of things. It really changed me to see people in very different disciplines all able to have a very good standard of living.

How did you then come to choose medicine and music?

Medicine has always been respected in my family. Doctors are a revered species in Hong Kong. They're pillars of society, pillars of learning and respect. But in high school I didn't really think of being a doctor. I read Shakespeare, I read French books, read geography, mathematics, all sorts of different things. I never thought of myself as a pre-med. And music . . . well, I've always studied music. I began studying piano at the age of four.

My mother wanted me to study the piano. She knew I had a good ear and a good musical memory because at age two I could sing all the songs that she sang to me with good intonation. I had a very rebellious nature and I didn't take well to teachers who rapped on my fingers and yelled at me constantly. For some kids it works, but it only works up to a certain level. If the pressure is external, if it's not from the love and passion for music which is internal, that kind of discipline only works on a child, I believe, until adolescence, when the child discovers independence and self-motivation and passion. At that time I think I needed more of a supportive, loving approach rather than a punitive approach. When I came to Canada I had just that. I had a teacher who really supported me and taught me a few things but did not overburden me and did not overly punish me. So that worked well for me.

How did you come to choose Harvard?

I was accepted to Yale, Harvard, University of Toronto and University of Western Ontario. At that time, my parents were in Hong Kong and I called them and asked where I should go. My dad and my mom finally just said "Go wherever you like and we'll support you." I remember that phone call very well.

I remember in particular that they didn't encourage me one way or the other; they left it up to me. Of course they would have preferred that I be near home and in Canada. I chose Harvard because of all the things I'd read about it, the people I met there, and the fact that I felt it would be an international experience. By that time, as a senior in high school, I had read widely. I thirsted for a bigger world. As much as I loved my family, I felt I needed to break out on my own, to experience completely what it's like to live on my own.

What was it like for you?

The burden of history is very exciting and humbling. As a freshman I stayed in dorms Henry David Thoreau had occupied. There were also some very important musicians who'd stayed there too: Leonard Bernstein, Virgil Thompson, Elliot Carter, Yo-Yo Ma. I was there eight years, for college and medical school.

How did you maintain your music?

Well, I conducted the Bach Society Orchestra as a junior and senior in college. I took conducting lessons and practised piano, took some theory lessons and attended Boston Symphony concerts.

That seems a tremendous amount of activity while carrying a full course load.

I didn't look at it that way because that implies a certain reluctant effort. That attitude is the worst sense of school. The best sense of school is of discovery. You read with passion, and you're doing things that you love so you don't notice that it's a heavy load. I was studying American history, French literature, mathematics, and conducting an orchestra, singing in an a cappella group. All these things were new and exciting and I forgot the number of hours it all took. "A change is as good as a rest." That's what my father says. He says for him a vacation is not inactivity but different activity or pursuit.

Was this love of the work something you developed on your own or was it something you got from your family?

Probably both. I think my parents had a strong work ethic. Their attitude is not 'bring home the trophy' or 'bring the medal or the marks', but study with joy and passion that which you love. I think it may be a little bit of an unusual ethos for a traditional Chinese family.

Singing in his bath.

Were you on a full scholarship at Harvard?

No one receives grants, only loans at Harvard. We paid our way through Harvard. That made it a difficult choice because Canadian universities offered full scholarships, and U.S. universities are very expensive. But I was the last child and my parents felt they could splurge on me. I worked every summer. My parents didn't expect me to contribute, but I felt obligated because I was placing such a financial burden on my family.

How did you come to choose medicine?

Senior year came and I had to decide what to do with my life. Now, this is a very difficult thing because after four years of liberal education you're qualified to think about a lot of issues, but you're qualified to do nothing in our modern, industrial society. It was a very painful moment for a lot of Harvard graduates. Probably eighty percent had no idea what to do. You can't just go to college again or just think about politics and art, or marine life and the Mediterranean. So I think a lot of people chose a profession without any clear idea about what they wanted to do. . . .

I felt a passion for learning in many fields—sciences I loved, music I loved, languages, history—but I felt that medicine was the right thing for me because you could do a lot of good for your fellow man, it's a field where you can do well and do good. I saw the study of the human body as an extension of my liberal education. I learned how the body functioned, how it's put together by bones, tendons, muscles and finally by molecules. That's all very fascinating. And how these things can possibly go wrong, the pathophysiology. And then finally, how you can alleviate or cure these things. Even more important, the things that you cannot cure and that remain an intractable problem and therefore suggest possibilities for research. Also, there is an example in my family, my brother, who went into medicine and loves it.

And music?

At that time, I did not see conducting as a professional reality. Frankly, the opportunities weren't there. Of course, with life, everything is paradoxical. The timing is always wrong, life is never a road you create but a road you happen to travel on. For me, when I decided to go into medicine, that's when I did most of my growing as a musician. I conducted community orchestras in Boston, I formed my own ensemble called the Boston Summer Orchestra and did all-Mozart programs. I was music director of the Bedford Symphony. I went to Aspen one summer to be a conducting fellow at the Aspen Music Festival and I worked with the New England Conservatory Youth Orchestra. I went to see Ben

Zander who became a kind of mentor, who took me through a lot of repertoire, and on top of that I did a lot of self-study all during medical school! It was during that time that I really grew.

Why conducting?

I think it's a natural extension of my training. I was trained in voice, piano, I took some violin lessons at one point, and I played tuba in the band. You play one line, monophony; but conducting is polyphony where you deal with many voices, many different possibilities of sound. For me the symphony is the world, it is the culmination of musical creation-symphony and opera. And as Mahler said, to create a symphony is to create the world. The symphony has endless interest and fascination for me. . . .

I'm basically a social person and I like to work with people. As a solo pianist I would spend many hours in the studio practising alone, or as a doctor, I must spend many hours reviewing cases alone. If I were practising medicine I would never have become a radiologist or a pathologist. I would want to see people and counsel them. I like to work with people and watch them interact. In conducting, you can study your scores in private, plan your rehearsals, and then go to the rehearsal hall and work with a hundred people.

How did you choose ophthalmology?

The eye is probably as fascinating an organ as any in the body. The eye is miraculous. Ophthalmology is a field where you can see everything that you are trying to diagnose and treat. If you're an internist, you can't see the liver, you can't see the heart. You can only see shadows of things by x-ray studies or ultrasound. But in ophthalmology you can see everything directly. You can see a cataract, you can measure glaucoma, you can see the retina using lenses, you can see the cornea–and that to me is very exciting. Secondly, you can do a lot of things for eyes. You can take out cataracts, you can alleviate glaucoma, you can treat diabetes in the back of the eye, you can repair a lot of trauma to the eye. You can do things dramatically and directly to the eye, whereas in other fields, like internal medicine, a lot of things are chronic, a lot of things are intractable, untreatable, frustrating.

Is it a field where diseases rarely, if ever, prove fatal?

It's true. You almost never die from eye diseases. There is the death of a sense, but not the death of the being. I don't like dealing with life and death on a daily basis; that's not for me. It's too much. Some doctors do and they tune it out or they have dissociation mechanisms or they feel it so heavily that it paralyses them. . . . I don't think dealing with the eyes is a trivial matter either. Surveys have shown that blindness, besides death, is the second greatest human fear. It's more than loss of hearing or loss of a limb.

When did you decide to give up medicine and devote all of your time to music?

Over the last three years, I've come to realize that I must devote all of my energies to this all-consuming profession of being a conductor. It's not just a profession, it's really a calling, a way of life. You have to know how to deal with an orchestra, how to deal with human beings—at the board level, at the orchestra level, at the staff level, and fund raising and all those things. I suppose I could carry on both professions, but I think I'd rather do one of them exceptionally well rather than both only moderately well. In order to do that I have to devote all my time to learning this very complicated art. . . .

This decision really goes against the grain, not just against Chinese society, but any society, to be trained in medicine and then walk away from it. Society has invested a lot of training and time in making me an M.D. To turn my back on that really goes against the grain. I wouldn't say people are giving me a difficult time, but a lot of things are unsaid and I feel them. In the end, I feel I am much more valuable as a conductor than as another ophthalmologist in overcrowded New York.

Have you had any doubts about the decision?

Living in New York keeps my faith alive. So many great orchestras and great artists come to New York, it's like being warmed by a fire constantly. Even though so many of my friends are bankers and doctors and lawyers, when I saw Von Karajan or Bernstein or when I see Zubin Mehta doing a Mahler symphony or Kurt Masur doing a Bruckner Symphony, I know I've done the right thing.

What would happen if tomorrow there were no more conducting jobs?

Well, that's a remote possibility, but at this time I'm not so worried about it. I think you have to be strong to weather the darker periods; it's really a long, difficult road. I always tell my youth orchestra, something that is worthwhile and great must be built over years, not over days. You have to apply constant steady pressure in this field; you can't lose your drive. I realize that to become a great conductor you have to soak in a culture and to learn a great many things over a great many years. But, as T.S. Eliot says, "The view is worth the climb."

If you had a choice, what orchestra would you like to conduct?

I would have to say the Vienna Philharmonic. The Vienna Philharmonic plays with warmth, suppleness, tradition and technical excellence. It's the ultimate. There are many orchestras that would be a great pleasure to conduct. Not to conduct, but to share with, because when you're dealing with a great orchestra, it's not that you're cattle-prodding them to play a certain way. You fuse your personality with that collective personality, and great orchestras do have collective personalities. Let's say the Vienna Philharmonic is cultured, warm and lush, then let's say the New York Philharmonic is brilliant and virtuosic. So when you conduct the great orchestras you don't really reshape them; you bring out those qualities and fuse them with your own.

Is that your next step, to get an orchestra of your own?

Yes. I would like to become music director of a regional or a city orchestra.

Is that what you're searching for?

It's not really done that way. People come to you. There's a general buzz in the business as to who's where and who's available. Of course, there are many ways to build a career. I think there are three ways to enter the profession: one is through being an assistant conductor of a great orchestra; another is by conducting a leading youth orchestra or young people's training orchestra; and the third is via competitions, if you win a big competition like the Von Karajan competition, or the Stokowski competition.

Why is it that conductors seem to have great long careers and live to great ages?

Because all the unhappy, obscure and frustrated ones died young and unacknowledged! Seriously, why shouldn't they? They live healthy, prosperous, active lives with opportunity to wield extreme power and prestige, high earnings, and they exercise daily. So why not?

Would you like to come back to Canada?

Yes, I think Canada is very rich culturally. I think Toronto has everything. It's got opera, a great symphony orchestra, theatre and dance. Everything. . . . I think the challenge for Canadians is to become an international force, so that the Toronto Symphony should be well known to the rest of the world, should be well represented in recordings that have worldwide distribution, should tour extensively and be recognized internationally, and become as well known as the Philadelphia Orchestra or the New York Philharmonic.

What makes you a Canadian?

I think first of all, I'm a citizen of the world. . . . I believe in mankind, the minds of men and women, and their artistic strivings. I think John F. Kennedy put his finger on it. I always remember going to the Kennedy Center in Washington and reading those inspirational words to the effect: Civilizations will not be remembered for their buildings or their war machinery. Rome has fallen and perhaps Washington one day may not be the centre of military power it is today. But they will, instead, be remembered by their civilization, the poetry, the art, the music, the plays they've produced, rather than by their sophisticated war machineries or their buildings of power. I think, therefore, that art is an opportunity to cut across national boundaries, economic and social boundaries. . . . Art has the possibility of cutting across all those artificial barriers erected by man. Of course, my home and family is here, and I love this country. But I think of myself as a citizen of the world, a citizen of art, and of humanism.

Samuel Wong made his conducting debut at the age of 28 with the New York Philharmonic and the Toronto Symphony. A graduate of Harvard Medical school, he is married to Hae-Young Ham, a violinist with the New York Philharmonic.

Samuel Wong in Hong Kong with his seventy-nine-year-old grandmother. She walked with a cane because her feet had been bound.

ADRIENNE CLARKSON

On television, Adrienne Clarkson appears warm and friendly with a smile too quick and subtle to be false. She says that the relationship with the camera is an intimacy with which she has always been comfortable. In person, it is her concentration, her ability to zero in ferociously on the aspect of a question that interests her, or to fix the gaze of the person across from her, that is most striking. There is a speed and an efficiency to this kind of rapport that is intimidating. It might be the sign of one who does not suffer fools gladly, or the brilliant mind of a complex personality shifting gear at high speed to deflect intrusion. Whatever the reason, she is a formidable and fascinating individual.

子曰知之者不如好之者
好之者不如樂之者

Those who know the truth are not equal to those who love it, and those who love it are not equal to those who delight in it.

I was born in Hong Kong in 1939. My mother was born in Hong Kong; her family were Hong Kong people from the time the British came. Originally they were Hakka. My great-great-grandfather was involved in business with the British and they had a large house on the Kowloon side. My father was an overseas Chinese born in Australia. When he was nineteen he returned to China but because of the civil strife then ended up in Hong Kong. His family had come from Canton province.

How did your parents meet?

They met in Hong Kong. My father had no money at all. He started from nothing but he was very athletic and social. He danced well and gradually fell into a circle of young people in Hong Kong. He met my mother's family and my grandmother liked him immediately—he was particularly handsome and debonair. My parents were married in 1934. They had a wonderful life, they were young and Hong Kong was, I think, an extremely civilized place to be. Indeed, I remember seeing home movies of my parents swimming and on the beach in Repulse Bay. My father was always interested in gadgets and technology and had purchased one of the first Bell & Howell 8mm cameras.

My father had had quite an interesting life before his marriage; he had become friends with the Canadian trade commissioner through his business activities, which is where our connection with Canada began. He came from a very, very humble background in Australia, from a small town which I have visited with him which he goes to almost every year now. He goes back to Australia every year because he still has all his brothers and sisters there. None of them ever went either to China or to Hong Kong. He comes from nine brothers and sisters—six brothers and sisters still living, and they're all over seventy-five. None of them married a Chinese except for him. He always felt his Chinese roots very strongly, I think, although he doesn't speak much Chinese. He didn't grow up speaking it though he spoke some dialect, I mean some Toisan [Taishan] dialect, and I think when he was in the village for that brief period he learned more. Of course living in Hong Kong he picked up some, but he has always spoken whatever Cantonese he has with an English accent.

What brought your parents to Canada?

The war. My father fought with the British in the Hong Kong volunteer reserve unit and was awarded the Military Medal from the British for valour—he was a dispatch rider on a motorcycle. He was a great sportsman, a great horse rider—Hong Kong was all gentlemen jockeys until after the war. It was that kind of life. He used to get up every morning at 4:30 and go and ride and then go to the office. I was born right near the Jockey Club in Happy Valley on Broom Road, a house that—surprisingly, considering how Hong Kong has changed enormously—still exists. It was an Art Deco looking house, a duplex with a roof garden. . . . One day my mother was looking out the window and she saw a Japanese hopping across the back yard—that's how she knew the war had begun. My father's unit was called up and my mother and grandmother and brother and I hid as best we could—in basements and such. It was a short, brief, terrible war lasting two or three weeks. We lived under the Japanese occupation for six months and then through some wonderful miracle we were put on a list as Canadians to be repatriated to Canada on a Red Cross ship in diplomatic exchange for Japanese from North America. My father even tried to get us out to Australia, but the war was so fierce in the Pacific at that point that he didn't hold out much hope for that. He had managed to get a letter out to one of his Canadian trade commission friends who was then in India but hadn't had a reply. Then suddenly out of the blue, we were informed that we were on a list to go to Canada, so we came. It was very much a fluke.

Do you remember anything of those early days in Hong Kong?

I was two when we left, so I have few memories. My earliest memory is from before the war, standing near a waterfall, which I've seen many times since, with my mother, wearing a matching dress to hers. Apart from that I have one memory from the boat coming over: I saw a whale, I mean everybody saw the whale and I had to look between people's legs to see it. . . .

We had no family here in Canada, we were just thrown into it, and I think it was particularly difficult for my mother. There wasn't a language barrier because my mother's education had been in English and my father had been born in Australia. But it was a tremendous adjustment to land in Ottawa in the middle of winter.

How did you end up in Ottawa?

My father was given a job by the Canadian government in the Trade and Commerce department. It was not exciting or well paying, but it was a job. As soon as the war was over he started his own import and export business. I think he thought we would only be in Canada for the duration of the war and then return to Hong Kong. But he went back to Hong Kong in 1946 and 1948, and when the Communists were successful in 1949 he didn't feel Hong Kong would have much of a future. A misjudgment I suppose. So then Dad decided that we should become Canadian citizens, which was not easy then. You couldn't become a Canadian citizen if you didn't have relatives in Canada and we had none. But he knew a lot of people and we were made Canadian citizens by an order-in-council in Parliament in 1949. I think that was unique.

What are your first memories of Ottawa?

Snow. I must have been three and I walked off the street car into this great big pile of snow. And I remember lying at the bottom of it and looking up and seeing the sky, a round circle of bright blue. I wasn't the least bit frightened and it wasn't even cold—it didn't feel cold . . . I remember the snow and the cold.

I thought it was a very nice place to grow up in. It was a very small town then. Really small town. Almost completely government. There were certainly not many Chinese. My mother did not find it as easy to make friends as my father did, and so, I think, she felt very isolated and lonely. She had to adapt to so many new things–she'd never even been in a kitchen before we came to Canada. One of the last things she asked her mother before getting on the boat for Canada was, "How do you cook rice?" and my grandmother said you put your hand down and let the water come over the top of it and that was all she knew. So she had to do all that—learn to cook, learn to keep house, learn to look after her children. I mean, they weren't particularly rich in Hong Kong but they had a driver, they had an amah for each of us and a cook and someone to do the laundry.

In those early years did you have the feeling that Canada was only a refuge, a temporary stopover after which your family would return home to Hong Kong?

No. After we became citizens in 1949 we were brought up very positively. I wasn't brought up with any sense of loss. We never had the sort of feeling that I've sensed in a lot of European immigrants, especially those from Eastern Europe and the Baltics, this sense of loss, of being deprived of something. My father said, "We're Canadians now, we'll live a Canadian life and we'll do everything we want," and that was it. I think both my parents took well to Canadian life. My mother was a very solitary person who liked doing aesthetic things, particularly sewing, embroidery, painting, playing the piano. She didn't enjoy company all that much and Canada was perfect for her. They took up sport fishing in a big way. We rented a cottage on Lake McGregor near Ottawa in 1947 and then built our own place in 1949. We spent all our summers there. That was one of the things they really loved about Canada; they loved fishing. My father always went salmon fishing in the fall in Northern Quebec with his business friends. And trout fishing; they were crazy about fishing, fly fishing, casting, spinning, you name it. It's said my mother caught the largest pike ever caught on Lake McGregor; it took twenty-two minutes to bring it in—everybody remembers it. Unfortunately we ate it; we should have had it stuffed.

I think the happiest part of the Canadian experience for them is the wilderness part. My mother didn't enjoy swimming; she never liked it in Hong Kong. Well, you know, Chinese women don't like to go out in the sun, they don't like to be dark. She didn't like swimming or sun bathing or anything like that, but she really enjoyed fishing. My earliest childhood memory of the cottage is hearing my parents get up before dawn and the put-put-putter of the $2\frac{1}{2}$ horsepower engine going out into the lake. If you went out with my parents you were the one who ended up rowing. You never got to fish. They were pretty strict. You couldn't talk. It was so boring and both my brother and I were great chatterboxes.

What else do you remember of Ottawa in those early years?

Ottawa was a wartime town with people from all over the world. I remember school as being lots of fun and having a wonderful time. I had wonderful teachers. I can remember all their names; I can see them now. I never went to a private school—we couldn't afford it and my parents never thought about it as a possibility in any case. My father is profoundly democratic and populist, and I'm very glad that I went to public schools—I enjoyed them.

Did you always do well in school?

Yes and it was expected of me. The only time I didn't do well was when I learned how to write. Actual penmanship. You know, printing I wasn't bad at but penmanship in grade five really stopped me. I had a darling teacher, Miss McRae with purple hair—I'll never forget—she was the first woman I ever saw with purple hair. And interestingly enough, she was one of the most vivid storytellers. We had a twenty-minute thing in the morning after the Lord's Prayer when she'd tell us Bible stories, and they were so much better than Sunday school.

Was it hard work or did the high marks come easily?

It came easily for me. I don't take any credit for it. I think there are natural things that happen to you that have nothing to do with intelligence. Like a good memory; it has nothing to do with intelligence. I have almost a photographic memory. I was also very good at mathematics. Most Chinese are very good at mathematics. My parents swear that I never learned to read at school, that one day I was just reading the newspaper at home when I was about four. I've read other cases of that. I mean, I don't think I ever learned to read. I can't remember when I couldn't read.

You said it was expected of you to do well.

Yes, but there was no pressure. The expectation was there because we were bright and it was assumed we would do well and go to university and have productive lives.

They were talking as much about quality of life as academic or professional achievement?

Yes. My brother was always going to be a doctor. At six or seven he was capturing bumble bees in jars and dissecting them. He was very focused from an early age. I wasn't; I was all over the map in my interests. I think the closest analogy would be with Jewish families where it's simply expected that you'll study and do well.

There is the argument that this high achievement comes from a sense of insecurity, a desire to protect oneself.

No, I don't think it was like that because my father is one of the most secure people in the world. He started to work when he was nine years old in total poverty. My father has never been unhappy. Things have happened to him that haven't been very nice and he's accepted it and moved on.

You speak so much of your father, your relationship is obviously close.

Very close, very close with my father and I think it still is. It's not necessarily close in the sense that we don't speak every day on the phone, but he's always there solidly behind me. I think it's an enormous advantage to a woman of whatever race to have a father who thinks of her as an equal, and gives her the passport to the world which is all male and makes it possible for her to function well.

WILLIAM POY,
FATHER OF ADRIENNE CLARKSON.
©1947 BY YOUSUF KARSH.

This is an enlightened position, certainly not the norm.

I don't think he looks at it is as enlightened, I think he simply thought I was more like him and therefore he didn't take any account of my being a girl. The other thing he always did, which I think was really important, was that I wasn't only an intellect to him. When he would go to New York on business trips he'd be sure to come home with three or four wonderful dresses for me, from Depinna's, which was a store on Fifth Avenue. We didn't have any money, I mean we had hardly any money, but he would always come back from a business trip with a doll or a music box.

Was your brother close to your mother in the same way that you were to your father?

I think so, and I think that he, being her first child and having been born premature and so on, I think that he had a special place in her heart. I don't think there is anything strange about that. And then he was alone for four years before I was born.

Were you always aware of being different. You were brilliant, a woman, Chinese. Did this make you especially aware of being different or an outsider?

Oh, I was always different. I've always felt different—I still feel different—and my parents encouraged that difference. My parents were both extremely attractive people. My father is very beautiful, he's extremely handsome, and in the photos of him when he was young he looked like a movie star. He's a legend, absolutely a legend, and he was a beautiful dancer and fun, you know. I don't have that seriousness in my background that a lot of European immigrants have. Whenever they had a little extra money my parents would spend it, perhaps buy my mother a fur coat. I wasn't brought up with the idea of hoarding money or saving.

They lived a lot for the moment. You know, we always went out to a restaurant once a week to eat. Nowadays people do it all the time, but in the 1940s and '50s they didn't. We either went to the matinee on Saturday and to Murray's for lunch, and my brother and I had the children's menu. Or we went to the early movie and then went and had Chinese food in the evening. That was the Saturday ritual for us.

Did you realize how exceptional this life was?

Yes, I did. I think I did because I had good friends and could see that they lived different lives. There was always a great emphasis on food in my house. My mother learned to make very good Canadian food—I mean she made brownies, she made pies, she made cakes, stews, that sort of thing. We always had a Canadian meal at lunch and Chinese food every night. And for Chinese food my mother was a perfectionist. We would have at least three dishes—one with vegetables, one with either bean curd or egg and one with some kind of fish, even if it was just dry cabbage with steamed fish, and it was always perfect every time.

Was there any discussion in the home about the Chinese Exclusion Act?

Well all I remember about that is that my father was always very clear to us about the fact that we would never go and live in Vancouver. All the overseas Chinese knew what Vancouver meant. I didn't go to Vancouver until I was thirty-two years old. And I still don't particularly care for it. You see, my father being a very intelligent person realized that what they had done to the Japanese during the war was only part of a larger racism towards Orientals.

It's very interesting that whole question of discrimination. It was very clear to me that I would make my life in a big city like Toronto. It would never be on the west coast which was filled with these evil people who would shovel anybody into concentration camps or cut off their pigtails or whatever. My father said it was important to live in a place where everybody was equal and where people take you for what you are. My whole attitude toward the west coast and Vancouver has been coloured by that. I've never been willing to be seduced by its beauty.

You said that during school your interests were all over the map. When did specific interests begin to enter your mind?

Well, this is an aspect of my parents that I think is very unusual, but they both had vaguely theatrical longings. My father thought that public speaking was one of the most wonderful things to do and he had done it even as a tiny child. He loved orating—he still does—and thought that I should go in a public speaking contest when I was in high school, which I did and I won. I had never paid much attention, but I realized that when my mother was young she had harboured dreams of being an actress. She had acted in some school plays and really liked it. Her temperament was very much like that of an actress. She was very emotional, like a roller coaster, and if she had had talent I guess that she would have been a classical stereotype of what an actress should be. She was very concerned that we be very poised and presentable in public, and one of the things she felt important was to learn dancing and piano. So I went to ballet class when I was about seven—ostensibly because I had terrible posture. I still do have terrible posture. The dancing lessons never helped with the terrible posture, but I loved them. I took ballet and I took tap dancing and so did my brother. We spent most of our youth from seven to about sixteen dancing.

Social dancing?

Oh yes! We used to dance at home, and my parents would take us out with them if there was a big celebration. To me the Canadian Grill Room of the Chateau Laurier is still the epitome of glamour. It has a lovely orchestra and, you know, I can still remember the texture of the rolls they served there. The headwaiter was called Fred and my father used to have his annual Christmas party there. We would take maybe ten tables and my brother and I were always included. I'd have a new dress for it and a corsage; it was wonderful. My parents included us in everything. They never went anywhere without us. We were never left with a babysitter. And we never had any rules in our lives. I never remember being told to go to bed or that it was bedtime. And I got a radio when I was ten and used to listen to it at night.

Is this perhaps a variation on how some parents in Chinese families feel they should simply let their children be, because life is going to be very hard anyway?

Probably, probably. I think it's a whole different way of bringing up children. We were allowed to eat anything. The only thing I was not allowed to eat until I was an adult—that is, sixteen—was coffee, for some reason. I used to dream that it was the most wonderful thing in the world and it was the biggest disappointment.

What else happened when you turned sixteen and became an adult besides drinking coffee?

Oh I'll tell you; I had my first gin and tonic. I hated it. I thought it tasted just like perfume smelled and I didn't see any point in that. So I never got drunk. I also had a cigarette. My father was a chain smoker, so I always used to say to him I can hardly wait until I'm grown up and can have a cigarette. He smoked five packs of cigarettes a day but cut it out when he was fifty, like that, when my brother said to him from medical school, "If you don't stop you'll be dead from lung cancer."

Those were the initiation rites of adulthood?

Yes, I guess they were. I didn't learn to drive until I was in my twenties. My brother learned when he was fourteen. I remember we went to Florida for Easter in the early '50s and he had just gotten his learner's licence, so he was allowed to drive—he was so small behind the wheel he could hardly see over it. We also had dogs; dogs were a very important part of our life. Again, that was something my mother really liked but something you couldn't really have in Hong Kong because it's so crowded. But we had a Borzoi called Snow White by the time the war broke out. We had pet chickens and rabbits. In Hong Kong they're dyed red for Chinese New Year. I remember a red rabbit. That's another early memory I have, of a bright red rabbit.

Did you travel a lot in Canada?

Yes. We knew a nice old Chinese guy who lived in Chinatown who was a kind of relative. He came from the next village from my father's family. He had a pre-war Ford and he used to lend it to us. In 1946 we went to Algonquin Park and in 1947 to Niagara Falls. And then I think in 1948 or 1949 we got our own car.

How did you end up choosing the University of Toronto?

My interest in literature began in high school with a wonderful teacher, Walter Mann. When I decided that was what I wanted to study he said I should go to the University of Toronto and enter Trinity College because it was the best. He was a decent, wonderful guy and he inspired me and I got a scholarship and went. My mother hadn't wanted me to go to Toronto. She wanted me to go to McGill where my brother was going. We used to go to Montreal all the time and I got to know it quite well. And I thought, I don't want that. I want to find something else.

My father had a business friend here and he and his wife invited me to visit one summer and I just loved Toronto. I loved the dry wonderful WASPy quality. I just liked it. Ottawa wasn't like that; it had a different feeling to it completely. And the country is so different, the rolling land and beautiful farms—whereas the farms around Ottawa, God, I mean, how did those people live! Everything was rock patches. I've come to appreciate it but at the time I just couldn't imagine how they survived. So I was quite set on Toronto and my mother was very against it. We had a fight, and my father was on my side. He said, "Look, if she wins a scholarship, then she can go," so I did. I would say that that was the decision that coloured the whole rest of my life. I don't think I would have had the career I've had, had I gone to Montreal.

Was it the University of Toronto or was it the city?

It was the University of Toronto. There was a tradition, an intellectual tradition at the U of T, which I liked. This was the centre—I didn't know it then but I felt pulled to the centre. This is the centre of English language life in Canada. Also I was part of a group born just before the war. During the war there simply weren't many babies being born. It made a lot of difference because there was a six year gap before anyone caught up to you. There was a whole group of us able to get into some very interesting positions after graduation in 1959, 1960. Barbara Frum and Peter Gzowski and many others.

Had you started writing at this point?

Yes. I wrote for the Trinity *Literary Review*. I was not a journalist then. I was not interested in the daily newspaper. I've never been interested in newspapers. I was writing short stories and poetry, you know, feeling my way around. Peggy Atwood and Dennis Lee were my contemporaries at Victoria College.

And you continued to your masters?

Yes, right away. I always thought I'd get my masters. My father had gone to night school during the war at the University of Ottawa and got his masters and I guess I always thought I'd get one, too.

Did you study with Northrop Frye at the University of Toronto?

I took Frye's literary symbolism course as a graduate student. I had two very influential professors at university. One was Arthur Baker at Trinity, a self-described Christian Humanist and a very great expert on Milton and Sir Thomas More. The other great influence was, of course, Frye. They were very different in many ways, but through them I came to be able to read from different perspectives and to have a deep understanding of literature.

You went to France after your MA. How long did you stay?

Two, three years. Something like that. I had been to Europe with my family the summer after receiving my BA and had fallen in love with France. So after my MA I went to Paris and enrolled in a course for teachers of French in foreign countries. I couldn't speak a word but I had taken French all the way through school. I loved French literature, I could read it, I could write it then, better almost than now—more literarily anyway—but I couldn't speak a word. After three months I could speak as well as I do now. I continued to write but not seriously. I was busy enjoying myself and learning about life in France. That's when France became branded on me. So years later, when I became Agent-General for Ontario in Paris, I felt that it was an important and logical step for me to take because it used a part of me that had been formed in France twenty years before.

What brought you back to Canada after three years?

Well, I got married to a fellow Canadian. We had been students together at the University of Toronto. And then I went back to university. I was a teaching fellow and then a lecturer at Victoria College. During my first year back in Canada I met a friend at a party who was a script assistant here at the CBC. She asked me what I was doing and I told her, but I said I really didn't think I was going to be an academic. I didn't know what I would do but I had to do something. And she said they were auditioning people to do book reviews on a daily TV program; they'd tried some professors but they were very dull, why don't you try? You know, why don't we audition you? And I thought, that sounds like fun. So I went into Studio 6 where I later spent ten years of my life and auditioned and I loved it. The minute I walked into the studio I loved it. I loved the darkness of it. I loved the womblike quality. I loved the cameras.

Theatre.

No, not exactly, because I don't like live audiences. I've never liked live audiences. I just don't find it as focused. When you're on television it's one person you're talking to. Just one. It's a very intimate communication.

Do you ever have any difficulty making that connection with your audience?

No never, no never. I think I've always been able to do it because I understood it from the beginning. I don't think it's anything you can teach people. I know some people who make their living doing it who are terrified by it. . . . It's very intimate. It's a very vulnerable thing. And you can always tell people who are really scared on camera. Even if they have a career on television there is a little veil, a cellophane barrier between them and the camera.

So from that first book review that was it for you?

Yeah, I loved it. It went well and they asked me to come once a week to review a book. I did it for a couple of months and then they asked if I'd like to try and do an interview. I did the interview and liked it a lot—asking interesting people interesting questions was fabulous. At the end of that season Anna Cameron, the host of the program, was leaving and I was asked to audition as her replacement. Dozens of people auditioned. I did my audition, which was an interview, and then I went off to France for the summer. About a month later they phoned and said I got the job and that's it.

And how long did you do Take 30?

From 1965 until 1973, and then I did *Adrienne at Large* for two seasons, and then *Fifth Estate* started in 1975.

What is it about interviewing that appeals to you most?

I've always loved interviewing. It still grabs me every time, it's quite amazing. I guess it's like a long sustained love affair with different partners—each time you're there with someone interviewing them, when you're in that light and it's happening, there's this intense light that surrounds you both. And it has nothing to do with the lighting. It has to do with intensity, and that's very rare. It spoils you for a lot of things. Makes other things seem mundane.

Do you have favourite or most memorable interviews?

Oh I have a number, I suppose. One is the Shah of Iran. People remember that and I certainly remember it. But also my literary interviews. I had a wonderful interview with Arthur Koestler. I mean a remarkable interview, just remarkable, fabulous. Laurens Vanderpost was another wonderful interview that I just felt uplifted by, just transported to another plane—I'm selfish about the interviews, I like the ones where I feel transformed. There are also the other interviews where you really get something or something happens that reveals the thing in all its enormity—the Shah of Iran type interview. There was also a wonderful interview with a man called Sir John Glubb who was an Englishman who ran Jordan under King Abdullah. After King Abdullah was assassinated he was thrown out of Jordan and ended up in a place called Poundtree Cottage. He was a scholar and was writing books and was a marvellous figure, you know, a person who had just lived a life of action and a life of the mind and spirit.

Your responses seem very literary. Your images and your composition of the response suggest that they have been addressed on some level, as if you have asked these questions of yourself many times.

Plato says the unexamined life is a life not worth living. I certainly agree with that. It should be over my door because I think that that's certainly been my motto and continues to be.

If we could go back a little bit and talk about your writing. What started it and how did it develop?

Well, I always liked to write. I always liked to record things, write things down and describe things. I loved composition in school. I liked that organization of words quite a lot, but I didn't know what I would do with it. I think in some respects I short-changed my own visual sense because everything that is visual I really love; I love paintings and sculpture and scenery. I like creating beautiful atmospheres. I'm very good at colour. I can remember colours. I can look at a wall and then go somewhere two months later and buy a cushion that fits the wall perfectly. Not the same colour but the right tonality. I think it's the visual sense that drew me to television, even though I've always thought of myself as literary.

T.S. Eliot said he never would have become a poet if he hadn't learned French. How much did going to France and learning French have to do with your writing?

I've always loved French literature. It's very different from English. It's a more rigid language than English, inflexible in what it will accept, and there's a certain intellectual rigour about it that I like. I find that there is a part of me that is only expressed when I speak French. There are aspects of my personality that come out when I speak French but not when I speak English. I think one's life is enriched by other languages. I speak Italian reasonably well now and it's had the same effect. Italian is a very easy language to speak badly, but it's extremely alive and much more flexible than French. It is really a reflection of the turn of mind and the kind of spirit of the people.

Who were the writers that influenced you the most?

Well, I read absolutely everything. But the novelist I still admire the most and re-read the most is George Eliot. I think she is the greatest novelist in the English language, and then Tolstoy is the greatest novelist in a European language. I have just re-read *Anna Karenina* and will re-read *War and Peace* next summer. I also adore Jane Austen. I don't read that many novels any more because there's just so much coming out all the time. I read my friends' works. I like a writer called Ward Just a great deal. An American writer living in Paris and he's just a fabulous, fabulous writer. Very tight, restrained; I think he's just a great writer.

You published three novels in quick succession 1968, '70 and '71. Why has nothing followed?

Well I don't think I had any more to say in that way. I think also my television life became very intense. I'll have something to say again at some point but not quite yet.

You've had such a public career for such a length of time. The media tends to fix an image of somebody like yourself, take them and put them up on a pedestal, shine all the lights on them and then yawn and shuffle them aside. But you've remained in the light for more than twenty-five years, in different manifestations. It has not been the same Adrienne Clarkson all along. How has that been for you?

Great. I think that's what you should do. I mean that's what I should do. I don't know about other people, but I don't like being bored and I don't like doing the same thing all the time. Again, that's where television spoils you because even when you work within a particular series there is the most enormous variety. There is huge variety. Programs about everything from dogs to Van Gogh. All my interests, which are extremely varied, are reflected in *Adrienne Clarkson Presents*. Even when I did something like *The Fifth Estate* it was not boring because there were so many things, so many interesting stories to be covered. What gets tiresome is the way of life, travelling all the time and never a moment of your own. It really was a dog's life. It was dreadful.

What kept you going?

Well, I don't know how to stop. I really don't know how to stop. I think I'm doing a very interesting job, I'm good at it and I have to earn my living. We don't work for two months every summer; we just go off and lie down somewhere. You don't get many jobs where you can do that. It suits my personality to work very hard for periods of time and then to take time off. I'm not a 9 to 5 type person—I'm not. And I find that very difficult. This is not to me an office. It's not an office because we are all creating something here. In most offices you don't create anything; you are just there to be in place, you know, so other people can find you. Whereas here we actually create things, organize programs; I watch stuff, I comment on it. I don't write most of my scripts here. I write them at home. It's just a different pacing.

But do you have a chance within the twelve month period to withdraw?

Oh yes, I do. I have to have that.

What is that time like, when you withdraw?

Well, it's very nice. I have a house in the South of France. I just spent four days there at the end of a filming trip to Europe, picking olives with my neighbours. It was just wonderful. I was picking olives for an eighty-year-old neighbour. She's a wonderful woman and she has three different little parcels of olive trees. There are usually about six of us working at a tree at once. You truly feel a part of things—a redemptive feeling.

I've had a house there for seven years now, right in Van Gogh country. I have many friends in the village. A lot of interesting people live there. It's always been very emotionally rewarding to be there; there's lots of interesting people and the countryside is absolutely beautiful.

Do you have a similarly intimate relationship to the countryside here?

Yes, Muskoka and Georgian Bay. Georgian Bay appeals to me particularly, except for the snakes. I don't mind the non-poisonous ones but I don't like a rattlesnake. I love Lake Joseph; I really feel a great attachment to that sort of atmosphere. I'm not fond of the Rocky Mountains; I'm not fond of mountains generally. I like the sea; I was born by the sea, I suppose that's why I like it.

It's about scale too. Southern Ontario and the South of France have features—rocks, trees, water–that are closer to human scale. The Rockies and the forests of the west coast overwhelm you with their presence.

Yes. Mont Blanc is a terrifying, huge presence. What does this mean? I don't even want to think about what it means. I don't understand that. It doesn't appeal to me.

How did the Agent-General position come about?

Well I got a message at my CBC office. A head hunter called me from Caldwell Partners and said he had been hired by the Ontario Government to talk to people about the agent-general position—they were opening the office—and my name had come up. They are very good headhunters, Caldwell Partners. So I went and talked to them, and then I talked to more people, and then there was a series of interviews with four or five people and I got the job. There was nothing political in it. Nothing.

What was it about the position that appealed to you?

Well I thought it was interesting because I would start the office. I would be promoting Ontario in France. And it was a way of living in France for a few years again, which I very much wanted to do. I had always had it in my head that at a certain point I would either buy an apartment in Paris or a house in the south.

How long were you there?

Five years. It was a three-year term and at the end of my second year they asked me if I could stay on for two years after the third year. I said okay, and then that was it because I really didn't want to be away from Canada too long. It's one thing to spend a few months of the year there and another to be an expatriate, which I don't want to be.

When you returned to Canada was there a similar sense of re-entry that you had after those three years after university?

It was different, I think. It was a whole different time. Canada in 1987 was changing slightly. Not as dramatically as it is now, not a crisis as it is now. But it was starting; you could feel the agitation. The first stage of Meech Lake happened in May of 1987, so there was a sense that something was really happening in Canada.

Was it a completely different country from the one you had left?

It was getting to be a little different. I felt that the 1980s were very bad for Canada because everything became money, money, money. For Toronto—I used to come back from Paris every six months for two weeks to work in the office here—and I used to think that Toronto was becoming disgusting for the money. I mean just awful. I never thought of Canadians or of Toronto as being a place just for money. I think that was really very bad for us and for our society. You could almost smell money. Ridiculous—horrible actually. I think that Hong Kong is a place like that, but I don't think of Toronto or Canada as a place like that.

Have you ever felt a part of or wanted to be a part of the Chinese community?

No. I would say it's never been an issue because there wasn't any community in Ottawa when I was growing up and because my mother and father came from such different backgrounds that there wouldn't be any meeting ground in that. My father came to my mother's world in Hong Kong and he fit into my mother's world. In a way I suppose the Chinese here would have been much more like what my father grew up with until he was sixteen or seventeen in Australia. They were these poor old men without their wives and all of that. My parents' friends were all Canadians, ordinary Canadians.

As you became well known, were you approached to become involved in political causes by the Chinese community?

Well, Dr. Joseph Wong got me involved after the CTV program, "Campus Giveaway." I thought it was a very bad thing and I thought it was wicked and I will always speak out against racism and injustice against the Chinese. I guess my not speaking Chinese and not having been brought up there and not having those kinds of roots to Hong Kong or China makes me different. I don't think I'm in the least bit lacking because I didn't have that kind of community. My community became what I chose it to be and what my parents chose it to be in the New World. I think that's true of a lot of immigrants whether or not they are Chinese. I'm very, very happy to have made the choices that I've made because it's made my life very rich and very happy. I'm not obsessed by being a woman or by being Chinese or by being my age or anything. I just wish to enjoy life and to live a full and enriching life and to contribute something and create something. That's what I really want to do, so I don't think about these other issues that much. If I'm asked to participate in a Chinese Canadian event I do, or I lend my name to it.

What would you say to the Hong Kong immigrants coming to Canada now as a result of the changes to come in 1997?

I think it's very important that the people who come here now from Hong Kong realize that Canada—even though we're going through a terrible crisis—is a wonderful country that has been created by a lot of struggle and hard work and political give-and-take. It is a social democratic society basically, a middle class, social democratic society. And I think that's hard for people from Hong Kong to understand. I do have many friends from Hong Kong. I think it's hard for them to understand this, but I think once they do understand it, they'll play by the rules because that's the kind of people they are. They're very decent, very honest, very straightforward and up front. They'll say to you, what are the rules? If you tell us the rules, we'll follow them. That's the way the Chinese are. If you say to somebody, "gee, I've heard at such and such a club they don't take Chinese," they'll say, "well, I'll phone them and find out." You know, they have that attitude. . . .

It's up to us Canadians who've been here a long time to say basically that this is the kind of society we have and that we welcome you. We should welcome everybody. We are a country of immigrants. The difficulty arises if you are uncertain of your own identity and then you feel swamped by all these different cultures. What must remain common between us, however, is a belief in English common law and the parliamentary system, certain givens, and we must say that this is what we really believe in and what we work for, and if you want to come and join us that's just great.

Do you have any sense of what might happen in 1997?

I don't really. I actually want to go to Hong Kong within the next year or so and find out what's going on. I always like it when I get there. I don't long to go there but I enjoy it while I'm there. I'd like to meet this guy Martin Lee. Whatever he says I really like and I think he's intelligent.

What about the future for you?

Well, I've always lived on not knowing exactly what's going to happen next. But I have to plan the series quite far ahead. The shows that you're seeing now were started in 1989–90. They take a long time to do. So I'm just carrying on with that for now and am quite happy to do so.

And for your children? What is different for them in the world today?

I think one of the things that's happening is that they are going to have to deal with a society which is by and large postliterate. Television has done that. Television and computers I think. There are still people who are twenty-five to thirty who have the sort of literacy I was raised to have, but I'm not so sure about the younger ones. Knowledge and understanding empower you in life and if you don't have them you really have nothing. You're stumbling around in the dark. We were lucky, when I think of it. I went through my Trinity College residence a couple of years ago when they were fund raising, and I went into a student's room and there was a stereo and television. You know, we didn't even have a radio. We got one clean sheet a week. We'd put the top one on the bottom and use the clean one on top. We didn't go shopping for a hobby. You bought your fall wardrobe in August, which would be a coat, a suit, two sweaters, three blouses et cetera, and that was that. We didn't have records. The whole thing was nice because that part of your existence was very restrained, so that you had the things of the mind or of the spirit foremost. That's what you concentrated on. There were very few distractions. Today, society's filled with distractions—consumer and otherwise—and I think it's more difficult. But that's a whole other set of discussions that one could have. There's sexual issues, there's consumer ones. All of that opened up after the 1960s.

Is there any way of getting past becoming a postliterate society?

Well, I think we're just going to evolve into something different. I'm not sure what that's going to be yet . . . I think, for instance, that it'll have a great deal of impact the number of channels we can get. It means that maybe the traditional way we make television is not meaningful any more because even people between the age of thirty-five and forty-five now only watch a minute and a half of each program. They make their own program. Everybody makes or stitches up their own program. The Gulf War was a real example of that. We never watched any single news program from beginning to end. We watched a minute of CNN and a minute of ABC and then a minute of CBC and then Newsworld for two minutes and then back again. We patchwork-quilted our global village together and I think that's going to happen more and more.

What do you hope for the future?

Well, I want Canada safe and one country and together. I think it's very important. And I want it to be decent and caring and full of policemen who say hi to you even if they don't know you. I was walking up from Women's College Hospital and I looked at a policeman—he was walking along—and he said hi to me. I thought, in France you'd never have a policeman say hi to you.

Perhaps he recognized you?

Perhaps. But even so it was just a very nice feeling, that feeling of decency and that feeling of what we are really like as a people at our best. It's something we share with the Scandinavians. They're the only people in the world we're really like. I wish we were more like that. That's what I really want for the future.

Why do you want the country to stay together?

Because I think it's important for us. I mean, it just won't be Canada without being the way we are now. This is what we put together as Canada. Otherwise we might as well become part of the United States, and that's not really what interests me.

Adrienne Clarkson, executive producer & host of Adrienne Clarkson Presents, the CBC's prime-time arts and culture series, has made an extraordinary contribution to Canada in broadcasting. A fervent Canadian who came to this country as a refugee, she is determined to show in her new series, the bilingual, multicultural richness and texture of Canada. She began her television career in 1965 on CBC television's daytime information series, Take Thirty, then became host and journalist with CBC's Fifth Estate. Along the way she won Actra awards in 1973, 1974, 1975 and 1981. In 1988, after five years as Agent-General for Ontario in France and two years as president and publisher of McClelland and Stewart publishers, Adrienne Clarkson resumed her television career.

Lee Kum Sing

The history of music and its traditions are passed down from master to pupil, from generation to generation. It was a long and curious journey from a resettlement camp in postwar Sumatra to the concert halls of Munich and London, but it was the desire to be connected to that long tradition that inspired Lee Kum Sing to leave his homeland. He studied in Australia, Europe and the United States before settling in Canada. Now, at the Vancouver Academy of Music, he has the opportunity to offer his students the knowledge and experience passed down to him by his masters.

子曰君子成人之美不
成人之惡小人反是

THE SUPERIOR ONE ENCOURAGES THE BEST QUALITIES IN OTHERS AND DISCOURAGES THEIR WEAKNESSES; THE INFERIOR ONE DOES THE OPPOSITE OF THIS.

I was born in Sumatra. My parents came originally from Malaya. My father was the manager of a British Company and was transferred to Sumatra.

What do you remember of your youth?

Before the war it was very fine. We had a great time and we had relatives visiting us regularly. It was very pleasant until the war broke out. I was five or six, old enough to remember the atrocities, and the suffering.

What do you remember?

Quite a bit, and for a long time afterwards I felt uneasy and nervous when I saw a big crowd gathering. During those war years, it meant that someone was being tortured or being executed. That was quite common, especially the water torture in the marketplace.

The Japanese did this?

Yes.

What other memories do you have of that period?

Apart from other horrifying events that took place every so often, two of my friends' fathers were taken away by soldiers in the middle of the night. I witnessed the agony that the families went through. Both mothers went berserk due to the mental strain. It was horrible. For a long while I did not have much confidence in mankind. I visited Auschwitz concentration camp during one of my recent visits to Poland, which only confirmed my feelings.

We human beings don't seem to learn from the past. The exploitation that continues to go on between individuals and between nations can only create more animosity and hatred, and these feelings cannot easily be erased. I think that by nature human beings are born with a feeling of insecurity, greed and weakness.

Tell us about your education.

I started kindergarten just before the war broke out. During the war, there was no education. In fact, my father had arranged for my brothers and myself to receive some form of education from a neighbour who was a teacher. This was absolutely illegal, and if we had been caught, the consequences would have been unthinkable. As children we were made to understand the situation and we conducted ourselves very maturely. When the war ended, we had to catch up with our education.

Did things get better after the war?

When the war ended, the Allies came. One of my uncles traded with them. Unfortunately, in Sumatra revolution broke out after the war. What my uncle had done was considered unacceptable by the guerillas. One day he was taken by the guerillas. My aunt came crying to my father for help. My dad had to call in the Allied troops to rescue my uncle. In so doing, my father placed himself in a precarious position. Although my father had disguised himself during the rescue, he was recognized, so our whole family had to flee, and we spent six months in a refugee camp. We left everything behind in our haste to escape. There were some very nervous and tense moments.

However, I might like to add that in the midst of these turbulent times, I had the opportunity to hear Sukarno speak. It was incredible. We waited for him for a long time. He was supposed to arrive at 2:00 P.M. to talk to us at the rally, but he was very late. There were at least 50,000 people present. In those days, that was a huge crowd. Sukarno was from Java—the Sumatrans did not trust people from Java—and they were sceptical about him even though he was the founding father of Indonesia. At the beginning, the crowd gave him a cool reception. Sukarno was fabulous. He was such a great orator. I remember, he did not have a script, yet as the speech progressed, we could see the people being magnetised by him. In the end, he stirred them to such a tremendous ovation.

What sort of schooling did you have after the war?

I went to a Chinese school. During the colonial days, the colonial powers built only one school, and of course there were many schools built by the missionaries. However, you had to belong to a certain congregation or religious belief in order to be admitted. The Chinese community realized that their children required education in their own culture and consequently built schools of their own. I went to one of them.

Was there a big Chinese community in Sumatra?

Not really, but big enough to warrant a school or two.

How long did you go to Chinese school?

I finished my formal education which was up to the equivalent of today's high school. I also had spent a few years in a Methodist and then a Catholic school, which were of course in English language. In those countries, the schools ran two sessions: morning session, which was from 7:15 to 12:45, and afternoon session from 1:00 to 6:00. For a number of years, I attended both sessions at different schools.

What led you to music?

I started music during the war years. My mother had a piano which she played. My eldest brother and my cousin, who had come to stay with us because of the war, started playing one year before I began. My first teacher was not good at all. After six lessons, I refused to go back to her. I was only around six or seven, but I was quite stubborn, and I refused to go back to her. I went to a different teacher later.

When did you realize that it was what you wanted to do? What age were you?

I realized it from the very beginning. I remember I could spend hours at the piano. It was a refuge for me—something that let me reach deep into my inner self.

What was the time from age ten to twenty like for you?

There were lots of changes in our lives as a family. The sudden uprooting from Sumatra to Malaya was traumatic, to say the least. It was a very hard time for the family. My parents must have gone through a great deal of agony leaving everything behind. Life was good before the war, but after the war my brothers and I had to grow up fast. It was a survival-of-the-fittest situation. Unlike today's 'peace time' teenagers, we had less opportunity for many things. But what we had we were certain to make the best of. We realized the value more, I think.

How did you motivate yourself to make up for lost time?

It was not a question of motivating myself in those days. The war taught us to make the best of whatever we had. To be alive and healthy were big assets. We were fortunate to have schooling at last. Moreover, if we did not want to study, there were always some kids who were ready to step into our places.

Were you aware of the disparity between those who had wealth and those who didn't?

During the war years most people had little. There was not much food, let alone other materialistic things. There was little or no employment for the men. Most of them were like my dad, lying low for fear of being arrested by the Japanese. There was a constant threat that at any given moment one could be picked up by the Japanese and taken away. Having wealth was immaterial. Unless one worked for the Japanese, there was hardly any employment that one was willing to expose oneself with.

Did music help sustain you through these years?

Yes, I think so. The piano was my friend, I suppose, and music was something I could get lost in—forgetting what was going on around me.

When did you give your first concert?

I was fourteen at the time. After that I had quite a few opportunities to perform both on radio and in public concerts. I also toured with my school orchestra in Malaya and Singapore. After school I applied and auditioned for an Australian government scholarship.

What were the biggest problems you faced when you went to Australia to study?

Language! Although I had English in schools, which was as a second language, my first language was still Chinese. We also spoke a few dialects and Malay.

What struck you most about Australia when you first arrived?

It was my first experience in a Caucasian society. Many things were new to me. The people were very friendly and helpful, and I enjoyed my first experience with opera. It was most exciting. It opened up many opportunities for me. The scholarship programme looked after me very well. Besides attending the University Conservatory of Music in Melbourne, I was exposed to a lot of concerts, operas and ballets. After a year or so of study, I began to play concerts and did radio recordings for the ABC, the Australian Broadcasting Corporation. I also taught while I was in Australia.

Did you like teaching right from the beginning?

Yes, I did. I had a wonderful teacher when I was young, Madame Tjong Tsze Yin, who was trained in Geneva, Switzerland. She made me an assistant at her school; I think I was one of her top students. She gave me not only beginner students but also older students who were older than I was but less advanced in their studies. I was most thrilled and enthusiastic. Madame Tjong was most helpful and encouraging but strict.

What is it that you like most about teaching?

I don't just teach the students to play the piano. Apart from teaching them the basics such as techniques or style interpretations, there is a wide range of topics to cover in order to properly understand the composers and their compositions. Don't forget that keyboard literature has over four hundred years of history. Apart from these factors we have to consider the individual character of the student, his emotional and psychological make-up and sensitivities. All in all it is a very complex and interesting subject. Teaching is also learning.

How long were you in Australia?

Two and a half years. Although it was a wonderful country I felt that it was quite removed from everywhere else. I left for Germany as soon as I got my diploma. I always wanted to go to Europe.

I had heard Hans Richter-Haaser in concert and I was very impressed with him. I had also heard his students in concert, which prompted me to go and study with him. Of course, I had to apply and audition, which was quite an experience. At the audition, the candidate before me, a German girl, came out crying saying that the jurors had suggested that she return in two years. After hearing that, I thank God that I was accepted. Can you imagine going all that way to be rejected?!

I went first to Detmold—Nordwest Deutsche Musikakademie. I did not stay too long, though. Richter-Haaser was a wonderful man and excellent musician, but Detmold was too small and I felt that I should expose myself to more cultural activities than Detmold had to offer. So I decided to move to Berlin. I was attracted to German music. After all, most of the major piano music composers I was familiar with such as Bach, Beethoven, Schumann and Brahms were German. It was logical that I stay in Germany for further studies.

How did you handle the language?

Not very well, but I managed well enough to get by.

Where did you study in Berlin?

I went to the Musikhochschule and began to look for a teacher. I asked the students in the school, but it was impossible to get a good grasp of who I should study with. One of the professors, Gerhardt Puchelt, had a recital two nights after my arrival. I went to hear him. I remember it was an all-Beethoven evening. Although it was not his best night, something in his playing made me feel that I should study with him. It was a good choice. The man was an intellect and an excellent scholar. He was also an experienced chamber musician and accompanist for singers. Of course, his fluency in English was an advantage to me. During lessons, he often made references to literature and art. Professor Puchelt was a generous man. He gave me long and extra lessons. He was particularly noted for his interpretation of Schumann and Schubert.

What was your life in Berlin like?

Very lively and interesting. Politically, Berlin was an island. In 1958 to 1961, the Berlin Wall did not exist. There weren't any restrictions for travelling between East and West Berlin. The East Berlin government in those days went all out to compete with the West in opera production in particular. They had two wonderful opera houses. Each of them presented first class productions. According to a good friend of mine from New York, who is a great opera enthusiast, East Berlin opera productions outshone those of the New York Metropolitan. I heard an average of four to five concerts a week. It was wonderful. I also had the opportunity to listen to not only the best assortment of artists of all instruments—including singers—but also almost all the conductors who came to conduct the Berlin Philharmonic and the Berlin Radio Symphony Orchestra. As you know, the Berlin Philharmonic is one of the greatest orchestras in the world, and so practically every major conductor of note in the world came to play concerts with the orchestra each year. I also attended numerous rehearsals and heard many debuts. Among them was the debut of

Canadian pianist Glenn Gould. It was an unusual experience for me. I sat in on his rehearsal and later talked with him and walked with him to his hotel. I remember his concert followed the one given by the great pianist Bachaus–the grand master of the German School.

Which part of Berlin were you in most of the time?

I lived on the west side of Berlin but my wife travelled to East Berlin daily for her ballet classes.

How did you meet your wife?

We first met in Singapore. She travelled to Europe with me and we eventually got married in Berlin.

Is she Chinese?

Yes. And she's a ballet dancer. She was trained at the Royal Ballet School in London. When we first met, she was on a tour of Asia performing. Later, she was in East Berlin for further training, at the same time she was dancing with the Berliner Ballet.

What happened after Berlin?

I returned to the Far East and made my home in Singapore. I became active as a pianist making tours in the region as well as being an accompanist for visiting artists. Among them were Joan Hammond, the Australian soprano, Kim Borg, the Finnish bass-baritone, Betty Allen, contralto, and Alfredo Campoli, the violinist. Alfredo Campoli and I made three tours during the 1960s. It was he who first told me about Victoria and Vancouver.

Did you teach?

Yes, I took in a few students. I found it difficult if not almost impossible to play the two roles well, especially since there was constant travelling involved, not to mention practising and rehearsing. However, among my students was Margaret Ling Tan, who went on to become the first woman to achieve the DMA—Doctor of Music Arts—from Julliard. Incidentally, she's now very active and doing extremely well in performing twentieth-century music.

Were you able to make a good living?

It was not bad at all. I had some forty concerts a year in those days. My wife was the founder of the Singapore Ballet Academy and ran a successful school.

When did you leave Singapore?

In 1962, I was awarded a State Department grant offered by the U.S.A. I went to the U.S.A. My aim was to get to know some big American music institution and at the same time do some studying there. I went to the Eastman School of Music at Rochester, New York. Eastman was one of the best known and most well established schools. They had excellent facilities, especially their library. But I was rather disappointed. Rochester is not Berlin. The entire cultural outlook was different from what I had been used to. Besides, the politics in the school were too much for me. In 1962–63, it was the height of the Cuban missile crisis. After having been through war, I was quite concerned about the situation. But I was astonished to find that my fellow students hardly concerned themselves with the issue and that upset me a great deal. However, I did manage to play a few recitals in Rochester and made my debut in New York during my stay.

You feel social awareness and activism are important?

Oh yes, absolutely. It's perhaps because of my wartime and colonial experiences. And, I am very interested in history. How could we interpret Chopin, Prokofiev, Beethoven, etcetera, if we are not aware of the conflicts during their times—political, social, personal—that resulted in the many wonderful compositions we enjoy today?

What did you do after you left Eastman?

I returned to Singapore and continued my career as a pianist and teacher. I wanted to do more than just the two careers then; I was trying to influence politicians and musicians to set up a music conservatory. I was appointed a trustee of the National Theatre. A few friends of mine set up a company to run concerts. However, I realized that the time was not ripe for such ventures. The country had many political and social problems. Art and music had to wait. In 1967, the French government offered both my wife and myself a grant to come to Paris. My wife was to study at the ballet department of the Paris Opera and I went to study with Magda Tagliaferro and Julius Katchen, whom I had known since 1955.

Lee Kum Sing with wife Soonee and children Horng Kher and Horng Dih in Paris in the late 1960s.

We were in Paris from 1967 to 1969. Paris was such an inspiring and beautiful city. Politically, it was also very exciting. It was during the time of General De Gaulle and the student uprising. I needed this time very much to study and think. I also took the opportunity to study orchestral conducting. From 1968, I began to accept more concerts. I gave concerts in England, Belgium, Italy and France and in Asia. I gave a concert in Florence and was re-acquainted with my professor from my time at Eastman, Orazio Frugoni, who had returned from the U.S.A to become the Director of a graduate school of fine arts in Florence. After consulting with him, I decided to pursue my graduate studies in Florence in 1960–70 while concertising in Europe.

It worked out very well. My family had returned to Singapore and I was alone in Italy. Life was extremely hectic, having to attend to my studies and travelling to give concerts in Europe, England and Asia.

What made you decide to come to Canada?

When I was living in Paris, the political situation in Southeast Asia was rather unstable. To make the story short, my wife and I decided to move to a country where we could bring up our two boys. I remembered Alfredo Campoli's high regard for British Columbia. It's heaven on Earth to him, and I think he was right, after having lived here for some twenty years. I had a good friend from my Berlin days by the name of John A. Young who had moved to Montreal. My wife and I liked the idea of a bilingual society, so we decided to apply to come to Canada. The Canadian Embassy in Paris took our application but they remarked that I would be better off if I had a graduate degree. Hence my move to Florence before Canada.

When did you go to Montreal?

We didn't. Remember the FLQ? It sounded very messy to us and our friend John Young had left Montreal and come to B.C. I must add that while I was concertising in Europe and England, I got an offer for a job performing and teaching in a college in England. My wife and I concluded that England was not the best place to bring up the two boys although music was wonderful there. We decided to come to B.C. I went home to Singapore in 1970 for a few months. I packed up and moved the entire family over.

What struck you about Canada when you first arrived?

We had no idea what it looked like. I thought it would be extremely cold. However, to our astonishment, we found so much greenery and the climate was most agreeable, except for the rain.

Did you have contacts here or a job?

John Young was my only contact. As for a job, there was nothing lined up. We just came.

What was it like at the beginning?

It was tough but both my wife and I were expecting it. I was quite ready to do anything to make a fresh beginning. From my past experiences, I have managed to cope, and I like adventure. We were met at the airport by the father of an ex-student who had immigrated and was living in the interior. The next day, we were introduced to another family from Singapore. Very quickly, I was introduced to a few prominent people who were interested in music. Among them were Mrs. Iby Koerner who was one of the founding members of the Community Music School which later became the Academy of Music. John Young, my friend, had asked me to contact the director, Jerold Gerbrecht, about the possibility of teaching at the Community Music School. When I called him, he told me that the school had only fifty students and they did not have a piano department, but was I prepared to start one? My answer was okay, I will start one for you. So I landed myself a job. Today there are about 1500, 1600 students attending the Academy.

Why do you think you've stayed in Canada?

I have lived here for twenty years. It is a good country, like Alfredo Campoli said, "Heaven on Earth." Truly, it is one of the best countries in the world although it has its problems. It's a young country. It's stable, the crime rate isn't high and the social programs are good. Apart from the rain, the weather is excellent. Most importantly, if one works hard, one can do very well.

Was your wife able to continue her career?

Yes. My wife has excellent credentials and she is also a fabulous teacher. Like everything else, the beginning was not too easy! She is now the head of the dance department at the Vancouver Academy of Music. She has trained a large number of very successful dancers and teachers who are pursuing careers in many parts of the world.

Have you done any recordings or released any records since coming to Canada?

I have done recordings for the CBC in Canada but have not released any records here. Although I have completed a few tapings at Wigmore Hall, London, and in Asia, I have refused to have them released so far. Somehow I do not feel that they are satisfactory enough. Most of my recordings were for radio in Asia, the CBC, and also for the BBC and in Europe. I have also done a number of TV programs, but mainly in Asia.

Someone asked me once if I felt I have wasted my time teaching students who never end up pursuing music as a career. My reply was that, first of all, I do not expect any of my students to be a musician unless they absolutely feel the 'calling'! For those, I have the enjoyment of teaching them. For the rest, I hope music will never leave their lives and that their experiences in music will prompt them to become a patron or sponsor of the arts. My work takes me to many countries not only in Asia but also in Europe. Currently, I am a visiting professor to China, Japan, Hong Kong, Southeast Asia and Poland. For the past ten years, I have been with the Victoria International Festival of the Arts.

We think of Beethoven, Brahms and Chopin—classical music—as being the height of western culture. How do you explain its popularity in the East?

It is a complex question. First, in the history of Chinese culture, music was never given the same emphasis as paintings, literature or porcelain and handicrafts. Music was seen as a pastime and not as a career. When the Chinese started to emigrate to other lands to seek greener pastures their first priority was to provide a living to support their families. There was no time to take up music. As they became more proficient in supporting their families, more effort was made to provide a better education for their children and this included music lessons. Many saw music as a symbol of social status. Secondly, you must remember that western music is seen by many first-generation Chinese as a foreign culture. Western music as a career choice was not encouraged. Eventually, all this will change as the idea becomes more acceptable. There's no doubt that there is a profusion of talent in music amongst the Chinese community. China has in recent years produced a flood of highly proficient and promising young violinists. Among the internationally known artists of Chinese heritage are Yo-Yo Ma, Cho Liang Lin, Fou Tsung and Melvin Tan, just to name a few!

What advice would you give someone considering a career in music?

Music is like the priesthood. You must have the 'calling.' It is not something that you choose—it chooses you. In my own opinion, education by and large is very narrow. Everyone is channelled towards getting a degree so that they are ready for the job market. This is not education but a preparation for a vocation. It is quite a pathetic approach. No wonder so many people in the world hate what they do.

How would you change the system?

It has to be a collective effort; individually, one can't do very much. The system is deeply ingrained. We can only try to make people aware of the situation by instilling in the students the virtues of being a musician and the responsibility one has to society.

You've talked about education. What happens when they leave school?

Canada is a big country. It strikes me that the provinces and cities are lacking in communication and cooperation. Canada is also a young nation. To speak of its own culture and heritage is perhaps a bit premature. In my own experience, to know my own ethnic tradition, culture and heritage helps me to understand, respect and tolerate others more readily. The consciousness of my own roots actually enriches those I have adopted. I remember when I was in Australia, some thirty-five years ago, the Australian Broadcasting Corporation ran almost the entire music scene and the attendance at their concerts was large. An important artist like Oistrakh could hold three recitals plus four orchestra concerts in one season in the same city and still pack in the audiences. This is amazing. The population of Melbourne was smaller than Vancouver's population today. I quoted Australia, because Australia and Canada have many things in common. Both are young countries and have people from different ethnic backgrounds.

How do you explain Australia's success attracting such audiences?

I guess their organization was good, programming and advertising were good, and most importantly, the young people and their families were encouraged to attend by means of youth concerts. I remember an excellent concerto competition held, first provincially, then nationally, each year. This brought a certain excitement and enthusiasm to the general concert populace. I must also add that the media were also most supportive. In a nutshell, Canada does not have the education to support and maintain the same kind of interest. Canada is a young country. To compound the problem, its citizens are made up of a cultural mosaic, and hence the tradition of concert-going has not been well established.

What should we do to improve this situation?

Something should be done to educate and stimulate the young audience. I believe they must be trained when they are young. We have many students learning music in every city, but where is the audience? Parents and educators must encourage the students to attend and support the arts as a complete music education. There must be more communication and cooperative links between music institutions such as the symphonies and the operas and the schools to encourage participation and involvement.

What is music? What does it mean? What is it in our lives?

Before humans can speak in words, there's sound. That sound is music. I think music comes first, then language. Look at the movies, the early ones—there's no talking. The music is sufficient. Maybe most of us are not conscious of it. Music soothes, excites and depresses. Music touches the deepest emotions and the soul. Personally, it is a major part of my life. I could do without a lot of things but I don't think I could do without music. It is not just a companion. It enriches one's life. To appreciate fine performance, one has to cultivate and educate oneself. The degree to which it touches us depends on how knowledgeable and sensitive we are. Good music never diminishes in quality and it always amazes.

Is there anything else you would like to say?

Canada is a fine country. It is a vast nation with an abundance of resources. We also enjoy a good standing in the world. It is noble to pursue a multicultural society, but there are some setbacks to that, in that it makes it so much more difficult for Canada to establish an identity. With the U.S. having such a large influence over us financially and culturally, and our many different heritages, classical music has so many distractions to compete with before it can establish itself as a mainstay of Canadian culture. I still believe that education is the key to building a new generation that is more aware and sensitive. Even though that may sound like Utopia . . . don't we always have to aim high? I believe that if we put out our best, we might receive something good in return.

There are a number of people who have had a tremendous influence on Lee Kum Sing's life and career and to whom he will be forever grateful. One special person was Mr. Val Elton of England who together with Julius Katchen and Mr. Heah Joo Seang of Penang gave Lee Kum Sing his first important break.

Lee Kum Sing with students James Parker and John Kimura Parker.

Alexina Louie

Alexina Louie is one of the few successful composers of orchestral music in Canada. She has been interviewed quite a number of times and so was neither uncomfortable nor inhibited by the presence of our tape recorder. We were delighted by her candour and the detail of her memory. The interview was interrupted after about forty-five minutes by a telephone call. When we began again we were horrified to discover that because of a bad connection the tape recorder had failed to record the interview. Alexina Louie calmed us and said she would be happy to start again. It seems that composers and recording artists learn to accept such technical problems with the insouciance of ducks to rainy weather.

The Master said, "If the scholar is not serious he will not be venerated and his learning will be shallow. Be loyal and sincere and have no friends who do not value virtue and learning as much as you. Do not be afraid to abandon your faults."

The part of my background I know best is from my father's side of the family. My great-grandfather was a man named H. Y. Louie who came to Canada from Canton province—actually both sides of my family came from Canton province. He came over to work as a farmer. He didn't speak any English at all, but he taught himself English from the people he met while sitting in his horse-drawn wagon delivering produce from the farm. Originally, he settled in Vancouver. My grandfather followed a few years later. My father was born in Calgary where he lived until he was about three, and then, through whatever circumstances, the family ended up back in Canton.

Eventually, at the age of about ten or twelve, my father and my uncle were sent back to Vancouver, which must have been a harrowing experience because they didn't speak English and they had to come over by themselves. They went to school and worked at the same time to save money to send back to China. Eventually, the entire family came over—quite a large family, too.

The last person out of China was my grandmother, who got stuck there when the Communists took over. I didn't realize this until after she died, but she was really an amazing character. When the Communists first took over, anyone who could be seen as a landowner was persecuted. My family owned a small plot of land on which they grew vegetables, which made them landowners. My grandmother was the only member of the family remaining. She was taken into the village square, a sack was put over her head, and she was beaten. One family took her in and hid her and eventually she tried to make her way out of China. At my father's end in Vancouver they were working on the immigration officials to try to get her out. The Communists wouldn't let her go. Finally, she hired a junk to get her from the village over to Hong Kong, but the night she sailed there was a big storm and her boat was blown back to the mainland. She was arrested and put in jail. When she got out she installed herself in the offices of the Communist officials hoping that her presence would become so irritating that to get rid of her they'd finally give her permission to leave. She was successful and I remember meeting her in Vancouver.

She spoke no English. She remained mysterious. She was our grandmother. I did not get to know her story until I began asking my father about all these things, wanting to discover who I was. It wasn't until after she died that I came to realize what an incredible woman she was. There was great remorse on my part for not having known her better and having her share her story with me directly.

How much Chinese do you speak?

Very, very little. I was born in Vancouver's Chinatown—that's where my father's business is—and we lived there until I was five or six. Until we moved, I used to go to work with my father and play in Chinatown. I have fond and terrifying memories of Chinatown. I would spend a lot of time with an extended family of my father's acquaintances and I would speak Chinese. I understood more Chinese than I do now and in fact I even went to Chinese school for a time. When we moved I lost a lot of that contact, with those older Chinese. It was a predominantly Caucasian area and I ended up having a lot of Jewish friends.

Just to wrap up the Louie story, my grandfather set up this grocery business, which became rather important in Vancouver at the time. To this day my father and his family have a company that imports and exports Chinese foodstuffs.

And your mother's family?

She was born in Victoria. Her story is rather different. My mother's family ended up in Saskatchewan, in a small town called Strasburg, then eventually in Moose Jaw. It was a typical kind of story. They were the only Chinese in a small town; they ran a family-operated café where all the brothers and sisters—and there were ten or twelve–worked.

Was it a Chinese restaurant?

It was Canadian and my grandparents baked great pies.

You still remember that?

Oh yeah. In fact, when I moved away to California to go to school . . . when I'd come home for a visit, they knew how much I loved their apple pies, so they would always make an apple pie for me when I came back.

When did you start studying music?

I was seven. I never asked for music lessons but my father decided it would be a good part of my education to learn how to play, so he bought a piano. When it came into the house I asked him what it was for. He said, "You're taking piano lessons."

I think the idea came out of a respect for learning, but also it was part of a genteel thing to do. My father had a tough life early on; I know he wanted a better life for us. I've been to the village in China where the family comes from and I can see how someone would leave a rural situation like that, I can see what their vision was. In spite of all the hardships in a new society—not speaking English, racism, all kinds of hardships—in spite of all this, the Chinese belief is that if it does not provide an immediate improvement in your life, you believe that for the generations down the road it will be better.

When did the music take over? When did it become a passion?

I think I was about twelve. At that age I switched to a really fine music teacher and that's what changed things. There came a point earlier on when I wasn't practising that much. Studying music is incredibly difficult. It isn't something you can do just before a lesson; it's part of your daily life, like getting up and washing your face. When you're a kid, it's really hard to have that kind of discipline and at a certain point my mother said, "Well, this isn't working out. You're not practising, so I think it's time for you to quit." She wasn't angry. When I thought about stopping lessons I was really upset and I started to cry. From that point on they never had to tell me to practise again.

When did you start to teach music?

I was fourteen. My teacher had me teach one of her students. I worked with him every day for half an hour. He was blind. She would give him his lesson and then I would practise with him. I worked with him for three years. It was a remarkable experience for me. I learned about patience and understanding and about disability. It was a different kind of teaching. Because he couldn't see, I had to work with feeling. Feeling the keyboard and teaching him how it felt to hold his hands properly.

Speaking of challenges, what kind of racism have you experienced?

I know that my father and his generation experienced a great deal of it. I have experienced relatively little. Perhaps it's because I care not to see it when it happens. And also I feel very comfortable being a Canadian so I don't really see a difference between myself and everybody else.

ALEXINA LOUIE
FIVE YEARS OLD.

Did you experience more racism when you moved out of Chinatown?

Yes. At the very early stages I remember being called names. I went to my father and asked him why this was happening and he said you must deal with this with a great deal of dignity. He said those people were ignorant and I should feel sorry for them. I think I'm really fortunate because he was able to impart that message to all of us.

How important was education to your parents?

My father's family is involved in business and on my mother's side they're professionals. Education was always important, and not just any education. We were encouraged to go to university for a profession. My father wanted us to be doctors and lawyers, and I turned out to be a composer.

You say you turned out to be a composer. When did you make that decision?

It's hard to say. When I was a kid I was really very shy and I had a hard time expressing myself. The only way I had to really express my feelings was to play the piano. Over a period I learned how to put everything that I was feeling into a beautiful phrase of Mozart. I just . . . music became a very important part of my communicating skills.

But at that point you were expressing yourself through the work of another composer.

Exactly. And at that point I never expected to be a professional composer. It was my father who unknowingly steered me in this direction. At the age of sixteen or seventeen he said to me, "Well, I've been paying for your lessons long enough. It's about time you started earning some money." So he bought me what is termed a 'fake book' in music. A fake book is a book that has melodic lines and chord symbols of pop songs and from this book you can improvise your own songs.

I said, "But Dad, this is not like playing Mozart." In Mozart, every nuance is written. He tells you when to play loud, he tells you how to phrase something, he gives you every single note. You learn how to make those black notes on the page into music. But this other kind of music, the fake book, is just bare skeletons and you have to fill in everything else. So I said, "I don't know how to do this," and he said, "Well, you're going to learn," and because I was such an obedient daughter, I began and I learned. . . .

Did you go to UBC to study music?

I took a general arts program with a major in psychology. After sitting through Psych 100 and 200 in huge lecture halls feeling completely alienated, I realized it wasn't for me, that I was getting much more fulfilment from the two music classes I was taking. I was much more interested in and engaged by music. I had a great teacher, one of those few teachers that you get in your lifetime where learning is very easy . . . you learn through osmosis. I wanted to study with him in my second year but the only thing he taught was composition. I started studying composition, not because of a need to compose, but because the teacher I wanted to study with taught composition.

And then gradually I realized that my great love of the classics led me to want to find out why a passage by Beethoven or Brahms would move me to tears. What was at the core of this work that was absent in the work of a lesser known composer? Because a note is a note. In order to learn what made that music great I studied analysis, which is a more intellectual approach to music, and composition, where you deal with the formal problems of writing. I thought that I could get inside the music by having to try to do it myself.

To understand where it comes from?

Yes. Instead of analyzing the result, search at the source.

And after you finished your undergraduate degree?

When I finished I didn't know what major to take. When I was an undergraduate my major was music history and I had several minors, one of which was composition. My composition teacher said something to me that really rang a bell. He said, "I just can't see you spending your life in a library doing research." So it was his encouragement that led me to choose a school where I was going to learn more about composition. I wasn't a serious composer as an undergraduate; I was learning the craft. My real self-expression still came from playing the piano. I went to graduate school for composition not knowing what to expect and feeling very insecure because I hadn't really written much music. That's how I ended up in California, at UC San Diego.

It was a totally different world for me. At UBC I was encouraged and I was a very good student. I knew all my teachers. It was a small music department, the student body was small, we really knew each other very well, and the professors were good. I could have stayed there for graduate school and everything would have been very comfortable, but I realized that just staying in one place is not the best thing for your development. So I ended up in California. The reason why I chose that school was because it was not primarily a faculty of performers with composition as a sideline. This department was wild because it was made up of composers, people who were actually writing music, not just lecturing about music. . . .

I was thrown into a world that was quite wild. It was California. It was 1970. I had to deal with a lot of different kinds of difficulties there. The cultural difference between Canada and the United States, especially California, is huge and unless you actually live in the United States, you don't recognize really what that is. I felt like a fish out of water for the whole ten years . . . but I met some incredible people and I think that had a great deal to do with my development. There were several very important things that happened to me there. One is that because of the cultural differences, I learned who I was. I was totally separated from friends in Canada, and when you're thrown into a situation that's alien and difficult, which graduate school is, you either succeed, and in the process learn much about yourself, or you're crushed. I succeeded. . . . I met some very interesting people. One was a set of Chinese twins who live in San Francisco and the other is Peter Salemi, who is an American of Italian descent. Peter was incredibly involved in Oriental music. He used to practise Japanese court music every night.

Was he the one who led you to discover Oriental music?

Partially, and that's what's ironic. While I was practising Brahms in one quonset hut, he would be in the next quonset hut practising this piercing, intense Japanese double-reed instrument which just struck at my heart. It was just incredible. I didn't even know this music existed. He introduced me to this whole world of Oriental music. I asked him what Chinese instruments would be interesting for me to learn. He suggested a Chinese zither. I took lessons in the instrument at UCLA. Not that I became very good at it, because of course it takes your whole lifetime to become good at an Oriental instrument, but I did learn the basics. . . .

Anyway, I got my masters degree in composition. It was not an easy degree to get. It took a lot of perseverance on my part, but during that time I injured my wrist. Suddenly, there went my means of expression. And because I could no longer practise, I was left with five hours a day to fill. I filled that void with composition. It became much more important to me when I couldn't play the piano anymore.

Is that when you began to see yourself as a composer?

I didn't write any music at all in the six years following my graduation. I didn't want to write for a couple of reasons. One was that graduate school had been traumatic; the other was that I hadn't discovered my own voice. For those six years I taught composition in Los Angeles. And all the while I continued to discover Asian music and philosophy and literature. Eventually, I realized that the reason a musician might want to play my music is if I have something unique to say. I realized that the interesting thing here is that I'm of Chinese origin but I was raised in the West. I thought, what would happen if I was able to take these techniques, or philosophies, and meld them together to come up with something that became my own personal language? Indeed, that's what happened.

The first attempts were really studious, self-conscious. But I was on some kind of interesting, exciting road and I felt really good about it. And at that point, from California, I submitted a grant application to the Canada Council. In order to apply for that, I had to send in some scores that I had written. I had these scores and a few taped performances, so I sent them in to the jury, and lo and behold, I was successful. I spent that time writing music and doing research. Through that kind of encouragement, even far away from home, I felt quite positive about what I was doing.

What happened when you brought this transformed person back to your parents and said, 'I am a composer'?

Well, by that time there wasn't anything they could do about it. I think they just accepted it; the arguments had long been put to rest. My parents had wanted me to go on and get my Ph.D. I wanted to be a composer and I felt that going on to another graduate school to get a doctorate wasn't going to teach me that much more about composing. My father didn't understand that kind of thinking. He thought the more degrees you had the better off you would be. I never did get my Ph.D.

Your parents had a chance to hear your music and enjoy it?

Sort of enjoy it.

Did the Canada Council grant bring you back to Canada?

No. I kept working in California and teaching piano.

What made you decide to leave California?

There were several reasons. By that time I was living in Los Angeles and most of the musicians I was coming in contact with were studio musicians making a lot of money playing jingles. These musicians were not interested in the philosophy of music or talk of Stravinsky; they were only interested in talking about how many sessions they were able to get and their residual and royalty cheques. I was looking for musicians I could talk to about the art of music making. The other thing was that I was becoming increasingly despondent about the kind of lifestyle one has to lead in the United States. In three separate incidents I had my life threatened by students because I didn't give them high enough grades. They said they were going to beat me up. I thought, do I really need this? The third thing was that I realized that at that point in time, the mid- to late-'70s, Canada really needed its artists, wanted them—which does not seem to be the case now—but at that time there seemed to be all kinds of opportunities. I felt if I were to return I would be encouraged here to keep going with my work. So I moved back to Canada in 1980 and settled in Toronto, which was much more of a centre of artistic activity than Vancouver was at that time.

I started teaching almost immediately. I taught at the Royal Conservatory. I had no piano, I had no tool with which to compose. I thought that if I got connected to the Conservatory, not only would I have some sort of income, but I would have a piano that I could write on. I wrote a number of good pieces during that time.

When did you feel that you had found your voice and were able to put it on paper?

It started happening about 1978, two years before I came back to Canada. In 1982 I was deeply affected by the death of Glenn Gould and wrote a piece called *O Magnum Mysterium: In Memoriam Glenn Gould*. It premiered in January 1983 as a commission from McGill University and in the fall of that year was performed by the Toronto Symphony, the Montreal Symphony and the Vancouver Symphony. It was broadcast across the country. It was that piece that brought my work to the attention of the music community. It's a very schizophrenic piece. It moves constantly from tortured sound or torment to sublime statements.

Six years old.

Like the impression of the man.

The piece eased the pain for me of the loss of one of the few artistic heroes this country has produced. It was also a rumination over the pain of the artist; he was only fifty when he died. He literally burned himself out. . . . His death made me think about the life I had chosen to lead, it made me think about the artist's life. What does it mean? You give your life to it and what do you have? After working through this in the piece . . . tormented sections, anguish, and then the sublime . . . the piece ends with a quotation from Mahler, it ends up in the atmosphere, it ends up heavenward. I found peace for myself and consolation over his death. The artist has a wonderful life. It's a life of real fulfilment. There is an inner paradise that one has that is yours, if you can keep going.

How did you meet your husband?

He commissioned my first professional piece.

Had he met you before he commissioned it?

No. I had a piece performed in Vancouver. I was living in California at the time. He heard the piece and wanted to commission something for his group. The name of the group was Days, Months and Years to Come. It was an ensemble of five or six musicians that performed contemporary music. He phoned me from Vancouver. I was flabbergasted because the piece was really a student piece. He wanted to commission a work from me and so we started talking on the telephone and corresponding.

How long after you met did you get married?

Oh, we had an ongoing relationship for a long time.

He's a musician?

And a conductor and composer.

Is he Chinese Canadian?

He's Ukrainian.

How did your family react to that?

Well, at the beginning when I started dating, I had terrible running battles with my father. When I went to university I belonged to a Chinese student organization. I dated some Chinese men but as my interests became more and more musical, I started to hang around with musical types, none of whom at that time were Chinese. So I started dating Caucasian men and my father hit the roof. I was the eldest in the family and the first to go through all this, so it was more difficult for me than for my siblings.

Why was it your father who was so upset and not your mother?

I think my mother's family was more used to Caucasian people, having been the only Chinese in a small town in Saskatchewan.

So the battle's over?

Yes. It was laid to rest many years ago.

What were your father's objections?

He never really told me. He just got very upset. But when he took the whole family back to China in 1973, I understood. I understood where we had come from. I understood his pride. I saw where my family had come from and how they had had to work to leave all that. . . . I saw the place where my great-grandfather and great-grandmother are buried on a very small knoll. I saw the house that my grandfather built, the road he built. I saw China—the people, their pride and self-worth—and I understood what my father wanted for me.

Are you able to make a reasonable living as a composer?

Yes. I live hand to mouth. I live from commission to commission, so if I'm not writing music, I'm not making any money.

Do you have an agent?

No. Nor do I have a publicist. So for me to have the success I have is a wonderful surprise. I thought I would have to wait until I was a senior composer before things would start to happen. But when I came back to Canada, the country was looking for a cultural voice. It turned to its artists and from there came my opportunities. The situation has changed; it's now quite bleak for artists, so I'm not sure I'd have the same success if I were starting now.

You're considered a prominent member of the Chinese community. What does that mean to you?

I think the most important thing for me is to be able to contribute to the culture of the country. I didn't set out to be a prominent Chinese Canadian; I set out to be a Canadian artist.

Do you see yourself ever leaving Canada?

I don't know. Maybe.

For what reasons?

When I went to the States I missed Canada tremendously, but I'm getting tired of the smallness of attitude: the western alienation, the Quebec separatists. . . . If I left Canada, it would not be without a heavy heart. It also disturbs me that the arts don't hold an important place in the society; it makes for a less rich environment. There's a certain spiritual malaise in the air.

Do you work at home?

Yes. That's one reason why we've been able to have a child. We have flexible hours; neither of us works 9 to 5.

What is it like to balance both being an artist and a mother?

It can be trying. The baby has to eat every three hours. I spend one hour feeding her and changing the diaper, then I have one free hour to work before it starts all over again.

Before you had the baby, how did you work?

I worked every day, almost every day. And I worked very long days. When I wrote the Toronto Symphony piece, I would start at 10:00 in the morning and finish at 2:00 in the morning. This went on for months. I did some other smaller projects in between, but basically I worked on that piece for a year. A year to produce twenty minutes of music.

What is the working process behind the creation of a piece of music?

Well, when you get a commission to write a piece of music, you have to conceive of the reasons for bringing the piece into the world. What are the expectations for the piece? What do I want to say with the piece? That in itself takes a long time. When I actually begin to write, I sit at the piano and I start to improvise and begin to pull the piece together. I get up every morning and have my coffee and start working and sometimes after hours of work there's still nothing there that's useful. But I continue. I stop when I get hungry, take a break, maybe read something to recharge my brain, but basically it's that kind of steady working that produces the music.

It must be difficult to do an orchestral piece since you can never test all the sounds in your studio.

Yes. You have to conceive, imagine everything.

Is there any way of hearing it before a first public performance?

That would cost you $20,000. You don't hear it until the first rehearsal. And I think contemporary music is much harder because it's a brand new language. It's not something already imprinted in the musician's fingers.

How would you describe your music?

I can tell you what it's not. It's not minimal and it's not twelve-tone. People have said it's expressive, that it touches them. They have also described it as impressionistic. I try to conjure up atmospheres.

There was a time in contemporary music when emotion and touching people's emotions was out of favour.

It has always been important to me. When I was a kid I was very shy. I could only express myself playing the piano. What I felt, I played. When I was in graduate school, when I injured my wrist I redirected that self-expression from the piano to composing.

Do you retain fondness for your work when it's finished, or do you push it out into the world and turn to the next?

I am very proud of my music. There are pieces of mine that are so personal that they move me when I hear them. Sometimes it's difficult for me to listen to those pieces because there is so much of me in the piece. . . . But, there are also pieces I hear and think, "You could have fixed that one and there is a little something there you could have improved on." . . . I feel very fortunate being an artist. It's a profession that grows with you as you grow. It's very difficult and you have to be very strong to survive, but I can't think of a better life to lead.

Alexina Louie composed the opening music for Expo 86 in Vancouver, The Ringing Earth; the piece was also played by the Montreal Symphony Orchestra under Charles Dutoit at the United Nations General Assembly during United Nations Day in 1989 and was broadcast around the world. Other compositions include Three Fanfares from the Ringing Earth, which opened the new National Gallery in Ottawa, and Scenes from a Jade Terrace, which opened the new Canadian Embassy in Tokyo.

BENI SUNG

When a Canadian general offered to be Beni Sung's sponsor in Canada, his family readily agreed. But the general lived in Trenton, Ontario, while the school the Sung family chose was Brentwood College, near Victoria, B.C. His parents assumed there was little distance between these places because both required the same postage. We conducted our interview with Beni Sung in his apartment/ showroom at the Colonnade, a well known apartment complex in the heart of downtown Toronto. This was the first interview he had done in some time, having taken a break from the bustle and glamour of the high profile life he once led. Now he has returned a more serious-minded and, in his own words, more "spiritual" artist, though not lacking in ebullient, infectious energy and wit.

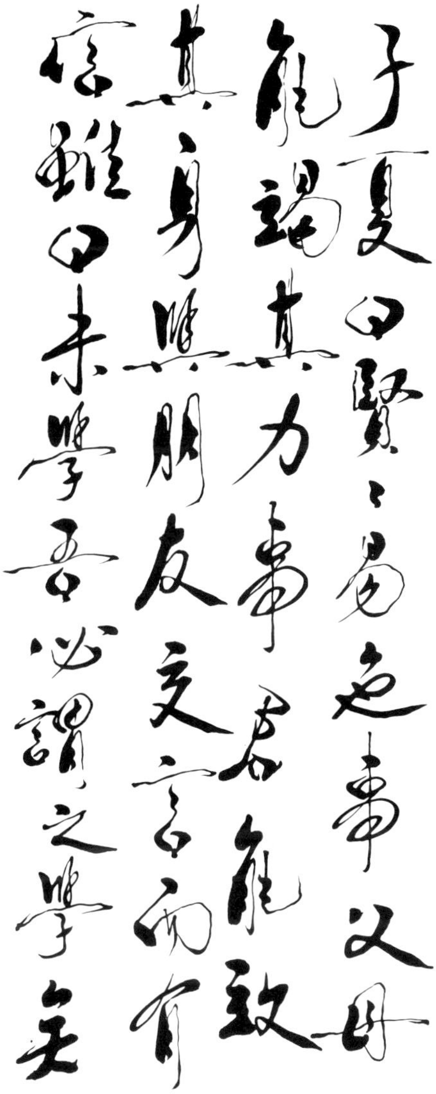

IF A MAN CAN TAKE HIS MIND FROM THE LOVE OF BEAUTY AND APPLY IT AS SINCERELY TO THE LOVE OF VIRTUE; IF HE CAN SHOW HIS GREATEST STRENGTH THROUGH HIS DEDICATION TO HIS PARENTS; IF HE CAN DEVOTE HIS LIFE TO HIS MUSE; IF HIS WORDS ALWAYS REMAIN SINCERE— IF PEOPLE SAY THIS MAN HAS NOT LEARNED, I WILL SAY HE HAS.

I was born in Hong Kong in 1952. My parents had left Shanghai in 1949. They lost everything and were forced to start over again in Hong Kong. My father started out doing some trading and then somehow got involved in the clothing business.

What do you remember from your childhood in Hong Kong?

My parents' business catered to foreigners—GI's and Canadian Armed Forces personnel. It was the time of the Korean conflict and they'd come to Hong Kong for R&R—I guess we had built up a reputation—they'd come to us to get some clothes made quickly so they could wear them during their R&R. We had a very prosperous business and we ended up having our own factory, a men's department and a ladies' department. By the time of the Vietnam War we had about three different stores. We were not rich but comfortable. I think at that time we had three cars. . . .

I've always had somebody to look after me and that's why I'm such a mess; I don't know how to organize myself. I am just such a mess. Sometimes I think, "Why did they do that to me? Why didn't I learn?" I've had friends who were just meticulous and so organized, they know where everything is. Sometimes I come across something and say, "Oh, this is where it is!" I'm just such a mess.

You blame this on your spoiled youth?

Yeah, I do, I do. I've always had money to spend. I'm not saying that I was rich or anything, but my parents always gave me money to spend even when I was a little kid. I remember I had, you know, $10 in my pocket; a chocolate bar was 50 cents or something like that. So compared to other kids, I was very well off.

What was it like, having contact with foreigners, GI's and others?

It had a great influence on my life and it's why I ended up being in Canada. I was always very involved in the shop. It was the centre. My name was given to me by an American GI. This captain said, "Does this kid have a name?" They said, "A Christian name, no." He said, "Well, can I name him for you?" "Fine." So he gave me Beni—Benjamin. . . . One time there was a group of generals from the Canadian Armed Forces, we were entertaining them and I expressed an interest in going abroad—I didn't care where. So anyway, one of the generals wrote to my dad and said, "If you're interested, I would be glad to be Beni's guardian in Canada." He was based in Trenton, Ontario, and when we got the letter, my dad said, "Now if you want to go I will let you because he's a general who is influential and has family and can look after you." But little did we know that he was in Trenton and the school I applied for was in British Columbia. In Hong Kong, the airport is half an hour away; everywhere is very close.

How old were you at that time?

Sixteen.

What were your experiences in school up to that time?

I went to Catholic school, a private boy's school. I was there for six years and then went to a high school called St. Francis Xavier which is run by Marist Brothers. Basically I was on my own. At that time my parents were very busy making money.

Do you have brothers or sisters?

An older brother. He was the black sheep of the family. He was sent to boarding school and he didn't like it so. . . . We never had a close relationship because he's nine years older. So basically I was a child by myself.

Before you came to Canada had you travelled outside of Hong Kong?

Only to Taiwan.

What did you think of Canada when you first arrived?

Oh God. It was cold; I remember it was raining, damp. No people around. I was used to a lot of people all the time, all my life. I was brought up in Hong Kong. I only know Hong Kong—dense with millions of people. I arrived in Vancouver at 6:00 P.M. and the streets are empty. And I said, "Oh my God." And then I flew to Victoria and the school was in the woods by the ocean. Brentwood College. A very good school. Very exclusive. There was a prince there and we had flying lessons and horseback riding. At that time the tuition was $4,000 a year. It's over $10,000 now. I was rubbing shoulders with the Southams and Woodwards.

It sounds like quite a culture shock.

Oh yeah, terrible. I had an ulcer when I was sixteen. I was the only Chinese there.

What gave you the most trouble?

The food, the language, everything.

How did you deal with it?

I was young. I adjusted. A lot of people liked me. I remember my mother gave me everything, all the clothes I could possibly wear. She even gave me a shoe polishing machine. It went off in my suitcase and there was a joke in the cafeteria that the Chinese had brought a bomb with him. Everybody came up to see me after prep, to my room and asked what it was. So I met a lot of kids that first night. Everybody was very nice and they all invited me for mid-term and Christmas—well, Christmas I went to my general's place—but they wanted to invite me to go on long weekends and stuff. I was very welcomed at that time and I felt very good. The problem came the year after when they accepted more kids from Hong Kong. There were problems because they didn't speak as well as I did, they didn't want to mingle, and I was caught between them and the rest.

How did that make you feel?

I was very resentful. At first it was hard to adjust. I think of Saturdays and Sundays. I used to cry. I used to sleep and I was depressed. I used to go to bed hungry because the food was awful. Oh, it was awful! I mean, you wouldn't want to eat it now. God, you know: sloppy joes and tapioca pudding you could turn upside down and it still sticks to the plate.

And it was always so cold and damp. And they made us run through the woods. It was just awful! I thought it was just terrible and I hated the tranquillity of the woods. . . . The view from our classroom was beautiful; it faced Mount Baker. The setting was quite incredible. . . . I managed. I survived. And I graduated with honours.

Why didn't you just pack up and go home?

I wanted to go home. I even had a return ticket but my parents said, "Don't you dare. We spent so much money!"

When you finished at Brentwood, why didn't you return to Hong Kong?

I came here for my education. At that point I wasn't thinking of staying in Canada, but I was going to finish my education here.

BENI SUNG AND MOTHER IN HONG KONG.

Where did you go after Brentwood?

The University of Victoria. No special reason. I didn't know what I was going to do but I had to make a choice. I wanted to go into arts but my parents objected. They liked the way children in Jewish families went into the professions—an architect or a doctor—that's what they wanted. I obliged. I took psychology, commerce and Japanese. I did well but I didn't excel.

Why did you take Japanese?

Because I loved the language and I knew it was very important for trading.

How far did you go in university?

One year. When I graduated from Brentwood, my art teacher told me that I really should pursue design or art because I had the talent. I guess I had become Canadianized from spending so much time with one of my friends' family in Vancouver. They said to me, "Beni, if that's what you're good at and it's your life to live, you should pursue it." His mother told me that there was a good school in Toronto—The Ontario College of Art. I took her advice. I wrote to them, I got an interview, and flew out from Vancouver.

I flew out for the interview and brought a portfolio. I was interviewed by three or four people. At the end of the interview I walked out feeling very confident that I'd be accepted. Two weeks later I got the letter saying I was accepted, but I wasn't sure whether or not I wanted to do it. My parents were paying for my tuition and they didn't want me to go into art, so it was a big conflict.

Did they know you'd applied?

No. I didn't tell them for a year. They thought I was still at the University of Victoria.

Didn't they notice the change of address?

They didn't know the difference. It was still a Canadian stamp. They were too busy making money. . . . But finally, after a year, I went back and told my father. I was prepared for him to disown me. I said, "You know, I've made a decision... I've decided that I want to take arts. I've been studying for a year." He said, "Well, how did you do?" I said, "I did very well." And he said, "If that's what you want to do, it's fine with me." It was the biggest shock but that was it.

How did you come to jewellery?

Well, at the art college you learn to do everything. It's like they drop you in a dark room and you search around and find what you want, then attach yourself to it. One day I was in the metal shop—I was doing some project—and I saw this lady. She was a sculptress from Australia. She was doing a commission for a museum, a neck piece of sterling silver. It was sculptural and textured and I was intrigued by the way she was working. So I started to imitate her work and got very turned on working with metal. I burned a lot of stones; I had no technique whatsoever. At that time, bangle bracelets were very popular so I started to learn to make them. But I was soon frustrated because the school was not really geared to making fine jewellery. So I enrolled in George Brown College at night. I studied at George Brown for seven years solid. Everything: gemmology—jewellery arts, enamelling, you name it—anything to do with jewellery—casting, everything.

What was it about jewellery that appealed to you?

I find it very therapeutic working with the metal. At that time I was very young and I didn't have a lot of patience. Actually, I wanted to design clothes because I've always been exposed to clothes ever since I was very young, and I love to look good. But the fact is I hate sewing. I don't have the patience to sew. I analyzed it and I think it's that I like things a little bit more permanent and jewellery is more permanent than fabric; fabric disintegrates. I had taken courses at Ryerson in window display, but I hated the fact that you work so hard and then it just gets dismantled. I feel really good right now because I have at least a thousand pieces of jewellery out there I call my babies that will be forever. Pieces of jewellery are very permanent; they last forever. . . . But it's curious because I'm not the kind of person who likes to stay in one place or have a permanent residence. I'm a Gemini and I love changes.

When I graduated from OCA I knew exactly what I wanted; if I hadn't got it I would have left Canada . . . I wanted to work at Secretts. At that time it was a very exclusive place. It was the only place that nurtured young designers and sold the kind of jewellery I wanted to design; much more artistic, not commercial. I admired the level of work and the calibre of people who worked there. It was a milieu that I wanted to be involved in. It was dealing with society, it was dealing with wealth and uniqueness and all that. But they didn't really need me; they just hired me as a joe-boy for the summer. I worked really hard and they kept me on after the summer. I worked there for four years.

I enjoyed it. We did window displays. At first I was basically the joe-boy running around, but I worked my way up and became a hotshot designer with lots of clients. People recognize talent.

At that time Secretts had seven designers and clients who spent lots of money. Society people, people who appreciate gem stones, people who appreciate craftsmanship and uniqueness. Their clients used to enjoy spending money and the designers did incredible work for them. You know, I thought if I didn't go to Secretts I would go to Paris. I've always liked French culture. I love the French language. Paris, my God, that's the epitome of design and beauty. My aspiration was to be the best.

Has your work become more or less complicated?

More.

Why?

Now I'm working with people in the Orient, and technically, the sky's the limit. Here in Canada labour costs are high and the expertise is limited for what I want to do.

What is jewellery about?

It's a very mystical thing. It's power, it's a statement of wealth, of social status, it's a reflection of the person's personality—their psyche, really. When someone comes to me for a piece of jewellery I have to get inside them and find out what they're about. That's why I'm so successful, I really give them what they want.... It's not just a question of buying a diamond brooch with lots of diamonds on it. This piece I did for a lady from New York, it took me forever to come up with the design because she wanted it to be dramatic and flexible. She wanted to wear it as a pin or a clasp—you name it. The only thing it doesn't do is fly. But I find that sort of commission exciting, a real challenge.

How did you start your own business?

Well, I'd been working at Secretts for four years and the boss said, "How come you're still here?" because he knew I was from a family that could afford to help me with my own business. At that time I think I was already a Canadian citizen, so I went back to Hong Kong and spoke to my parents. They gave me about $30,000 to get started. I came back and bought stuff. I started out with antiques and things like that. I didn't have a store; I worked out of my apartment.

Did your clients follow you from Secretts?

Oh, yes. They were very supportive. They followed me and then there was also word of mouth. I was doing very well. I expanded a couple of times until about five years ago when I was approached by Tom Creed. I agreed to open a store in Creeds. I took over the Cartier boutique. It wasn't good for me because I ended up being a shopkeeper. I didn't like that. And I was under a lot of pressure, doing a lot of PR and being pretty high profile. I was in the newspaper all the time and went to all the functions. I didn't enjoy it in the last few years because there was too much financial pressure. I had won a few awards but had little time for creation.

How do you compare Canadian high society to high society in Europe or Hong Kong?

Canadian society is mostly new money. A lot of them have worked hard in the last twenty, thirty years. Most of Canadian society is very conservative. They don't want people to know that they're wealthy. So you know they're wealthy, but not how much.

Do they ever ask you to design something so that it looks like it isn't worth very much money?

Yes. I have people who want to wear a stone but they don't want it to show, they want it understated. It's difficult because—well, it's not difficult to make it flashy—but it's very difficult to make something fabulous look insignificant. . . . The favourite saying is, "I want to wear it night and day, and day and night." You don't wear your clothes night and day, but because they're spending $10,000 on a ring, they want to get mileage out of it. But then they'll go out and spend $4,000 on a gown that they'll wear once; they wouldn't be caught dead in it another time. I find that most of them lack self-confidence. It's not like in Europe or in Asia where people have such *savoir-faire*, such confidence.

It's understandable when you speak of Europe, but we usually think of money in Asia as being pretty new. Where does their self-confidence and savoir-faire come from?

I don't know—maybe their instincts. They have a certain instinct for knowing what is suitable for them and what is not. And they're very aware, they follow the trends very closely, and they're very quick to accept new ideas. They know proportion, they know scale, they have an instinct, just like I had an instinct when I was young: what looks good on me and what I like and what I don't like. I could walk into a shoe store and know exactly which shoe I would want to buy. I think it's just the way you're brought up, I guess. Exposure. I don't get confused. When I walk into a store, a store like Barney's or something, I could pick out what would look good on me and I walk out. I don't spend time trying on different things.

What jewellery stores won't you go into?

Well, I can't say that because my attitude towards jewellery has changed. I used to be a snob and say well, this is terrible workmanship and this is terrible design. Most of the pieces I see nowadays are poorly made, but on the other hand, I have come down a few notches because it's a matter of dollars and cents. By working in the Orient I realize I can make a lot of money. It's kind of sad because I think to myself, I don't ever need to design jewellery to make a lot of money. I could go and pick out things that I could turn around and sell to the appropriate market and make hundreds of thousands of dollars without doing hardly anything.

How much of your time is spent designing and how much selling?

I design and sell all at the same time.

Does it give you as much pleasure to sell as to design?

Oh, I can sell anything! Anything, anything. I can turn stone into gold. As long as I truly believe in what I'm doing. . . . Actually, some of my pieces are really art pieces. That's why I find it limiting working in Canada because I know that if my pieces were exposed to the right people, I could charge much more money. A lot of my clients don't know what they've got; they are artistic pieces, one-of-a-kind pieces. They are what you call miniature sculptures, like Fabergé and Cartier. But the thing is, I didn't get as elaborate as I would have liked because Canadian society does not want elaborate pieces. They want pieces they can enjoy and wear all the time.

Are there some fabulous jewellery collections in Canada?

Oh yes.

Artistically?

I would say more on the stone side, great stones. Canadians prefer stones.

Why?

Its intrinsic value. But you see, the thing is, you really need a very sophisticated person to have a collection of really rare stones. There are ladies in the States, heiresses, who have different sets of pearls—black pearls, white pearls, evening pearls, and fantastic collections of gemstones.

Do Canadians like jewellery as much as anybody else?

Jewellery is the last thing they would buy. The first thing they buy is a house. When they get married they buy a house, then a car, then all the gadgets, and then they buy some art when they get a little money—art and antiques. Then they buy a cottage, they buy a boat, and the last thing they do is they buy jewellery.

What would the order be in Hong Kong or Europe?

Oh, jewellery; everybody loves jewellery. Young girls want to buy jewellery. It's a different mentality; gold and jewellery always maintained an intrinsic value, so in times of war they could always leave with their jewellery if nothing else. Canadian society has been so stable—no one ever had to flee. So Canadians find diamonds very flashy, they don't want to wear them. . . . I think people like emeralds, but then they say that emeralds are too fragile, and there's always a reason, you know . . . there's always a reason. . . . And sometimes, you can get much better prices here in Canada than in other places because there isn't as much demand. People here are still wearing silver and costume jewellery. There's nothing wrong with that it's just that it's a different ball game. . . . Some people are happy with reproductions but others want Louis XIV or nothing.

Is it changing?

Changing in the sense that people are much more educated, yes. People are much more aware, but it's still not a priority—they have to send their kids to school first.

What would a major collection of jewellery in Canada be worth?

A couple of million, but that's nothing. I was in Monte Carlo and I was looking at a ring that was $1.5 million, just one ring. I was there to see a collection and they had pieces that were in the millions, $950,000 for a strand of pearls, $2 million for a necklace. But they sell to Arabs, they sell to real wealth. I'm not saying that people here don't have money—a lot of people here have a lot of money—but it is a different investment and a different kind of attitude about wealth.

Why wouldn't somebody with $50 or $60 million not have a jewellery collection worth $3 or $5 million dollars as part of an investment portfolio?

Why? Because unless they are international people who travel a lot, who go to parties in Monte Carlo or Gstaad, they don't need it. In Monte Carlo, people wear stones that are ten, twelve carats. Here, they don't want ten, twelve carats. They find it gauche, they find it nouveau; it's a different mentality.

But what about for investment purposes?

To be a really good investment it has to be something you can sell and there's not a ready market for jewellery unless it's really expensive, of an international calibre, which you could take to Geneva to auction it off.

How has living in Canada influenced your thinking?

When I first came to Canada I was with some very wealthy people, but they were very down to earth. The thing that impressed me so much was that nobody wasted food. I was so surprised. They took leftovers and made soup. I thought, oh my God, it's wonderful. That's what I loved about it. . . . I could have gone back to Hong Kong a long time ago; my parents wanted me to move back. But I didn't like the phoney society, I didn't like the labels—even though I was brought up with labels. I had come down a few notches. To me it doesn't mean anything anymore. I think I have become a little bit more spiritual. . . . I used to want to be very well known and I wanted to be important and accomplish a lot for Canadian society, be a member of this club and that club. It's not important to me anymore.

I guess I realized life is very fragile. I'm not chasing the rainbow. I used to have so many interviews and I was very high profile and it interfered with my personal life. People had preconceived ideas of who I was before they even met me and I resented that. It was all very good for business and that's important, but I really resent how it distorts your personal life.

What happened? What caused this change in attitude?

My life came to a standstill last year. I closed my shop, my health went to the pits, I went into a big depression, and I was in a lot of debt. I thought I'd failed. And I looked around at all these things that surround me and I felt like, oh God, so what if I have two hundred ties. Do you know what I mean? It's only things.

How did you find your way out of it?

With a lot of help and support from my friends. . . . I had completely lost confidence. I didn't know what I was doing, I didn't know how good I was or how bad I was. I was just lost. I've had so many relationships that just went down the drain because I killed it. Because I was more interested in my career. I want to share, but on my terms. . . . I'll tell you one thing: I think it's a challenge. When I want something I go after it until I get it and once I get it I don't want it anymore. I want it because it's a challenge.

Like a little kid.

Yeah. I was involved with a person I never thought I'd be involved with, but I worked at it and I got it. I couldn't believe it. And then I just dropped it. It's sad, really it's sad. I went out to dinner with a friend of mine, who's also a Gemini, and he said, "You know the problem with us is that we want relationships just on our own terms. You want someone to be home when you want them to be home. You can't have that. You've got to compromise."

It's much more complicated than a career.

Not only that. I find myself to be in constant conflict because I'm half-Chinese and I'm half-Canadian. I spent my first sixteen years in Hong Kong; I was brought up with the Chinese traditions and philosophy of life. When I first came here I became very western and now I'm getting very eastern. I'm reversing my whole philosophy. I realize how wonderful our Chinese culture is, how sophisticated, how subtle and refined. Canadian is really a non-entity.

I'm sorry, but there is no identity. If you were asked, "What is typical Canadian food?" what would you say? Pea soup? . . . But on the other hand, I find myself to be very western in my attitude and outlook in life. I'm much more down to earth, which I think is a Canadian attitude. I'm very relaxed. My values in life are such that I want to be happy, I want to be healthy, and I want to do the things that I want to do.

Do you see yourself ever leaving Canada?

Not permanently. I have been given a lot by Canadians and from Canada and I want to be known as a Canadian, but I am often working outside the country.

Would you have done a lot better if you had gone to the United States?

I think I've overspent my time here in Canada to be honest with you. If I had spent the last ten years in New York I know I would have had great success and been very well known internationally. I've been told over and over again, "Beni, what are you doing in Canada? You're too good, really." I don't know what they mean by "too good." I've been comfortable here. I'm spoiled in the sense that I've had a good lifestyle. I've been a big fish in a small pond.

But you said that doesn't seem to be so important anymore.

Now it doesn't. At first it was very important. I wanted to go to New York. I wanted to be there, but New York is very tough because our business is not just the talent; you've got to have backing, you've got to have financing—a million dollars worth of jewels is nothing.

What's in the future for you?

I still want to be international. I would like to have my base here, but I want to be international, by working in the Orient a few months of the year and developing my own line, selling them. Then coming back here to look after my clients here.

BENI SUNG WITH HIS PARENTS IN HONG KONG THE NIGHT BEFORE LEAVING FOR CANADA.

How many active clients do you have here?

I don't know exactly. Some people might have a lot of jewellery done at one point, then they get tired of it and maybe they go through a divorce, or sickness. So they quiet down for a while, then make some more money and get interested again. But my circulation of clientele is a thousand.

How many do you have that spend big dollars each year?

It depends on the economy and it's always only a small percentage that might spend $60,000 or $80,000. I had one experience with a man who wanted to buy something special for his wife for their anniversary. I had this bracelet that was $85,000—this was five years ago. I put it on a tray and brought it in to show him. He said, "I'll take it!" I said, "Don't you want to know how much it is?" "No, I'll take it ... I just love it! I just love it!"

You know, it's wonderful because yesterday I had a client that I've known for ten years and she still buys pieces from me, small pieces, all the time. What is so rewarding is to have people who appreciate your work—this is my gratification, not because they spend the money, but to have someone who appreciates my work—I think that's very important for an artist or for anybody. I would hate to work for somebody who took me for granted. That's what I don't like. I really appreciate the people who work for me. I treat them as jewels, I treat them as very rare jewels because it's so hard to find good people. . . .

Beni Sung was the first Chinese student accepted by Brentwood College on Vancouver Island. He was also the first Chinese student to be a school prefect and the first recipient of the Senior Citizenship Award. In 1984 Beni Sung won the De Beers International Diamond Award representing Canada.

Der Hoi-Yin

Der Hoi-Yin was born in Hong Kong shortly after her parent's escape from mainland China. Her father left China reluctantly; his sadness was such that he named his new daughter Hoi-Yin—the swallow that returns to the nest. When the family arrived in Canada her mother gave her the name Amy, hoping it would help her fit into an English speaking environment. Interviewing a professional journalist—Der Hoi-Yin is national business correspondent for The Journal *on CBC–TV—can be an intimidating prospect. We were surprised to find her as nervous about the interview as we were. Fortunately, this shared apprehension had a calming effect and set us off on a conversation of surprising intimacy and candour. We interviewed her at her home in Mississauga, Ontario, in the company of her husband Patrick and their three young sons.*

子游問孝子曰今之孝者
是謂能養至於犬馬皆能
有養不敬何以別乎

WHAT IS THE DIFFERENCE BETWEEN THE SUPPORT PROVIDED BY A DOG OR A HORSE AND THAT PROVIDED BY A CHILD TO A PARENT? WITHOUT REVERENCE THERE IS NO DIFFERENCE.

I was born in Hong Kong in February of 1954 and immigrated to Canada with my parents in December of 1956. My father named me Hoi-Yin, which means swallow that flies over the seas. The swallow always flies back to the nest, back to China, which, as far as my father is concerned, is still his homeland. Even today, if my mother would agree, he would spend half his year in China.

Is he a Canadian Citizen?

We're all Canadian now. The irony is that my children are the first generation born in Canada, even though my great-grandfather on my mother's side came to Canada in 1890. He came in his late teens, worked in a logging camp near Rossland, B.C., saved some money and went back to China to marry. He returned to Canada in 1899 and again settled near Rossland. He worked hard and this time saved enough money to open a sawmill. Subsequently, when Prince Rupert was named the western terminus for the Grand Trunk Railroad, he moved there, bought property and opened a grocery store.

The family remained in China?

Yes. But by 1911, my great-grandfather had saved enough money to send for his wife and son. I remember her feet were so tiny; they'd been bound as a child, and she used to walk about with a funny shuffle. She used to chase me around the house, beating her cane on the floor. It was a game she and I played. I was four years old when she died. I remember that night. Everyone came to my grandfather's home to pay their last respects, to say goodbye.

When your great-grandparents came to Canada, did they pay the head tax?

No, because my great-grandfather was classified an entrepreneur. But because of the Chinese Immigration Act, my grandfather, like so many young Chinese men, returned to China to find a wife. He married but returned to Canada alone because Chinese wives were not allowed into the country during this period, even if they were the wives of naturalized Canadians. My mother, uncle and aunt were all born in China, and they only saw my grandfather once every few years when he returned to visit. In an attempt to get my grandmother to Canada, my grandfather bought a birth certificate from a Canadian-born Chinese woman. My grandmother travelled to Hong Kong; all arrangements had been made for her to come to Canada; but she changed her mind at the last moment. She decided she could not leave three children in China with relatives for an indefinite period. That's the way my grandmother was. She always sacrificed herself for everyone else in the family. So my grandmother and the children stayed in China, separated from my grandfather, until after the Second World War.

How did your parents meet?

My father met my mother at Huang Pao/Chiang Kai-Shek School. The school was affiliated with the Huang Pao military academy, which had been relocated to Nanjing. My parents corresponded after my mother left China for Canada. She wanted to return to marry him, but my grandfather forbade it. My mother, being a very strong-headed woman, returned to China against my grandfather's wishes. It was a very difficult situation. My father's family had gone through a lot of pain and suffering in China when the Communists came because they were wealthy landowners. My paternal grandfather owned mines, highways and businesses. He died just before the Communist takeover, which everyone agrees was his good fortune, because of the atrocities committed against the family.

My paternal grandmother, my father's eldest brother, two uncles and all their wives were tortured and killed. And yet, my father said, "This is my country. I want to stay because I believe in China." My father had just completed a degree in international trade and economics from Zhong Shan University. He was part of an elite group of young people being educated under a Kuomintang program to help China modernize. After the Communist takeover, he was still determined to work for the country. He was young, idealistic, loyal and very committed to seeing China develop and have a bright future, a place on the world stage. In spite of what happened to his family, China was still his country. He had been assigned to the civil service of Beijing.

How long had your mother been in Canada before she went back to marry?

Three years. This was the time of the Communist-instigated land reform movement. My father was forcibly taken back to his home village, imprisoned, humiliated and tortured. That frightened my mother a lot, but everything calmed down and he was released. My mother, who was carrying me at the time, said "Who knows if he will be arrested again. I can't live with this uncertainty, and I certainly don't want to bring a child into such a world." So my mother and father left China on a visitor's visa saying my grandfather had left money in Hong Kong and that they had to go in person to collect it. They went to Hong Kong and never returned. That was 1953. My grandfather had friends in Hong Kong. But it was very difficult for them.

What did your father do during this period?

He did some part-time office work for the Shell Oil Company; a great-uncle was a senior executive there. But basically, my father was recuperating from tuberculosis, which was very common in China at that time. When his health improved, we came to Canada. We went to Prince Rupert where my maternal grandfather was.

He was still active?

He was very active. I remember him as a strong-willed and proud man, but very understanding, too. As a granddaughter, I didn't carry his name, but we had a close relationship because I was his eldest grandchild. Whenever he came to visit, I would bring him a scotch, then play the piano for him. He loved to listen. He taught me how to drive, he bought me my first camera. He loved the news, the CBC News. Even as a child, I can remember him always tuned in to the CBC, or reading the *Vancouver Sun*. He was one of the few people in Prince Rupert who subscribed to a Vancouver paper. He loved talking about world affairs. He spoke and wrote English well, but he also spoke and wrote Chinese, a real feat considering his age when he came to Canada. His father had sent him to Vancouver, to study Chinese.

My grandfather was a real entrepreneur. In Prince Rupert, he developed what would be considered today a prototype of the supermarket, complete with a fresh meat department, fresh produce and canned foods. He also had purchased investment properties, rental properties. And he owned a restaurant, which he leased out, and which he gave to my mother and father to run. Anyway, my parents settled in Prince Rupert. My father, who did not know anything about the restaurant business, made it a success. I think it was remarkable, considering he did not know how to cook and was often at the mercy of the people who worked for him.

He hired Chinese?

In the kitchen, yes; but not the waitresses. He had over twenty people working.

What are your earliest memories of that period in your life?

I remember my father and mother working very hard. I especially remember how alone my father felt at times. He did not even speak the dialect my maternal grandparents spoke. My father came from Ching Yuen in the northern part of Canton province and he spoke Cantonese and Mandarin. My mother's family came from Taishan, and spoke Taishanese. So my father, when he first came to Canada, had a difficult time communicating with my grandparents. He picked it up over the years, but it wasn't easy. As well, he had to raise a family. Very quickly the children came and soon we had six in the family; I have three younger sisters and two younger brothers.

What was it like growing up in Prince Rupert?

It was a wonderful town, not too small, not too big, a friendly place with lots of friendly people. It's on the west coast, in northern British Columbia, just south of the Alaskan Panhandle. When I think of Prince Rupert, I always remember the bright pinkish-red sunsets over the ocean, one of the most beautiful sunsets in the world.

Were there many Chinese in Prince Rupert?

My grandfather's family was the first Chinese family to settle there. Other Chinese arrived later. There was a sense of community, tight-knit but never large. My father helped build the first Chinese cemetery. We had an altar where we would pray to our ancestors, and burn incense and money for them to spend in heaven. My father also helped establish the first Chinese school. We all went to Chinese school in the evenings, from 4:00 to 6:00.

What did you think of that?

Half the time, I felt it wasn't quite fair when my classmates in English school could go out and play while I would have to go to Chinese school. In retrospect, it was good for us, but that is in retrospect.

When did you come to realize that you were Chinese, or different?

I always knew I was different, not really different, but that I was Chinese. I did not feel any animosity from the other children, my classmates. They did not discriminate, probably because there were so few of us. And my grandfather always taught us not to make waves, not to make trouble, because when he was in Vancouver studying Chinese, he witnessed the riots against the Japanese and that made a great impression on him. He felt that since we were a visible minority, we should all try to go about our lives as quietly as possible so as not to offend the majority. Many Chinese Canadians of his generation felt the same way. I felt different in that I had to go to Chinese school; but I also felt different in that unlike most of my classmates, I had to take piano lessons, which had nothing to do with being Chinese but meant I had to stay home and practise when they were outside playing. My mother loved music; she played the piano and she wanted all of us to learn. Even to this day, you see a lot of Chinese children who play and excel at the piano. Right now, I'm teaching my eldest son.

Was the family close?

It was very tight-knit. Lots of family and extended family around, a warm and wonderful childhood. We would go through Christmas and the New Year, but we would also have Chinese New Year, Chinese celebrations, the moon festival, spring cleaning of the cemetery and worshipping of our ancestors. My maternal great-grandfather's body was sent back to China, but my great-grandmother was buried here, so we'd go and visit her grave twice a year as part of the Chinese ritual.

Did you ever have to explain or want to explain the differences to your Caucasian friends?

Not really. We were raised in a community where there were very few Chinese people, so although we maintained a lot our Chinese heritage, we also had to assimilate. We did not have a Chinese enclave per se—there were not enough Chinese people to create one. There was an excellent relationship between the Caucasian and Chinese communities. One of my grandfather's brothers became a city alderman and the civic centre is named after him.

Did you do well in school?

Yes. I think that was part of my Chinese upbringing, that you had to do well and excel because you were new in this country.

Do you think you had to prove yourself?

That's very much part of the Chinese drive, the immigrant drive, to prove ourselves because we're in a new country. But if you look at Hong Kong, you can see the extremely competitive nature of the Chinese there, for a whole different set of reasons. I think most of it depends on your parents; if your parents are driven, the children are driven, too. But it's certainly not cast in stone. And the drive appears to be lost after a few generations, sometimes even after one generation.

But where does it come from?

I can only speak from my own experience. My father came to this country very well educated, but he had to start afresh. He believes his children also have to prove themselves, work hard, do well. My mother has the same drive; in many ways, she's even more driven than my father, but as I said, I think it's in part that immigrant drive.

Being driven is not necessarily about a particular goal; it's a general force through your life. When did it become focused on something specific, a career?

Not until after high school; up to then, my parents basically laid down a path for me to follow. To do well in school, to be the top of my class, and to do well in my piano. When I was fourteen years old, they sent me off to a private girls' school on Vancouver Island, again to get the best education they could afford. My father had been educated at the best schools in China; he wanted his children to have the same opportunity.

Was that a great sacrifice for him?

Of course it was. First I went away to Queen Margaret's, then two of my sisters followed, and my brother was sent off to Shawnigan Lake Boys' School. Then there were all the extra-curricular activities. For example, my brother coxed the

Shawnigan Lake rowing team at the Henley Cup in England. And I took music. In those days, room and board alone cost more than $5,000 per child. That was a lot of money. But they wanted what they thought would be the best for us.

What was private school like?

I was the first Chinese girl to be accepted into the school. The school was very British, high Anglican. Most of the mistresses were from England. We had morning prayers, prep every evening, and academics were stressed. There were no cooking or sewing classes or useful things like that. But we had an active sports program—grass hockey, tennis, swimming. The school was also well-known among the horsey set for its indoor and outdoor rings and stables.

Did you ride?

Yes, but I was never any good at it. The school was also known for its music program, which was what my mother was interested in. I studied voice and pipe organ at school. As well, my mother arranged for me to study piano in Victoria with Robin Wood, head of the Victoria Conservatory of Music. It was part of her plan to have the children well-rounded both academically and in the arts.

Was this to prepare you for marriage or prepare you for a profession?

In my parents' view, it was to help us adjust in Canada, which meant we had to excel not only at our school work. My mother started me off on the piano when I was four and a half years old. My brothers and sisters were all involved in music too; my youngest brother and sister studied with Lee Kum Sing at the Vancouver Academy of Music.

When did you start to talk about what you wanted to do after school?

I'm not sure. My goal was simply to do the best I could. We had mark reading every month, where your grades were read out, and it was important to me to do well. I worked so hard that when I graduated, I didn't even have a date for the spring ball. My headmistress, Miss Glide, phoned the headmaster of Brentwood College, Mr. MacKenzie, and asked him to recommend an escort. He apparently told her she'd waited so long to call that I'd have to do with the bottom of the barrel. My escort turned out to be Beni Sung, who's now a jewellery designer in Toronto.

Were you top in your class?

I was when I graduated. I won the scholarship trophy; and through the time I was there, I would never come below second. I was one of the headmistress' favourites because I worked hard and did well.

Did this create any resentment?

Not really. The girls at my school were quite open-minded. In my first year, I shared a room with three other girls, from Vancouver, São Paulo, Brazil, and Seattle, Washington. We were all so far from home that we found security in each other and became good friends.

Did you ever feel any racism?

I suppose there was what one might interpret as reverse racism, when the girls would say, "Look, if there's ever a war, we'll shelter you." They said that because there was a constant reminder—the school had built a bomb shelter during the Second World War for fear that the Japanese would bomb the west coast, and we were using it as the pool change room. We also knew about the internment camps Japanese Canadians had been sent to. So in effect, I think the girls were saying, "If there's a war with China, don't worry, you're one of us." That's a kind of reverse racism, but there were never any blatant concerns that I was Chinese because I was also very much Canadian.

Where did you go after you graduated?

I went to Queen's University in Kingston. My headmistress applied for me. A lot of boarding school grads ended up at Queen's. She decided; I didn't even know where Queen's was. I'm not sure why she chose Queen's. I've never asked her. I should go back and ask her one day! She's retired now. But I truly do not know. She applied for me and I never thought to ask. Again, she was sort of a mother figure to me. She taught history and I excelled at history.

At Queen Margaret's School, Vancouver Island.

Was that your favourite subject?

It was. She also applied for scholarships for me at Queen's and I received two. In total, they paid for my tuition.

How much of a role did your parents play in all of this?

My parents accepted everything my headmistress recommended, and when she decided to enrol me at Queen's University, my parents thought it was a wonderful idea, so off I went. At school, my headmistress basically orchestrated my life. While she did a good job, one of the things I dislike about boarding schools is that you totally entrust the upbringing of your children to someone else. I had a very dear girlfriend at school whom my headmistress did not approve of and she wrote to my parents because I would go out on weekends with my girlfriend and her parents. My girlfriend's father is a prominent lawyer in Victoria who, at that time, had just won the largest civil settlement in the British Commonwealth. But my headmistress didn't approve of my girlfriend; she thought she was a bad influence on me. So she wrote my parents and said she did not think I should spend weekends with her in Victoria. My parents agreed. But my girlfriend and I remained close throughout the years, and even though she later moved to London, England, she flew back to Vancouver for my wedding, to my parents' dismay. At any rate, my headmistress decided what was good for me, what was bad for me, and as I said, Queen's was totally her decision.

What were those years like for you? Were you scared?

It was a big adventure. While I had been away from home since I was fourteen, there was a sense of independence in going away to university.

Queen's was and still is a very small campus. At that time, there were about 8,000 students. I got to know many students quite well; most of us came from a long way away. We arrived there fresh and ready to meet the challenge, the freedom, the experience, and Queen's gave us all that. I graduated in two years, majoring in history.

What do you remember the most about those years in university?

Queen's offered an excellent education, and again, I worked very, very hard. I suppose I remember that more than I remember having a good time, although I do remember frosh week, I do remember my first and only football game, the Golden Gaels against the Varsity Blues.

When did you start to think about what you wanted to do with the rest of your life?

It was a gradual process that began the summer I graduated from boarding school, when I worked as a reporter for the Prince Rupert *Daily News*. My mother knew the owner, David Radler, who had just founded Sterling Newspapers with Conrad Black. David had gone to Queen's University; I was about to go to Queen's. And he had held one of the scholarships I was holding. Sometimes, when you think back about how things fall in place . . . whatever the reasons, David gave me my first job right out of boarding school. Without any experience, I suddenly found myself a reporter, a photographer, I even had to develop my own photographs. I did everything and I enjoyed it, I loved it.

That's when you decided to make a career in journalism?

It was a gradual evolution. While I did some freelancing for the student newspaper and for the Kingston *Whig-Standard* during university, I wasn't sure if I wanted to become a full-time journalist. But the more I thought about it, the more I thought, well, it's certainly a fascinating area. Those were the Watergate years, and like so many university students, I became swept up by the tide of Watergate—the idealism, the adventure, that you could do something to change the world, bring down presidents. I thought journalism would be an excellent way to learn more about the world, about people. So after I graduated, I applied for a reporting job with the Victoria *Times*.

In hindsight, it was a pretty daring, gutsy thing to do. I only had a smattering of experience, yet there I was, applying to a leading newspaper in a provincial capital. I wrote a long letter to the managing editor, Gordon Bell. I don't have a copy of that letter any more, but I do remember including some brazen statements like "you have nothing to lose if you hire me." I told him I was aggressive, intelligent, that I would break stories, that working hard was part of my nature, that if hired, I would do him proud, that I could do just about everything, even review music; that I played the piano and pipe organ, that I sang Italian operas and German lieder. Gordon Bell said he didn't need a music critic. But he did hire me as a court reporter. He later told me it was the highly unusual and unconventional tone of my letter that clinched the job for me. I worked there for eleven months and then I moved over to the *Vancouver Sun*. I stayed with them for ten years, until I joined the CBC.

What did you write about over those years?

The Victoria *Times* hired me to do court reporting. I spent every day in provincial court covering all sorts of petty crimes and a bit of Supreme Court reporting. But basically it was the crime beat. When I went to the Sun, I worked graveyard, again doing a lot of the crime reporting and the kinds of things all young reporters did in those days to cut their teeth. In the evenings, one of my tasks was to go to the police station to check the list of arrests, to look for prominent names, interesting cases. I was sent out on a lot of shoot outs and rough and tough assignments, since I had a reputation for being fearless and they knew I would always deliver. One of my most memorable stories during this period was the so-called case of the Five Dragons, five Hong Kong police officers who had fled to Canada after it was learned they had been on the take in Hong Kong. The Hong Kong government was trying to have them extradited. My assignment was to track them down and interview them. I managed to find two of them, interviewed none of them, and almost got my photographer assaulted in the process. But I did deliver a story on the hunt. After about a year and a half of this, I wanted to cover other things, too, stories with more substance. So I got onto the afternoon shift, then regular shift, doing general assignment reporting, plus the occasional crime story. I enjoyed it well enough, but I wanted to specialize. I moved over to the business pages.

Why?

There was an opening in the business pages; I applied and got the job. That was in 1978. Since then, I've been covering business and economics exclusively. I started by writing personality profiles on various business leaders in the community, people like Jimmy Pattison, Samuel Belzberg, Edgar Kaiser. It was a great introduction to business. There were ten of us in the business pages and we all had beats to cover. I was about to be given financial institutions, but the reporter who had the investment beat didn't particularly enjoy it. So I asked if I could have it. And I got it.

Why did you want investments?

The main reason was because investments transcends all the beats. As long as what I wanted to write about involved a publicly listed company, I could write about it, from an investment perspective. I also wanted the beat because the investment reporter got to write a weekly "investment letter," a kind of quasi-column which I thought, over time, I could use as a launching pad to become a full-fledged financial columnist. With this in mind, I found people in the business and investment community to teach me how to analyze financial statements, which is somewhat different from sector to sector, how to look at things like price-earnings ratios, market capitalization, basically how to cut through a lot of financial mumbo jumbo and get at what's important. With economic forecasting an integral part of the investment beat, I knew I needed a lot more than what I'd learned at Queen's, so I audited several more courses at UBC. I also got to know all the leading economists in Canada; every week I'd talk to a couple of them about economic trends, the dollar, interest rates, the deficit, all of which were issues then, and are issues now. I eventually got what I wanted. I became a full-fledged columnist writing eighteen column inches four days a week, with one of the columns running simultaneously in the *Financial Times* of Canada and syndicated across the country on the Southam business wire.

What is it about business that interests you?

The economy interests me. Trends interest me. Business people and their constant drive, their quest for a place in the structure of this country interest me. There are so many business people who came to this country with virtually no money, without even an adequate command of the English language, yet they made something of themselves. What makes them tick? Why have they succeeded? That's fascinating.

In a way, we've been asking you that same question. When you're asking people like Jimmy Pattison, Edgar Kaiser, Samuel Belzberg and others, what makes them tick, are you surreptitiously asking yourself that question?

When you're doing your work, when you're engrossed in your work, I don't think you ask yourself such questions. Perhaps subconsciously you do, but you're asking it of people you interview. But perhaps you're right. Perhaps you do, subconsciously.

What about your goals? Now, as you're becoming a mature woman are you asking yourself what you want out of life or was there a point when you did?

I have what I want, and I know what I have will continue to grow. I have a strong relationship with my husband, I have three dear boys and a good family life, and I have a career, a job where I'm paid to learn about people, issues, life.

And how did you get to the CBC, The National *and* The Journal? *How did you go from print to television?*

There was a six-week strike at the Vancouver Sun in 1984. So I moonlighted for the local CBC–TV supper hour show, covering business. The show's executive producer, Helen Slinger, was on maternity leave and head office in Toronto flew in a replacement, David Bazay. David had been a distinguished foreign correspondent in Europe and had just returned to Canada. He liked my work during those six weeks and offer me a full-time reporting job in the Vancouver show when the strike was over. At the time, I was still very involved and stimulated with my newspaper work and didn't want to leave it. So I declined. That year, I won the National Business Writing Award for top financial columnist. In the meantime, Helen Slinger's maternity leave was over, David Bazay had returned to Toronto to become executive producer of *The National* network news. He again approached me and said, "Look, I'm not offering you local news. This time, I'm offering you reporting at the network level, to come to Toronto and become our national business and economics reporter." He said his boss, John Owen, wanted to set this up as a new specialty beat, that although I would be stepping back, so to speak, in becoming a reporter again, I would, by virtue of working for *The National*, be the premier business and economics reporter in the country.

You have to know David to fully appreciate his use of words. But I wasn't sure if I wanted to move. I had a young son, my family, my husband's family were all in Vancouver, whereas we had no relatives in Toronto and knew very few people there. As well, I loved my work in Vancouver. My husband, who's always been extremely supportive and encouraging, finally said, "Look, if you don't take up this offer, perhaps this window of opportunity will not be open again. And personally speaking, I can still move for you, but in a few years' time, it will be extremely difficult for me to give up what I'm building here. So if you want to try this new endeavour, you have to do it now." I thought about what he said, and decided he was right. We moved to Toronto and I joined The National in August 1985. My husband, a chartered accountant, joined Coopers and Lybrand and is now a partner of the firm, heading up its mergers and acquisitions division.

Let's go back a bit. Did you always date Chinese men?

No. That's why my parents were never happier than when I brought home my husband-to-be. Patrick was introduced to me by his brother, and when we married, for good luck, we gave him the Chinese matchmaker's fee. Patrick was the first Chinese boy I brought home. I'll always remember that first day. My grandmother, who just died a few months ago, came out to the front hall to take a good look. She toddled out in her own unique way, poked her head around the corner and then, a big beam broke across her face when she saw Patrick. She already had her fingers crossed, hoping we would marry, that her eldest granddaughter would marry a Chinese. To her that's what counted. My parents, of course, wanted the same. But they also were charmed by Patrick's character. My parents think of him as their own son and Patrick treats my parents as his own.

How had they reacted to the Caucasian boys you brought home?

They would not open the door—literally—let alone their hearts. They were very Chinese that way. They would give me endless lectures. They would say "How could you? You must think of the children." To them, that also meant the grandchildren, and generations yet to come. It was important to them, at least when I was dating, that their grandchildren be Chinese. Mind you, my brother later married a Caucasian girl and they have a son who my parents adore. But there was considerable pressure on me to marry a Chinese, even though I wasn't a son, probably because I'm the first born and the first child to marry.

What did they think would happen if you married a Caucasian?

It's so difficult to understand what one's parents might be going through, what their logic might have been, but I think part of it is their recognition that they are an ethnic minority, a visible minority in this country. And being a visible minority, much of their security is drawn from the comfort of knowing they could associate with their own people, and have their children and grandchildren as a part of that community. While they believed the children should grow into well-adjusted citizens of this country, while they sent us away to schools where we became more Canadian than they ever wanted, they still expected that we would act and think like Chinese. I don't believe there's anything wrong with that, but I believe they also have to understand that Canada is our new home. This is where my children were born. This is where my grandchildren will be born. They are Canadian, truly Canadian.

What about you? What if one day one of the boys brings home a Caucasian girl or Black girl and says, "Mommy, this is the woman I want to marry?"

My husband and I have discussed this. First and foremost, they must be happy. Although my husband and I would be more comfortable with a Chinese daughter-in-law, our sons must be happy, and whatever colour or race, we have to accept it. We have seriously talked about it and we have seriously said to ourselves, we'll accept it, as long as whoever our sons go out with are good for them. We also have the choice not to accept. But then, we have to weigh the risk of alienation. It's judgmental and subjective, and we hope we will not be interfering parents, at least, not too much.

You said a number of times that you want your children to be truly Canadian, but they were born here. What do you mean?

I mean they are truly Canadian because they were born here. After a family history of more than a hundred years in this country, they are the first generation born here.

What do you want for your children?

I want to offer them every opportunity to adjust and assimilate, but yet to accept that they are Chinese, to know what their heritage is, because they must be secure first in where they come from. From that they can expand. We talk about bilingualism and multiculturalism in this country and there's been a lot of criticism of late as to whether these are routes we should be taking as a nation. My eldest son is quadrilingual, which I think is part of being Canadian. I've been hiring Mandarin-speaking nannies, so my children will speak Mandarin and Cantonese. I know they will never speak Shanghainese, my husband's dialect—that's asking too much—but at least they can speak Mandarin and Cantonese, the Hong Kong dialect. As well, my son goes to French school, not French immersion but total French. He's going into grade three this fall. At home he speaks Mandarin and Cantonese; out in the neighbourhood he speaks English. I've taught him to read English. He started with the Dr. Seuss books and is now onto the Hardy Boys and Nancy Drew. He also reads beautifully in French. Being the kind of Chinese parents we are, I try to find out where he stands in his class; I'm told he's in the top five in the French school.

Are there dangers to this? You're very conscious of these questions.

My husband and I are also very careful not to push our son too hard. If he did not adjust well in French school, we would have withdrawn him, put him in French immersion. We don't know if our second son will have the same ability with languages. So we'll decide what to do after we assess his progress in kindergarten. But it's too early to tell. He's only two years old.

Do you think you have to do twice as well because you're a visible minority?

You have to understand—twice as *hard*. We would be fooling ourselves if we believed we are the same as Caucasians who immigrate to this country. We are a visible minority; we are not like the Germans or Scandinavians or whatever who are going to blend into this country. But this country is also changing. There are so many racial groups now that are non-Anglo-Saxon or non-Caucasian. I believe we must all be comfortable and secure in our past, if we are to help forge a new future, to help build a new Canada. But it's not easy. My parents gave me an English name, Amy, when we came to Canada. I was called Hoi-Yin at home, but Amy in school. When I graduated from university, I decided to revert to my Chinese name. And when my eldest son was born, I felt that Canadians were tolerant and understanding enough that I could give him a Chinese name only.

But it was my mother who finally said, "Please, I beg you, don't do that. Children can be very cruel. That's why we gave you an English name, to help you through this stage. Give your son an English name now, and when the time comes, on his own, if he wants to, he can drop his English name and use his Chinese name." So at home, my three boys are called by their Chinese names; everywhere else, they use their English names. When they're of age, it'll be up to them to decide which name to use. That was my mother's wisdom. Just last year, my son came home and said, "Mamma, boys at school say I'm a China boy." So I tell him the kind of tales many Chinese parents tell their children, that the Chinese invented spaghetti, gunpowder, fireworks, that we have a proud history in China and also in Canada, that we are as much a part of this country as anyone else, and perhaps even more so than some of his classmates.

You work very, very hard at your job and your husband works very hard. The children have a nanny. How does this affect them? You have a very busy life. How do you fit it all together? You're not like your mother was.

My career is important to me, but my children are extremely important as well.

If you had to choose? Can you see a time when you might decide to spend the next five years at home—could you do that?

I would do it if I felt it were necessary, if I felt my children were suffering because of my career, but I don't believe they are suffering. In fact, I believe my children are better off without me home twenty-four hours a day. When I am with them, I happily dedicate myself to them. When I am at work, I happily dedicate myself to my work. I also spend every Christmas, spring break and summer with the children, so when they're not in school, I'm home with them, to be with them, to drive them to French camp, swimming lessons, whatever is necessary.

Do you see a difference between the way you and Patrick have your household and other non-Chinese households?

Perhaps we strive harder.

What is it you and Patrick are striving for?

We want our children to be better than us.

Is it really all focused on the children? Is there something else you want? Is there some material thing you want . . . ?

We are very content with our life; we are healthy; we have what we want; we can buy what we want; we can spend what we want, of course within reason. If we had more money, it wouldn't make much difference; in fact there probably would be a lot more pressure on us. What is important to me is that my children have a good future in this country, that they feel adjusted. I keep talking about feeling adjusted and being a visible minority, and that may be because of what my parents and grandparents have passed on to me, a legacy I carry because we are a minority. But even so, while my husband feels totally at ease both in Canada and in Hong Kong, I never feel more ill at ease than when I am in Hong Kong.

Why?

It's because I have become so Canadian. I actually feel more Canadian when I am in Hong Kong than when I'm in Canada. But then, I've never made an effort to live in Hong Kong. My sister lives there. She's married to a Hong Kong Chinese and has made a life there. So I suppose I could, if I had to.

What's going to happen to the Chinese community in Canada with 1997 approaching? Some say forty percent of the population of Vancouver will be Asian by the turn of the century.

The fabric of the country is changing, not only in Vancouver, but across the country. You will notice there are three Chinatowns in Toronto, four if you count the suburbs.

But you see how complicated this is for your average Caucasian? Suddenly we're talking about Chinese and Shanghainese and Mandarin. . . . What are we talking about here?

That's what Caucasians in Canada don't understand. There are divisions within the various communities, be it Chinese, East Indian or whatever. It's all broken into little cliques; and then you've got divisions between the ethnic groups. What we must try to do, is to help bridge the gap, so our children are not ethnocentric but multicultural, cosmopolitan. Some people argue that multiculturalism is bad for the country. Some people point to the United States and say "that's a melting pot and not like the Canadian mishmash of multicultural groups." But I don't believe the U.S. is truly a melting pot. It has its ethnic diversities, too; Spanish has even become the second language. But the Americans are very different from Canadians insofar as having a sense of national identity to help hold the country and people together. Regardless of colour or race, they celebrate being a nation as one, as American. They have their Stars and Stripes, their bands, their heroes, their holidays. They have their authors, their musicians. Throughout the last two hundred years, they've developed a real culture, a soul, a kind of glue that helps bind the people into a nation. That's what we lack. We're still searching as a nation for a national identity, and if we don't find it, it's going to speed up the fragmentation of this country.

How can Canada find its national identity?

That is part of the quest that is going on currently with the constitutional talks. And there are no easy answers. But I believe one of the fundamental problems is that we simply do not celebrate enough as a nation in a way that can link up all the ethnic groups, tie them together. How do we celebrate Dominion Day,

Canada Day? Certainly not with the kind of pride and fanfare the Americans display when they celebrate their Fourth of July. Do we celebrate Sir John A.'s or Sir Wilfrid Laurier's birthdays? What about Jacques Cartier? And it's not just to bond the new ethnic groups in the country. You know, perhaps if we had more common holidays with French Canada, more common ground to celebrate, there might not be such a deep line between French and English Canada.

It's an extremely difficult question, a very difficult one to answer. . . . I believe it's a quest that we as Canadians must make if we are to draw the country together. We have to be proud of ourselves as a nation. We're seeking our identity; no one knows at this stage what will unfold. My husband and I believe in a bilingual, multicultural Canada, and that's why we're bringing up our children the way we are. Yet what is that one string that draws us all together, or are there many strings? I don't know, but we have to find that, we have to, and we have to be so proud in this country that we can develop a culture and identity that is uniquely Canadian.

From a business perspective, what's going to happen to this country? There's a lot of concern about Canada going down the tubes because of free trade, because of the dollar, and other reasons. What's going to happen?

As I always say, no one has a crystal ball. This country has so many forces in play—socialist forces, free enterprise forces and various shades in between—all in a massive tug-of-war.

There is great potential in this country. The people, the resources, the wealth of knowledge, the ingenuity. Yet we are losing our competitive edge internationally. Our productivity is declining. And, as a country, we're living beyond our means, with the size of our federal debt, and the cost of servicing that debt. This all has to change if we are just to maintain our standard of living, let alone see it improve. If we want to maintain our social programs, if we as Canadians pride ourselves as a nation with a social conscience, then we have to put our own house in order. Some say, "Well just tax the rich, tax the middle class, tax the corporations." While I believe most Canadians have a sense of social justice and are prepared to pay more taxes than other nations, I don't believe Canadians are prepared to see a constant increase in taxes without fiscal responsibility. And we have to be careful not to tax to such an extent that the entrepreneurial flair in this country is dampened. The incentive to work, to create jobs and wealth is what will make this country grow and what will pay for all the social programs we hold so dear. What we need is the political will.

What do you want?

I only want my children to grow and prosper in our new country. They are not like my father, who yearns to spend half his year in China. They are now Canadians, albeit Chinese Canadians.

If right this instant, you were struck by lightning but somehow you had the chance to say something, leave something, a message for your children, what would it be?

Be proud that you come from a Chinese heritage, but be proud of being Canadian.

I want them to work hard in this country, excel in this country. This country is theirs now. Regardless of what others may say about them because they are a visible minority, they are a part of this country. Their children, their grandchildren, their great-grandchildren—my great-great-grandchildren—will forever be a part of Canada. While they may look Chinese, while they may speak Chinese, all of which is important, I know they will never be truly Chinese. They will be Canadian, Chinese Canadian.

But as their mother, from your heart, what would you say to them?

Enjoy yourselves. Love this country. Do well. Work hard.

What message would you give to Patrick if you had to leave a message?

For Patrick, I do not have to leave a message. My husband is so secure in himself; he believes that his generation, his classmates from Hong Kong, regardless where they decided to settle, be it in Toronto, New York, London, or wherever, they have done well, succeeded, because they are in a sense global people. To a certain extent I agree with him. We are a new generation of global travellers, global participants who can do well, succeed, excel, in whatever environment we are placed in.

But again, from your heart to him, what would you say?

Take care of my children. My children are so important to me. Take care of my eldest son, Yuen-Zong, his name means bearer of honour; and my number two son, Yuen-Kai, bearer of victory; and my number three son, Yuen-Han, bearer of wisdom. The children are the next generation; they represent our future, a new future in this country. That's important.

Der Hoi-Yin was the first Chinese Canadian to become a national network correspondent. She won a National Business writing award for Top Financial Columnist in 1985. Hoi-Yin is married to Patrick P.L. Chan, who is a partner in charge of mergers and acquisitions at Coopers & Lybrand, Toronto.

The Next Generation

Most of the people in this book have filled their narrative with stories illustrating the major events in their lives. They have told these stories many times over the years and have learned to delete insignificant details and emphasize the interesting. Fiona Huang was born in Toronto; Selwyn Au-Yeung was born in Hong Kong and immigrated to Canada in 1982 on a student's visa; Alec Chan was born in London, England, and immigrated to Canada with his parents in 1967. One of the most interesting aspects of conducting this interview was that it became clear that these three young people are still discovering who they are and what they think and feel. They are not yet shaping their stories for an audience, as they are too busy living them.

子曰後生可畏焉知來者
之不如今也四十五十而無聞
焉斯亦不足畏也已

WE SHOULD NOT HOLD PEOPLE OF FORTY OR FIFTY IN AWE IF THEY HAVE NOT BY THIS AGE DISTINGUISHED THEMSELVES; UNTIL THAT TIME WE HOLD THE YOUNG IN AWE FOR WHO IS TO SAY THEY WILL NOT EQUAL OR SURPASS THE PRESENT GENERATION?

SELWYN: My name is Selwyn. I was born in 1967 in Hong Kong. I came here in 1982 as a visa student and went to a boarding school called Appleby College, in Oakville, Ontario. In 1983 my parents and my brothers came to Canada and so I moved to Toronto with them. I went to Brébeuf College School for the next couple of years. When I graduated from Brébeuf I went to the University of Waterloo and studied accounting. I graduated in May of 1991 and am now working full time in an accounting firm called Deloitte and Touche.

FIONA: My name is Fiona. I was born in Toronto in 1971 and I went to the Bishop Strachan School in Forest Hill. I am now going to the University of California at Berkeley and am taking a semester off to study at Columbia University in New York.

ALEC: My name is Alec. I was born in London, England, in 1964 and came to Canada in 1967. I graduated from George Henry Secondary School in North York in 1983 and then went to the University of Western Ontario for three years and did a BA in statistical sciences. I worked for two years in a general insurance company called Gerling Global and then I went back to York University for a Master's degree in business. I worked for my mother's small clothing firm for one year and am currently working at *EYE Weekly*, a division of the Toronto *Star*, as operations manager.

Alec, how did your family get to England?

ALEC: My father was studying architecture in England and my mother was working as a fashion model for Christian Dior. We went back to Hong Kong for a year when I was young while my father came here to Canada to check it out. I had aunts and uncles who had already moved here and said it was a really nice country to live in.

What made your father decide that Canada was the place to come?

ALEC: I guess the environment. It was a very nice atmosphere. And at that time they were actually asking immigrants to come over. This was in 1967.

Do you speak Chinese?

ALEC: No, I understand a little.

And at home, do your parents speak Chinese or English?

ALEC: They speak Chinese between themselves but more and more they speak English.

How big are your families?

SELWYN: Two younger brothers, that's all.

ALEC: I am the eldest; I have one sister.

FIONA: Two sisters and a brother.

Have your families held on to all the Chinese customs or have they let some go.

SELWYN: It's almost the same, I can't think of any main differences except that we don't celebrate Chinese New Year as much as we used to in Hong Kong because we don't have as many relatives to visit.

What did you notice first about Canada when you arrived?

SELWYN: Lots of space. It is one of the major differences. I didn't speak English very well. I still don't. I spoke very little English when I first came so it was kind of hard to adjust, but it worked out well because the people I met were very nice to me.

Did you feel any discrimination at all?

SELWYN: Not that I noticed. In my school there weren't too many Chinese; I think there were between seven and ten and some of them were Canadian born. They were fairly friendly in my school. I didn't really feel any discrimination. Oakville is a fairly small town, and because Appleby was a boarding school we actually had a lot of people from all over the country, and from the States and from Europe.

Are most of your friends Chinese?

SELWYN: Mixed.

What about you Fiona?

FIONA: I have no Chinese friends.

Alec?

ALEC: All my friends in high school were white. It was weird. I used to be scared to go to Chinese restaurants. It was weird because where we lived there were very few Chinese people. I was one of maybe two Chinese students. Sometimes when I was young I didn't even realize I was Chinese. Then at university I joined a Chinese students' organization and started to get a lot of Chinese friends, some from Hong Kong. Half the organization was made up of Chinese Canadians and the other half was made up of Hong Kong Chinese, and we set up two committees where we'd meet and try to integrate the Canadian Chinese and the Hong Kong Chinese.

What made you want to join the Chinese student's organization?

ALEC: Just to get to know people because at Western I was new and unfamiliar.

What was your experience, Fiona?

FIONA: When I was in high school I didn't want to be Chinese. I wanted to be white because all my friends were white. When I was younger there weren't many Chinese people and I didn't want to be different. When you're a teenager you want to be like everybody else and I looked different and my grandmother didn't speak English. I just wanted to be like the Jewish girls. I'm not like that anymore. I would love to meet more Chinese people.

Did you feel isolated in high school?

FIONA: At the beginning of high school there were two of us. Then a whole lot of Chinese students arrived, but they didn't like us very much.

Why?

FIONA: Because we were Canadian. We were Chinese but we didn't speak Chinese. I understood Chinese, and we would sit in the cafeteria and I would hear them say things about me.

Did they reject you?

FIONA: Not really. They all stuck together. It wasn't like I ever had any interaction with them. The only way I knew how they felt was because I could understand Chinese and I could hear what they were saying about us. But other than that everyone was oblivious to each other.

How did that make you feel about being Chinese?

FIONA: My values were different in high school. All the things I was ashamed of are the good things.

What were you ashamed of?

FIONA: Just being smart. I hated being smart. All the Chinese people did well in math.

ALEC: It was the same in my school. I remember I was a loner. I had lots of different friends but I was basically by myself. I didn't really join a group per se.

Why were you a loner Alec?

ALEC: I think it was just me.

But when you went to university you joined a Chinese students organization?

ALEC: Yes. And I started to go out with Chinese girls. My parents never forced me to date Chinese girls; it was my conscious decision.

They never said things like it would be easier for you?

ALEC: No, it never came up. I actually asked them and they really didn't care.

Selwyn, did you ever date a Caucasian girl?

SELWYN: Casual dates, nothing serious. My parents don't know, they don't care.

They never showed a preference?

SELWYN: I don't think so because they always got along with my white friends from high school. I never get any positive or negative feedback on the things that I have done so far.

There seems to have been a point for many of the people in this book where it was important to look back at their family history and the meaning of their culture. Has that happened for any of you?

FIONA: I was to go back to Hong Kong the last two summers but I've chickened out at the last minute.

Why do you keep chickening out?

FIONA: I think everything is going to be so different. It scares me more to go to Hong Kong than to go to France.

Are you ashamed to go back as a foreigner?

FIONA: Yes, a little, but that's not why I don't want to go back. I don't know—they'll all look at me funny because I don't speak Chinese.

ALEC: There is also a different look. You can tell Canadian Chinese from Hong Kong Chinese.

SELWYN: Can you tell from me?

ALEC: It's hard. There are some people who are very integrated.

Tell us more about this look?

ALEC: I think they just dress different and they have a different look.

How is it different?

ALEC: Canadian Chinese seem to be always more preppy. That's how I notice the difference. I find a lot of them to be kind of snobby towards other Chinese people. It's weird.

Fiona, you're going to university in the United States. You're a Chinese Canadian in an American university, does that make you feel doubly different?

FIONA: Just the Canadian part.

You feel more Canadian at Berkeley than you feel Chinese?

FIONA: Yes.

How?

FIONA: It's just the way I was raised. I know now that I was all wrong to sit there and be ashamed to be Chinese. I was only sixteen.

What does it mean, then, to be a Canadian?

FIONA: I can say things like, "Oh, we don't do that in Canada."

Alec, do you have any desire to visit Hong Kong?

ALEC: I'd like to go. For me it's hard right now. I'm in the work force and it's difficult to pull out and go back for a decent amount of time. The only time I could go back would be for a vacation. I would like to see Hong Kong before 1997.

Selwyn, how did you come to choose accounting as your career? It seems to be a very popular choice for many Chinese students.

SELWYN: It wasn't really the case when I started. There were not too many Chinese in my university, in my program anyway, but a year later it was all Chinese. I guess a lot of Chinese parents feel that being a visible minority in Canada makes life more difficult and so it's better to have a skill or profession. I think being a doctor or a lawyer or an accountant makes you more independent. I didn't like the sciences so for me I chose accounting by a process of elimination.

Was there a language question, too? Certain professions require more language skills than others.

SELWYN: I would think so. If I had been a lawyer I might be too slow because sometimes I think in Chinese and sometimes I think in English; it's something I really don't have any control over. When I'm around my Chinese friends I think in Chinese.

FIONA: You know how you tell which language is your best? It's the one you add and subtract in.

SELWYN: That's interesting. One of the things we often do is inventory counts and I often find myself counting in Chinese.

ALEC: Or Chinglish—a combination of both.

SELWYN: You twist the meaning of an English word to fit it into a Chinese meaning—that's really interesting.

Alec, how much of an influence did your parents have in getting you to go to university?

ALEC: It was a basic assumption.

What did they tell you?

ALEC: They wanted me to find something that I liked. It's weird because many Chinese parents prefer that you go into a profession like medicine or dentistry because they're so stable. The sciences are the most stable. And then come the lawyers and the accountants and the engineers. All the professions are really popular.

What do they think of what you're doing now?

ALEC: Well, they're happy that I am doing what I like to do. I think the reason why I ended up where I am is because I was introduced to Junior Achievement. This was when I was in grade eleven. Junior Achievement is a non-profit organization that teaches students about business by letting them start up their own business. They provide counsellors to teach them how to start up the business, run the business, make and sell the product and liquidate the company.

That's where I got my interest in making things and that's why I wanted to get into business.

Fiona, what about you? How much of a role have your parents had in your choice of interests?

FIONA: I want to go to law school now; at least I'm ninety percent sure. When we were little my parents used to say now you're going to be a lawyer, and you're going to be a doctor and you're going to be an engineer. I wanted to do everything. I was even going to go to Hollywood and be a film maker, a producer, and I wanted to get into advertising. I don't know, I guess they've just been telling me so long that one day I just woke up and said, right, law's the right thing. And my sister is headed for medical school. It's strange that they predicted it when we were young.

Is there anything more than prediction?

ALEC: Your parents were good judges of character.

How important are your careers? Do you have major goals, a five year or a ten year plan?

SELWYN: I had a five year plan back in 1986 when I first started and it's up next week because I'll find out the results of my exams. I think once I find out I'll probably make another five year plan because getting your CA is only the beginning of a long learning process. It's like getting a degree in university. And now I'll open myself up to different possibilities. Like I am planning to go to Hong Kong in December to do something quite different from what I'm doing now which is auditing.

What would you like to be doing in five years?

SELWYN: I am hoping that a CA will enable me to do other things than accounting. Maybe start a business. Maybe working in a public accounting firm. Maybe something else. I don't know. I haven't really quite decided.

How important is money to you?

SELWYN: Not extremely important. I only need enough money to make me happy, and doing things like going to a movie can make me really happy, so I don't think I need a lot of money.

Fiona, do you have your life figured out for the next few years?

FIONA: Finish four years of Berkeley. This summer get a job in a law firm. Finish Berkeley and then I'm going to apply to law school.

Where?

FIONA: I can't say because if I do I'll jinx myself.

Osgoode Hall?

FIONA: No.

American. Why American? Why not Canadian?

FIONA: You cannot get a Canadian degree and practise in the States, but you can get an American degree and practise in both Canada and the States.

And after?

FIONA: I decided recently that I'd like to come back to Toronto.

What kind of law will you practise?

FIONA: Either corporate or criminal law. Well, that accounts for my time up to age thirty-five.

Where are you going to be when you are thirty-five?

FIONA: I don't know, but I have to get married in between all that.

You want to get married and have children?

FIONA: Yes.

How many children are you going to have?

FIONA: Two. Because it's mean to have only one because they have no one to play with and I couldn't handle more than two.

But what if your husband wants boys and you have girls? Will you just keep trying until you have boys?

FIONA: You must be joking!

Alec, what about you. Have you such detailed plans?

ALEC: I used to.

At what age?

ALEC: Starting with university, I knew that working for two years after university was standard if you want to go into business school. I used to have lists for getting married, too.

And when were you going to get married?

ALEC: Twenty-eight actually. Now I'm twenty-seven, everything's changed.

Do you have a clear idea of the kind of woman you want to marry?

ALEC: I used to have a list for this girl. My dad used to make fun of me.

You had a list that contained all the qualities of the woman?

ALEC: Yes. Canadian Chinese was one of them.

Canadian Chinese, not Hong Kong Chinese?

ALEC: Yes, but that can change, too.

What were some of the other things on the list?

ALEC: Wow! I think I'd have to have it on a computer disc. My dad used to actually think it was really funny that I had this wonderful list and he would tell me how no, no, it doesn't work that way. When you find the person you like you throw away your list.

What were some of the things on the list?

ALEC: Chinese for one thing. Career oriented.

Did you expect this woman to have children and stay at home, or have her own career?

ALEC: No. Not that traditional. Somewhat traditional.

FIONA: Every guy wants a wife to stay at home.

ALEC: No, that's not true. Actually I have always wanted my wife to work. I just thought it would be kind of boring for the conversations we would have if she did not work, if she was staying at home all the time.

But you want her career to be secondary?

FIONA: Yes. You want her to work but you don't want her to be as successful as you are.

ALEC: Okay, I'll admit that before I used to think that way, but now I do not think I would mind being equal.

FIONA: If your wife is making double what you are, you would have a problem with it!

What about children? Are you prepared to have them raised by a stranger? I mean if you're both working?

ALEC: I have not thought of that.

If you're on equal footing with your wife, who stays at home to raise the children?

ALEC: My mother always worked so we kind of took care of ourselves. She had a regular job so she was always home at night; it was only while we were at school that she was away.

But who's career gets put on hold for four or five years while the baby is raised?

ALEC: That is a biological question.

Which? Carrying the child for nine months or raising it for the first four or five years?

FIONA: People automatically assume you are supposed to stay home with the kid because you had the baby in the first place.

ALEC: I guess that way I am more traditional.

You would expect her to stay at home?

ALEC: In the early years, yes.

But what if she said, my career is more important than yours, so you stay at home. Would you give up the four years?

ALEC: I would have a problem. You got me there.

FIONA: I just think it's going to end up that way no matter how I plan it. I am going to end up staying at home with my kids. Someone has to do it, and I know my husband is not going to do it, so I know I will end up doing it.

And it makes you mad?

FIONA: Yes, because I have to do it. I don't think I have a choice.

Would you stay at home, Selwyn?

SELWYN: No, I don't think so.

What are some of the other problems you face? Besides this question of who is going to stay at home with the baby?

FIONA: All professors are sexist. Not all—that is a generalization—but a lot of them are. They think you're stupid.

Because you're a woman?

FIONA: Yes, I think so.

And how do you deal with that?

FIONA: You don't. You just be yourself.

Is this how you deal with unfair treatment? The reaction is to bury the anger and just prove yourself to be better? Do you face the professor and tell him to go jump in the lake or do you bury the anger and say, I don't care, I'll show you?

FIONA: I bury the anger.

ALEC: I am like you, I just absorb it. I think Chinese people don't ever really say too much. They just do it, or do whatever it takes to get it.

What do you think about the stereotypes used for the Chinese?

FIONA: The way they stereotype us is a good thing even though they hate us for it. Like hard working, stealing their jobs, being smarter than others . . . Chinese people cannot drive.

What do you think about that one?

FIONA: It is true.

ALEC: Why is it true? . . . Maybe it's because in Hong Kong they drive on the other side of the road. It is so stressful to drive in Hong Kong. I have only been in a taxi in Hong Kong and it was very stressful. Maybe it's just too relaxed here, so you fall asleep. . . .

Is it normal that Chinese kids live at home until they get married?

FIONA: Even after they are married.

SELWYN: Especially if you have both the wife and husband working, you need to have the parents to take care of the kids.

FIONA: But you learn so much when you live on your own.

ALEC: This is true.

What were the first things you had to face when you were on your own?

FIONA: I did not know how to do laundry.

ALEC: I guess that was my first thing, too. Cooking, too.

None of you have a problem living at home into your thirties?

FIONA: I don't want to.

What about your social life, entertaining, having friends over for dinner?

ALEC: I don't actually do that too much, to tell you the truth. I try to spend time with my parents as well. I find that because I am working seven days a week right now it's difficult, but on Sunday especially, I try to have dinner with them, which I don't think is normal for Caucasians.

What do you get from being with them?

ALEC: Well, there was a time when I was younger when my parents would tell me all sorts of things, like the lectures my dad gave me.

SELWYN: I never had that.

ALEC: You don't get lectures? Well they seem like lectures—they just talk and talk and talk.

SELWYN: Don't you have discussions, talk back?

FIONA: I tried that, but it does not work.

Is it a monologue?

FIONA: No. He always has to be right. It doesn't matter what he says—I don't remember half the things he says–but he would always be right in the end.

SELWYN: Mine is different. I just do the things I want. The thing is that you find out later they were right.

But when you think of your parents, what is it that they give you?

ALEC: I guess they give me almost everything. The guidance, my values.

Is it a warm feeling? Is it a comfort to go home?

ALEC: Oh yeah.

It replenishes you to go back?

ALEC: I guess I am very lucky in that I have a very good relationship with my parents. It is not like they are always telling me what to do. They give me overall guidance and they let me have my freedom to do what I want to do. But I only take in the things that I think are good. But we have interactive conversations; they listen to me, too. I think that is what good parents do.

Have any of you ever reached some disagreement with your parents that you couldn't overcome?

FIONA: Well my dad lets you break it so much and push and push and push and do all these stupid things that bother him but if he finally says NO—well it's a big no.

ALEC: I agree. There are different types of no. We have always had good discussions and sometimes we end up mad at each other, but we always come back together again afterwards. Especially with my mother. Sometimes I talk to my father through my mother. She is sometimes the mediator.

Is she a mediator, or is it just an easy way to avoid a confrontation?

ALEC: In a way I am closer to my mother.

What are the big problems facing you and your friends? A job? Money? Relationships? What?

ALEC: What do we talk about? Relationships. It is the most fun thing to talk about.

But is it the thing that gives you the most trouble?

ALEC: Yes, when it is unstable it does.

Every generation seems to have a crisis or a problem that preoccupies it. What is it for your generation?

ALEC: The future. I think we are all worried. The economy.

Is it the world economy, or just Canada's?

SELWYN: Canada. Whether it can be as competitive as the rest of the world—that is what my friends in the accounting firm worry about. Everyone is talking about international transfer. Working elsewhere. Everybody wants to leave.

Everybody wants to leave?

FIONA: Society is so good here. Now that I've lived in the States for a few years I realize how good it is.

SELWYN People want to get a better job. People think, well, maybe travelling is the best way to do it. Just to see what is being offered outside the country. To take a look around.

FIONA: Are you talking just the United States, or Europe?

SELWYN: My first step is to go to Hong Kong. I might end up going back there permanently. I might just stay for a year to get some experience.

Do you feel that you are a Canadian? That you will come back eventually?

SELWYN: Yes, definitely. Most of my friends are here. My parents are here and they like it a lot. I can't see myself considering any place else as home besides Canada, or Toronto specifically.

Alec, would you think of leaving? How do you see dealing with these problems?

ALEC: For me it is hard to change. It is hard to do great deeds. I think every person should do their own small deed in the area they can best affect. You can only touch so many people, you can only help so many people. It is just *how* you help them.

SELWYN: It is hard to be optimistic when I see major clients with losses projecting further losses in the years to come.

FIONA: My problem is do I want to pay seventy percent tax?

SELWYN: But there is no tax if you are out of a job.

FIONA: It will go back up soon, the economy.

SELWYN: I don't think we are being competitive enough. People don't seem to see the problems we are actually facing in terms of economic recession. I still see people who work from 9 to 5—leave right at 5 no matter what. If there is an unfinished order, they still leave right at 5. If I am talking to someone at 10:15, at 10:16 they leave for coffee break—sorry I have to take coffee break right now for ten minutes, I'll come back later. That attitude is very difficult for a lot of Canadian business.

What does that mean to you?

SELWYN: I am getting upset. I mean we are in a recession right now and people do not really care as long as they have their job. And then they start complaining that they are not being paid well and they want more pay. The pie is getting smaller but everybody wants a bigger share.

FIONA: The government has a lot to do with it.

SELWYN: That's right.

What do you think about politics, and the politics in this country?

SELWYN: I have a friend who is French Canadian from Quebec City, and when we talk about unity he does not understand why it became a problem in the first place. I guess our generation doesn't see it as a problem.

A lot of it has to do with language. What if somebody came along and said you couldn't use the Chinese language, or made it very difficult for you to use it?

SELWYN: Well, I do a lot of Chinese things. I watch Chinese TV, I listen to Chinese music. If somebody came along and said, sorry, you cannot do these Chinese things for the rest of your life, then I would get really upset.

What do you feel about the future?

SELWYN: I think the Chinese immigrants who will eventually become Chinese Canadian citizens will have to put more effort into the community. I have seen a lot of people come from Hong Kong who see Canada as being more a shelter than a home. They just want to stay away from Hong Kong until after 1997 to see what is going to happen.

FIONA: Your kids aren't going to be like that. Your kids are going to be Canadian. When you have kids they are not going to want to do all the Chinese things. They'll think you're old fashioned for dragging them to all those Chinese events.

Do you think there will soon be a new wave of immigration from Hong Kong?

SELWYN: I think the great wave has already occurred. I think that most of the people that could leave Hong Kong have already left.

FIONA: They come for five years and they get their citizenship and they go back to live.

SELWYN: I am sure in 1996 or 1997 they will all come back. I think we are going to see a huge Chinese influx.

Fiona, when you come back to Toronto after your studies and set up your law practice, do you see yourself dealing mostly with the Chinese community?

FIONA: I think I am going to make more of an effort to try to get involved. To not be so narrow minded. I am going to have all kinds of friends and I am never just going to be secluded with one group or the other.

Is there any final thing you would like to say? Some idea or message, a hope for the future?

ALEC: This thing about whether Canada has hope. I do have hope for it. I think it is going to have to be a team effort with everyone involved. I would like to quote Mother Teresa; she said, "It is not the size of the deed that you do, it is how much love you put into it." I think everybody has to put their heart into making Canada more competitive.

SELWYN: I agree. I have great hopes for the country. Even though I am planning to leave for a while I will definitely come back. One general comment is that I hope Canadians will stop complaining about things and do something, be active rather than passive. Don't let something hit you, then ten years later react to it—react to it right away. In very general terms, I think we should try to play a leading role.

FIONA: I know you think the Hong Kong people are always going to retain their values, but I don't think that is going to happen. I think in a couple of generations it will be gone. I understand Chinese, I can't really speak it, but my brother knows nothing. It's important to keep some heritage. It might not be lost to the community, but I feel lost. I feel like there is something missing.

Are you optimistic or pessimistic?

FIONA: I am optimistic. I don't know.

But you are coming back after you finish your studies?

FIONA: Yes. You just have to stick it out, that's all.

Essay:
The Chinese Minority in Canada, 1858-1992: A Quest For Equality

Peter S. Li, University of Saskatchewan

Chinese immigrants have been coming to Canada since 1858, yet Chinese Canadians remain a foreign population in Canada in two senses. First, as recently as 1986, seventy-one percent of them were born outside of Canada, and of these eighty-five percent came to Canada after 1967 (Statistics Canada, 1986). Second, in the eyes of the Canadian public, Canadians are usually equated with Caucasians, while Chinese Canadians and other non-white Canadians are seen as foreigners. These two factors—one based on fact, the other on prejudice—colour the general public's view towards Chinese Canadians. Immigrants in general and Chinese in particular are blamed for social maladies, such as unemployment and housing cost (Tienhaara, 1974; Li, 1979a; Angus Reid Group, 1989). Other times, such bias surfaces as a romanticized version of an exotic culture that tends to distort the Chinese Canadian heritage and patronize its people. The historical experiences of the Chinese in Canada, however, suggest that neither primordial culture nor ethnic distinctiveness has much to do with the particular course followed by the Chinese minority. Much of its historical path has been paved by forces of Canadian society beyond the control of the Chinese. To understand the demographic and social features of the Chinese community in Canada, and the reaction of the general public to this racial minority, it is useful to review the thirteen decades of history of the Chinese in Canada.

The first nine decades were characterized by legal discrimination and institutional exclusion targeted towards the Chinese. Prior to 1947, the Chinese in Canada were legally denied many of the entitlements taken for granted by white Canadians, including the right to vote, the right to travel freely in and out of the country, and the right to enter into certain professions and jobs (Li, 1988). The harsh treatment accorded to the Chinese minority defies natural justice, especially when the contributions of Chinese labour to the building of many pioneer industries in Western Canada is taken into account. For almost a century, the Chinese worked and lived as second-class citizens in Canada. It was only after the Second World War, in 1947, that the discriminatory legislation against them was repealed, and the Chinese began to gain basic civil rights. But it would take them another twenty years before Canadian immigration policy was revamped to allow the Chinese to immigrate to Canada under the same criteria and conditions as other groups.[1] The entrenchment of the Charter of Rights and Freedoms in 1982 and the enactment of the Canadian Multiculturalism Act in 1988 helped to heighten sensitivity towards minority rights. Yet, despite these legislative advances, the Chinese minority remains an occasional target of social distrust and hostility. In metropolitan centres such as Vancouver and Toronto where most immigrants reside, there have been renewed concerns about the Chinese presence and resentment of their economic success, especially as more affluent Chinese, mainly from Hong Kong, have begun to immigrate to Canada after a change in immigration policy in favour of business immigrants.[2] Despite their long history of settlement in Canada, and despite the economic, social and scientific accomplishments of many Chinese Canadians, the Chinese as a minority have yet to gain social acceptance and full-fledged citizenship in Canadian society. Looking back, it is appropriate to think of the history of the Chinese minority in Canada as a quest for citizenship and equality, albeit the past voyage was stormy and the future course remains precarious.

The History of the Chinese in Canada

One way to understand the history of the Chinese in Canada is to view it as three periods which roughly correspond to the major shifts in Canada's legislation towards the Chinese with respect to civil rights and immigration. The first segment covers a period of sixty-five years from 1858, when the Chinese first immigrated to Canada, to the passage of the Chinese Immigration Act in 1923. This was a period in which the Chinese became victims of institutional racism and were intensively subjected to legislative controls. The second period of twenty-three years, from 1924 to 1947, was an era characterized by exclusion, because as a result of the Chinese Immigration Act, no Chinese were allowed to immigrate to Canada, and the Chinese in the country continued to face legislative exclusion and social animosity. The third period embraces the years from 1947 onwards in which the discriminatory laws against the Chinese have been repealed, and Chinese Canadians have gradually gained their civil rights and enjoyed an improved social status. Throughout all three periods of this history, the Canadian government's policy towards the Chinese and the social reception accorded to them largely determined the structure and direction of the Chinese community. In this sense, the distinction between periods has less to do with any natural process of change within the Chinese community, than with broader forces within Canadian society to which the Chinese community was compelled to adapt.

First Period: Development of Institutional Racism (1858-1923)

The initial wave of Chinese immigration to Canada began as a result of the discovery of gold along the Fraser River. Some of the original Chinese pioneers came from California, where dwindling yields in the gold fields led them to contemplate new opportunities in British Columbia. Large scale immigration of Chinese did not take place until the Canadian Pacific Railway was constructed, between 1881 and 1885. In 1881 and 1882 alone, more than eleven thousand Chinese arrived by ship in Victoria from China directly (Royal Commission, 1885: 397-9). This second wave of Chinese immigration substantially increased the number of Chinese in Canada, which more than doubled in official census counts from 4,383 in 1881 (Department of Agriculture, 1886: 48) to 9,126 in 1891 (Department of Agriculture, 1893: 134).[3] By 1901, the number of Chinese in Canada had reached 17,314 (Statistics Canada, 1941: 684-92).

Like other international migration, the emigration of Chinese from their native land was propelled by two sets of forces. On the one hand, disruptions brought about by foreign invasions and internal revolts,[4] as well as problems of declining farm productivity and rising population (Perkins, 1969), forced many Chinese in the coastal provinces of Guangdong and Fujian to migrate overseas. On the other hand, the industrial development of Western Canada in the latter half of the nineteenth century required massive labour power that was not readily available from existing white workers (Timlin, 1960). Since Chinese labour was available in large quantity and at low cost, it was attractive to railroad contractors, manufacturers and employers in Canada.

From the outset, neither the Canadian government nor the Canadian public looked upon Chinese immigrants as permanent settlers. The Chinese were considered useful to the development of Western Canada but not desirable citizens. The subsequent public outcry against Oriental labour and the state's policies of Chinese exclusion reflected a utilitarian mentality towards what was considered an inferior race.

It is no surprise that the first federal legislation against the Chinese was passed in 1885, when the Canadian Pacific Railway was completed. It came in the form of a 'head tax' of $50 applied to virtually every Chinese entering the country (Statutes of Canada, 1885, c. 71). Prior to the completion of the railroad, Prime Minister John A. Macdonald was unwilling to take any measure that might jeopardize the project. As he frankly put it to the House of Commons in 1883: "It will be all very well to exclude Chinese labour, when we can replace it with white labour, but until that is done, it is better to have Chinese labour than no labour at all" (Canada, House of Commons Debates, 1883: 905). The head tax was raised to $100 in 1900, and to $500 in 1903 (Statutes of Canada, 1900, c. 32, 1903, c. 8).

In their first four decades in Canada, the Chinese had helped to build up many industries in British Columbia. The usefulness of the Chinese labour in mining, railroad construction, land clearing, public works, market gardening, lumbering, salmon canning and domestic service was well recognized by many employers and witnesses who appeared before a royal commission in 1885 and in 1902 (Royal Commission, 1885, 1902). The Chinese were welcome as cheap labourers in pioneer industries where other labour was not available. As long as they accepted their menial positions and avoided competition with white workers for higher-paying jobs, they were tolerated in times of need. But as white workers were attracted to expanding industries and as labour disputes surfaced, the Chinese became the target of racially based attacks for, at least in the minds of their accusers, causing various economic and social woes.

Between 1875 and 1923, the Legislative Assembly of British Columbia passed numerous laws against the Chinese (Li, 1988: 27-33). For example, a bill in 1884 disallowed Chinese from acquiring crown lands and diverting water from natural channels. The Coal Mines Regulation Amendment Act of 1890 prevented them from working underground. The Provincial Home Act of 1893 excluded Chinese from admission to the provincially established home for the aged and infirm; they were prohibited from being hired on public works in 1897. The Liquor License Act of 1900 stipulated that they were not entitled to hold a liquor license. Since their names were excluded from the provincial voters' list, Chinese were also barred from obtaining a hand-logger's license. The Chinese were excluded from the professions of law and pharmacy. The 1920 Provincial Elections Act reaffirmed that all Chinese were disqualified from voting.

Between 1885 and 1923 the Canadian Parliament passed four statutes regulating Chinese immigration, culminating in the Chinese Immigration Act, the most comprehensive legislation to exclude Chinese from entering the country and to control those already here (Statutes of Canada, 1923, c. 38). The Act stipulated that entry to Canada for persons of Chinese origin, irrespective of citizenship, would be restricted to diplomats, children born in Canada, merchants and students; all other Chinese were in essence excluded. The Act also required every person of Chinese origin in Canada, regardless of citizenship, to register with the Government of Canada within twelve months and to obtain a certificate of such registration. The penalty for failing to register was a fine of up to $500 or imprisonment for up to twelve months. Furthermore, every Chinese in Canada who intended to leave the country temporarily and return at a later date had to give written notice before departure, specifying the foreign port he planned to visit and the route he intended to take. Those who had so registered would be permitted to return within two years. The impact of the Act's provisions was virtually to stop Chinese immigration to Canada until its repeal in 1947.

Second Period: Exclusion and Adaptation (1923-1947)

By the time the Chinese Immigration Act of 1923 was passed, Chinese immigrants had paid $22.5 million of revenue to the Canadian government for entering and leaving the country; most of it had come from the head tax (Li, 1988: 38). The cumulative effects of exclusionary policies and discriminatory legislation against the Chinese had effectively reduced them to second-class citizens in Canada. Institutional racism against the Chinese was entrenched in economic and political institutions; unequal treatments were legally and officially sanctioned. The Chinese were denied many basic rights, including the right to pursue a living in many occupations. They were frequent targets of political demagogy. Considered to be an 'inferior race', they became marginal to Canadian society.

This institutional racism produced a hostile social environment in which the Chinese struggled to survive. Like other oppressed minorities deprived of the basic means to improve their disadvantaged positions, the Chinese were forced to respond by mobilizing whatever resources were available, including the reliance on sometimes remote clanship ties in organizing ethnic business and voluntary associations. These networks were not seen as an extension of an old world culture transplanted. Rather, they were a response to institutional racism and legislative exclusion.

The restriction on citizenship rights and their legal exclusion from certain jobs placed the Chinese at a disadvantage in the Canadian labour market. Although they were indispensable in building many industries of British Columbia, the Chinese were excluded from the core labour market by the 1920s (Li, 1979). The available data on occupations held by Chinese indicate that between 1885 and 1931 there was a percentage decline of Chinese workers in the industrial sectors, accompanied by a corresponding increase in the ethnic business sector. For example, in 1885 the number of Chinese engaged in laundry, personal service and restaurant work was estimated to be less than five percent of all employed Chinese. But by 1921, servants, cooks, waiters and laundry workers rose to thirty-two percent, and by 1931, forty percent (Li, 1988: 48-9). These statistics indicate that as racism and discrimination made it increasingly difficult for the Chinese to seek employment in the core industrial sector, they retreated to an ethnic business enclave where they thrived on marginal enterprises such as laundry and food services to avoid competition with white workers. The restaurant business, in particular, was a survival haven for many Chinese before the Second World War, and it remained an important sector of employment and self-employment for Chinese after the war, even when opportunities in professional and technical occupations became available (Li, 1990).

Another consequence of institutional racism and restrictive immigration policy towards the Chinese was to retard the development of the Chinese Canadian family. Like other pioneers in frontier societies, Chinese immigrants who left China to come to Canada in the latter half of the nineteenth century were mainly men. Economic hardship and uncertainty of the future made it difficult for many Chinese men to bring their families with them. With the imposition of head tax in 1885, and its steep increase to $500 in 1903, it became financially impossible for an average worker to be able to afford the passage money and the head tax for his wife and other family members. Oftentimes, they had to borrow money to cover the transportation cost and the head tax. Social hostility and rampant discrimination against the Chinese also tended to discourage them from bringing their families with them (Li, 1988: 58-62). Chinese quarters were sometimes targets of racial attacks, as in the anti-Oriental riots of 1887 and 1907 in Vancouver (Morton, 1974). After 1923 and until 1947, the Chinese Immigration Act excluded practically all Chinese from immigrating to Canada, thus making it legally impossible for Chinese men in Canada to sponsor their wives to join them.

As a result of these financial and legal hardships, the Chinese Canadian community, unlike the other pioneer ethnic communities, remained a predominantly male society. Data from various Canadian censuses indicate that in 1911, among the 27,831 Chinese in Canada, the sex ratio was 2,800 men to 100 women; and in 1931, the sex ratio remained 1,240 to 100 women among the 46,519 Chinese. Throughout all the census years before the Second World War, the unbalanced sex ratio among the Chinese population was the most severe among all ethnic groups in Canada (Li, 1988: 60-62). In the absence of Chinese women, many Chinese men in Canada maintained a married bachelor life. Those who had the financial resources to do so would take an occasional trip to China for a sojourn with their wives and families. However, they could be away for only up to two years, otherwise they would lose their permission to return to Canada. Many Chinese would have to wait for decades—until the repeal of legislation in 1947—before they had a chance to reunite with their family after the Second World War when changes in immigration policy permitted Chinese family immigration. The absence of wives and family also meant that the growth of a second generation was delayed. For example, by 1931, despite a seventy-three-year-long history of immigration, Chinese Canadians born in Canada made up only twelve percent of the total Chinese population (Li, 1988: 61). It was only following postwar changes in immigration policy that a more balanced sex ratio was gradually restored among the Chinese community, and a sizable second and third generation of Chinese Canadians began to emerge.

Throughout their history in Canada, and especially before the Second World War, the Chinese organized many voluntary associations as a means to answer the needs of the immigrant community amid a hostile social environment. These associations provided important functions to the Chinese community, such as organizing social services for those in need, mediating internal disputes and dealing with pressures of discrimination and segregation. The way in which the Chinese formed associations in Canada showed an ingenious use of limited resources for mobilizing collective efforts. Common locality of origin, common surnames, principles of fraternity or common Chinese heritage were used as bases of organization. No doubt, the denial of family life increased the need of the lone Chinese to rely on the community for support. As postwar Chinese immigrants entered Canada in larger volumes, they gradually altered the structure of the Chinese community. Correspondingly, the importance of traditional Chinese associations has declined as they have failed to meet the needs of these new immigrants.

Third Period: Gaining of Civil Rights and Chinese Family Immigration (1947 onwards)

Towards the end of the Second World War, the discriminatory policy towards the Chinese had become an embarrassment for Canada, since many Chinese Canadians had contributed to the war effort and China had been an ally during the war. In 1943, the United States repealed its Chinese Exclusion Act and permitted a quota of 105 Chinese to be admitted annually (Li, 1977). The denial of civil rights based on race also contradicted the charter of the United Nations. In 1947, the Parliament of Canada repealed the Chinese Immigration Act, lifting an exclusion of Chinese immigration to Canada that had lasted for twenty-four years. The Chinese in British Columbia were allowed to vote in 1947, and those in Saskatchewan in 1951. By the 1950s, most of the discriminatory laws against the Chinese in Canada had been removed (Li, 1988: 85-6).

Although the exclusion of Chinese immigration was lifted, the Canadian government did not consider Chinese immigrants as equals of European and American immigrants. Admission of Chinese and other Asian immigrants before 1962 was restricted to spouses and minor unmarried children, as compared to relatively free migration from Europe and the United States. As a result of a change in immigration policy in 1962, Chinese could apply as independent immigrants to Canada, but the policy still had a discriminatory clause which permitted a more restricted range of sponsorship than for those applying from Europe and America (Hawkins, 1988: 125-6). It was not until 1967, when Canada adopted a universal point system of assessing potential immigrants, that Chinese were admitted under the same criteria as people of other origins (Li, 1988: 91).

In the years immediately after 1947, few Chinese actually came to Canada. Between 1949 and 1955, 12,560 Chinese immigrants were admitted, about sixty percent of whom were wives and children, now able to be reunited with their husbands and fathers after years of separation. In the two decades following 1947, a total of 40,593 Chinese immigrants came to Canada, many immigrating as a family unit. After 1967, Chinese immigration to Canada accelerated. Between 1968 and 1984, 170,720 Chinese immigrated to Canada, fully eighty percent of the total of 212,374 Chinese who had immigrated to Canada since the Chinese Immigration Act was repealed in 1947 (Li, 1988: 92-4). This wave of postwar Chinese immigration increased the Chinese Canadian population and restored a balanced sex ratio, and a second and third generation of Chinese Canadians grew apace. Immigrating mainly from Hong Kong, Taiwan and Southeast Asian countries, postwar Chinese immigrants came from a more diversified occupational and educational background, many with a sophisticated urban culture. These postwar Chinese immigrants transformed the demographic and social features of the Chinese community, and contributed to the multicultural composition of Canadian society.

Largely as a result of changing immigration policies, the Chinese population increased substantially after 1967. In 1971, the Chinese Canadian population was 124,600; by 1981 it had expanded to 285,800 (Statistics Canada, 1971, 1981). By the time the 1986 census was taken, it had increased further to 412,800 (Statistics Canada, 1986).

Among the many changes in the Chinese community was the emergence of a new middle class made up of postwar immigrants who came as professional and technical workers, and second-generation Chinese Canadians who moved into managerial and professional occupations (Li, 1990). For example, in 1981, there were 44,450 Chinese Canadians who belonged to the new middle class[5], constituting about twenty-six percent of all Chinese in the Canadian labour force (Li, 1990). By 1986, the new Chinese middle class had increased to 63,400 or twenty-seven percent of total Chinese in the Canadian labour force. Among those in middle-class occupations, Chinese Canadians were more likely than other Canadians to have a university degree. However, the earnings of Chinese Canadians still lagged behind other groups, even after differences in schooling, age and other factors had been taken into account (Li, 1987; Li, 1990). These findings suggest that despite mobility into the new middle class and parity in education, Chinese Canadians continue to encounter income discrimination in the labour market.

The Chinese also continue to face social obstacles in their quest for equality in Canadian society. In 1979, in reacting to a public affairs program, W5, which depicted Chinese as foreigners taking away university places from white Canadians, Chinese Canadians across the country demonstrated and protested against the CTV television network. After months of intense lobbying, the network finally issued a public apology. In 1984 the increase in Chinese population in Scarborough, Ontario, led to a racially based public outcry against the Chinese, blaming them as the cause of parking and traffic problems in the area. The racial tension prompted the mayor to appoint a task force to investigate and to mediate race relations (Li, 1988: 123-4).

More recently, as immigration policy was changed to accommodate business immigrants, and as more wealthy Hong Kong residents moved to the affluent west side neighbourhoods of Vancouver, such as Shaughnessy and Kerrisdale, there was increasing hostility towards the opulence of the Chinese and the glamour of their mansion-style homes.[6] There is little doubt that Hong Kong immigrants have been the major supporters of the business immigrant program introduced by the federal government in 1978 and expanded in 1985, and that the new arrivals have brought substantial capital into Canada.[7] For example, about 23,000 Hong Kong emigrants, roughly half of those who emigrated from Hong Kong in 1989, are estimated to have come to Canada in that one year alone, among whom 5,300 came under the business immigration program (West, 1990). In 1990, 455 immigrant visas were reported to have been issued to Hong Kong residents as entrepreneur immigrants, one of the categories of business immigration; their aggregate net worth was $658 million (The Province, 1991). This new wave of immigrants from Hong Kong has injected a huge amount of capital into housing and business developments in Canada, particularly in British Columbia. It has even been suggested that British Columbia has escaped the economic recession of the 1990s largely because of the importation of offshore capital by immigrants (The Province, 1991). However, as they increase their presence on the west coast, the Chinese have also become the target of new racial antagonism, and are continuously blamed for destroying the traditional neighbourhoods of Vancouver by building what are referred to in the media as "monster houses."[8]

It is difficult to speculate what the future will be for Chinese Canadians. The historical facts suggest that the road towards equality has been hazardous and precarious. It would appear that despite the economic and occupational advances made by Chinese Canadians in recent decades, they have yet to cross the social barriers to full acceptance into Canadian society.

Peter S. Li is a full professor of Sociology at the University of Saskatchewan, where he is engaged in research in the area of race and ethnic studies. His recent books include Racial Oppression in Canada (with B. Singh Bolaria), Ethnic Inequality in a Class Society and Race and Ethnic Relations in Canada. In addition to his writings, Professor Li has lectured in China at the invitation of the Chinese Academy of Social Sciences, and in Taiwan at the invitation of Academia Sinica.

I WAS NOT BORN WITH KNOWLEDGE BUT I AM FOND OF HISTORY AND WILL SEEK IT THERE.

NOTES

1. The changes in immigration policy in 1962 permitted, for the first time since 1923, Chinese who had no relatives in Canada to apply as independent immigrants, but applicants from China or other Asian countries were not qualified for sponsored immigrants to the same extent as immigrants from Europe and America (Privy Council, 1962–86). Further changes in 1967 resulted in a universal point system of assessing potential immigrants, irrespective of country of origin (P.C. 1967–1616).

2. The *Immigration Regulations* of 1978 (P.C. 1978–486) allowed the admission of entrepreneurs without being assessed on the basis of occupational demand or arranged employment. The 1985 amendments (P.C. 1985–3246) expanded the admission of business immigrants to include entrepreneurs, investors and self-employed persons. To qualify as an investor, a person must have a net worth of at least $500,000 (P.C. 1985–3246, s. 3b).

3. Several factors would account for why the cumulative number of Chinese arriving by ship is larger than the number of Chinese reported in the 1891 Census. An undetermined number of returnees went back to China, especially after the railroad was completed, which left many out of work. Deaths during construction of the railroad and potential larger error margins of earlier censuses also may add to these discrepancies.

4. China was defeated by Britain in the Opium War (1839–42), a war over Britain's claim to trade opium in China. Between 1839 and 1900, Britain, France, Germany, Austria, Japan, the United States and Russia engaged in a series of wars with China in her territories and succeeded in securing unequal trading rights and privileges from the Ch'ing government of China (Wakeman, 1975; Hsu, 1970).

5. The new middle class is defined here as composed of those engaged in managerial, administrative, professional and technical occupations.

6. For example, two opinion polls in 1989 found that over sixty percent of respondents in B.C. agreed with the statement that "immigrants are driving housing prices up," as compared to thirty percent of the respondents nationally who said so (Angus Reid Group, 1989: 14).

7. The uncertain political future of Hong Kong resulting from Britain's agreement to return the colony to China in 1997 has prompted an exodus of emigrants from Hong Kong. The bloody suppression of the student demonstration in Beijing in June 1989 also shook the fragile confidence of Hong Kong residents towards the government of China.

8. In 1989 and 1990, *The Vancouver Sun* carried many articles on this subject. Some examples are: "Curbing monster houses," p. A9, 14 November 1989; "One man wields unique sword at 'monster' houses," pp. B1–2, 25 May 1990; "How we saved Shaughnessy from monsters," pp. D10–11, 23 June 1990.

REFERENCES

ANGUS REID GROUP

1989 *Immigration to Canada: Aspects of Public Opinion.* Report prepared for Employment and Immigration Canada.

DEPARTMENT OF AGRICULTURE

1886 *Statistical Abstracts and Records Canada.* Ottawa.

1893 *The Statistical Yearbook of Canada.* Ottawa.

HAWKINS, FREDA

1988 *Canada and Immigration: Public Policy and Public Concern.* 2d. ed. Kingston and Montreal: McGill-Queen's University Press.

HSU, IMMANUEL C. Y.

1970 *The Rise of Modern China.* New York: Oxford University Press.

LI, PETER S.

1977 "Fictive kinship, conjugal tie and kinship chain among Chinese immigrants in the United States." *Journal of Comparative Family Studies* 8: 47-63.

1979a "Prejudice against Asians in a Canadian city." *Canadian Ethnic Studies* 11: 70-77.

1979b "A historical approach to ethnic stratification: The case of the Chinese in Canada, 1858-1930." Canadian Review of Sociology and Anthropology 16: 320-32.

1987 "The economic cost of racism to Chinese-Canadians." *Canadian Ethnic Studies* 13: 102-13.

1988 *The Chinese in Canada.* Toronto: Oxford University Press.

1990 "The emergence of the new middle class among the Chinese in Canada."*Asian Forum* 14: 187-94.

MORTON, JAMES

1974 *In the Sea of Sterile Mountains: The Chinese in British Columbia.* Vancouver: J. J. Douglas.

PERKINS, DWIGHT H.

1969 *Agricultural Development in China, 1368-1968.* Chicago: Aldine.

ROYAL COMMISSION

1885 *Report of the Royal Commission on Chinese Immigration: Report and Evidence.* [Ottawa.]

1902 *Report of the Royal Commission on Chinese and Japanese Immigration.* [Ottawa.]

STATISTICS CANADA

1941 *Census of Canada, 1941: General Review and Summary Tables.*

1971 *Census of Canada, 1971: Public Use Sample Tape, Individual File.*

1981 *Census of Canada, 1981: Public Use Sample Tape, Individual File.*

1986 *Census of Canada, 1986: Public Use Microdata File on Individuals.*

STATUTES OF CANADA

1885 An Act to restrict and regulate Chinese Immigration into Canada. Chapter 71.

1900 An Act respecting and restricting Chinese Immigration. Chapter 32.

1903 An Act respecting and restricting Chinese Immigration. Chapter 8.

1923 An Act respecting Chinese Immigration. Chapter 38.

THE PROVINCE
1991 "The Asia factor." Pp. 35, 38, 21 July 1991.

TIENHAARA, NANCY
1974 *Canadian Views on Immigration and Population: An Analysis of Post-War Gallup Polls.* Ottawa: Department of Manpower and Immigration.

TIMLIN, MABEL F.
1960 "Canada's immigration policy, 1896-1910." *Canadian Journal of Economics and Political Sciences* 26: 517-32.

WAKEMAN, FREDERIC JR.
1975 *The Fall of Imperial China.* New York: Free Press.

WEST (MAGAZINE)
1990 "The orient express." WEST 2: 41-51.